CHAINS TO BE BROKEN

To my parents
who first introduced me to service of God and people

and to Christine, Niall and Michael
who have shared so much of this pilgrimage with me.

ARCHBISHOP
ROBIN EAMES

CHAINS TO BE BROKEN

A personal reflection on Northern Ireland and its people

Weidenfeld and Nicolson, London

First published in Great Britain in 1992 by
George Weidenfeld & Nicolson Ltd
91 Clapham High Street
London SW4 7TA

British Library Cataloguing in Publication Data:
A catalogue record for this book is available from the British
Library

ISBN 0 297 81150 9

Photoset by Selwood Systems,
Midsomer Norton, Avon
Printed in Great Britain by
Butler & Tanner Ltd, Frome, Somerset

CONTENTS

ILLUSTRATIONS

Unless otherwise shown, pictures are reprinted by kind permission of Pacemaker Press International Ltd

INTRODUCTION

Armagh
June 1991

Many books have been written about Northern Ireland and its problems. In fact, if those problems could have been solved by the written word they would have ceased to exist years ago.

When I was invited to write this book early in 1990 I felt at first that little purpose could be served by yet one more publication on a subject which appeared then to be defying any attempt at solution. With many others I was beginning to wonder if there was much evidence that people really wanted solutions: did the vast majority sense they were coming to terms with a situation which was inevitable?

As a Church leader I had seen a great deal of human suffering and frustration. My position granted me the privilege of meeting and knowing many people actively involved in the affairs of Ireland, North and South. But I was beginning to realise that, with other colleagues, I was failing to face up to those fundamental questions which lay behind the problems and the events we had to deal with: we were in danger of losing the capacity to face real questions about people's attitudes, aspirations and, above all, prejudices. Instant reactions to events, condemnations of violence, calls for peace and understanding and attempts to heal the wounds of a troubled society were all part of the daily work of the churches. But had we honestly given enough attention to the reasons for those attitudes and reactions? 'Reconciliation' is probably the most overused word in Ireland's vocabulary. Yet do we know what it means – and do we want it enough to pay the price involved? I was finally persuaded to write these reflections by the impression shared by others that the credibility of churches in Northern Ireland and their ability to make any difference to what is happening has been challenged.

There are questions which I feel individuals must face themselves before we can really expect institutions to respond helpfully to what people are experiencing: the institutional churches of which they are members and to which they look for leadership are affected by what the individual believes or does.

The events of 1968 and what was to follow have shown us a great deal about how people react to situations, how often individuals feel they are powerless in the course of events. Powerlessness leads to frustration, and frustration can breed prejudice.

1968 was a significant year for Northern Ireland, and as I write, 1991–2 could turn out to be of even more significance as we see the first faltering attempts to engage in political dialogue here for over a decade. Still, little will change unless ordinary people want it to change. Legislation alone will not bring reconciliation; it will be ordinary people doing ordinary things who will in the end determine the success or failure of what leadership decides is possible. There are chains to be broken ...

I am most grateful to all who assisted me with this book. In particular I acknowledge the help of my secretary, Roberta Haffey, for all her care in the preparation of drafts, Elizabeth Gibson-Harries, Church of Ireland Press Officer, for her assistance in tracing original material and the supply of photographs; from my publishers, Robin Denniston and Christopher Falkus, for their patience; and Hilary Laurie and Natalina Bertoli whose expertise and advice have been invaluable; and finally Christine, Niall and Michael for their support and encouragement.

R.H.A.E.

Author's Note

This book refers to various traditions, groupings and religious denominations. At times their full technical name is used – for example, the Roman Catholic Church, the Protestant traditions, etc. However, the more popular 'Catholic' and 'Protestant' are also used for clarity in some contexts.

1
ORDINARY
PEOPLE

A slight breeze brought ripples to the otherwise placid waters of the Mediterranean in the long bay off the Cyprus port of Larnaca. The beach was almost deserted – tourists had yet to invade the island in large numbers that year.

We had paused to gaze out across the waters in the direction of Beirut. Somewhere over there, always 'over there', lay that sad and strife-torn city, and somewhere among its ruins Brian Keenan was held hostage. His two sisters were silent. We had gone over in our conversation as we walked all we had found out, all we had heard and all we imagined we had heard, about him.

A Belfast school teacher at the American University of Beirut, he had been kidnapped on his way to work one morning and no one had claimed to be holding him: there had been no demands and no videos on TV. He had joined the familiar names of Waite and McCarthy and all the others. He was almost four years missing and we had come to Cyprus because it seemed a good place to talk to people who might know. At least we felt we were 'doing something'.

There was no sound from Beirut that evening. People told us they sometimes heard the sound of shells. But that evening it was as though there was nothing over there beyond the horizon. It was Brenda who broke the silence. 'It's strange, isn't it? We've heard so much about what Beirut's like. Somebody said to me yesterday it's just like Belfast.' The name of Belfast has become synonymous in the minds of much of the world with violence and strife. The media has made such mileage out of the bombing and the killing. Then they go away. They go away because there's a lull and people aren't interested in the lull.

What the media have left behind are people going about their everyday lives, picking up the pieces, living in an atmosphere of normality which is unbelievable because it *is* so normal and wondering when and where the next outrage will happen. Then, if it's bad enough, if there is enough damage done or sufficient deaths caused the media will be back. Once more the tragedy will be on the front pages and people all over the world may pause for just a moment to wonder what's it all about.

It is well-known that the Northern Ireland people dread the questions 'What's it like?' or 'What's it all about?' The truth for many is that if they can't understand it themselves, how can they possibly make sense out of it for strangers? All major community upheavals encourage people to generalise and simplify. They often slide back into oversimplification and generalisation which is much easier, after all, to justify in conversation than stating the simple human truth that the Irish problem has no clear source and therefore has no ready solution. 'It's about Catholics fighting Protestants' is a common explanation from the observer who arrives by air in the morning, has analysed the problem by lunchtime and by dinner is wondering why solutions are so difficult to find or accept.

'Why can't you people up there get on as well together as we do here in the South?' is often asked by people from the Republic of Ireland with its large Roman Catholic majority and its small Protestant population.

'I just wish you'd solve your problems and stop killing British soldiers or using up our money,' comes from the lips of many on the British mainland.

In the light of those events which make the headlines and cause many a Christian to express at the best dismay and at the worst frustrated anger at what he or she perceives is happening in Northern Ireland, it must seem outrageous to pay tribute to the decency, the honesty, the courage and the normality of the vast majority of people who live there. Yet this is what many visitors have seen when they have stayed longer and become more than the proverbial 'twenty-four hour expert' on Ulster. They have been amazed at the resilience of a people who have endured so much, and continue to live and even plan for the future of their families. At times it has amazed, to the point of incredulity, those who work among such people that anything resembling normality and human decency is possible.

It is those people who, behind the headlines and behind the smokescreen of the troubles, are the real side to a story that the world should hear.

This is the reason for so much that is difficult to explain or understand. For it is among those same decent people that the seeds of division, the suspicions and the enmity exist which make it possible for terrorism, racketeering, alienation and mistrust to haunt relationships and destroy lives.

To listen to these people is to understand something of what uncertainty which leads to fear is really like. To live as one of them is to risk becoming so identified with their prejudices that objective judgement becomes an impossibility. Perhaps the greatest danger is that you fail to see that there are lessons to be learned from what is happening. Lessons there must be, for this story is not just about violence and bigotry. It is about people. It is their story.

One evening at a time in the late 60s when local church bodies responded to growing unrest and communal confrontation by organising street patrols of clergy and laity to try to diffuse situations of tension, the group in which I was working came face to face with a mob which had surrounded a home in a predominantly Protestant area. Clearly, their intention was to evict the Roman Catholic family who had lived there for some time. How they proposed to do so was not yet clear, but despite the confusion and anger it was soon clear to us that, short of physical force, nothing would stop them. Someone whispered to me that the home was empty except for a child who had been seen running into the back garden. I slipped round to the back of the home without any clear idea of what I could achieve. There was no sign of any child but my attention was drawn to the sound of crying coming from the coal bunker. I opened the door and found a terrified eight-year-old girl hiding behind a pile of coal. Without thinking, I lifted her out and ran. Many years have passed since that night and many of the issues I try to address in this book seem far removed from the frightened eyes of that child. But the events of that night have never left me.

The troubles in Northern Ireland have a long and agonising history. The ingredients are complex and the suspicions and divisions which have manifested themselves have brought great suffering and tragedy to this community. The complexities of religious and political alienation, the divisions between and within communities have at times amazed, disgusted and caused total disbelief to the outside world.

Attempts to find solutions have varied from the dramatic to the urge to make progress slowly. Successive governments in Great Britain and the Republic of Ireland have become involved. Issues of security, questions of political judgement, grandiose schemes of reform, policies of fair employment, changes in educational programmes and methods of allocating homes have all been attempted. Terrorism and paramilitary activity have brought death and suffering to so many homes and families. Intimidation and protection rackets have produced distrust and instability. Atrocities such as the bombing of the La Mon Restaurant and the Enniskillen massacre have focused world attention on the Province. Generations of children have grown into adulthood without experiencing what would be called 'normality' in other parts of the United Kingdom.

My own ministry has been exercised in this atmosphere of tension and division. I have seen acts of unbelievable human courage; shared days of immense human sadness and suffering; seen political manipulation and expediency as well as individual acts of great vision. I have talked and listened. I have experienced moments of hope and moments of despair. Where does the future lie? What real hope is there for a people who can show degrees of warmth, compassion, understanding and generosity second to none and yet find themselves prisoners of a situation where the judgement of the world is that they seem to tolerate violence, division and bigotry?

Conflict is a fact of human history. But conflict is not always a negative in human relationships. It can be positive and it can point the way to human stability and understanding. The lessons of the past twenty-five years in Northern Ireland may not always appear to be appreciated by the people most involved. But lessons there are in plenty. To see the problems of human relationships in Northern Ireland as essentially parochial is understandable if you live and work here, but I cannot escape the conclusion that what we are experiencing has implications and meaning on a much wider canvas. Finding a solution for a community in conflict, however small, involves the largest human problems: identity, communication, community confidence and the human spirit as well as 'reconciliation'. The ingredients of reconciliation have proved to be as elusive and apparently contradictory as the conflict it seeks to address. Issues which would appear to have little connection in areas of peace and harmony suddenly take on a new urgency when people are dying at the hands of assassins because of their religious or political identity.

It is in this seemingly endless scenario of contradiction, misunderstanding and suspicion, that ordinary people live their lives of hope, ambition, love and fear. They deserve a future which has so far eluded them. Their hopes are themselves an amalgam of what they have inherited and what circumstances beyond their control mean for their daily lives. At the end of the day, we are talking about ordinary human beings – we are talking about people, but we are thinking about people who have experienced difficulties which deserve to be placed in a wider context if the world is to begin to see any long-term purpose in what they have endured.

I sometimes wonder what became of that little child hiding in a coal bunker. She was part of the scene. Her future lay in hands other than her own. She was a victim of events, feelings and emotions which lie far back in history. But her right was to inherit a place once termed 'the land of saints and scholars', which has become the very antithesis of what most would describe as a Christian country.

2
1968 QUESTIONS

The year 1968 marked a significant point in the recent story of Northern Ireland.

Picture a typical motorway with traffic flowing freely and in order. Suddenly a car crashes into the central reservation and is immediately struck by another. The drivers are eventually lifted out of their crashed vehicles and transported, gravely ill, to hospital. For a time they are in intensive care, where the finest and most sophisticated treatments then known are available and provided for them. Gradually, their condition improves and they are moved to a general ward in which relatives and friends are able to visit them. The line of visitors is long. They file into the ward and offer sympathy and advice: 'We are extremely sorry about what happened. It's good to see you improving but, you know, it should never have happened.'

Day after day the visitors call into the ward and time and again the same words are spoken. Soon the visitors begin to think that the words of advice are falling on deaf or indifferent ears, and so they stop calling. Instead, they start to comment on the crash from a distance. Soon the two victims are well enough to be released. Shortly afterwards, they are well enough to resume driving. The motorway has not really changed. But now more people are watching them. More people have ideas on why everything went wrong in the first instance. The advice the drivers received rings in their ears. Part of it seems important – part of it seems totally irrelevant, though well intentioned.

In a sense this scenario represents much of what happened to the Northern Ireland community in 1968–9. What had been gradually boiling up over years came to the point of impact: neither community would really want to accept responsibility for what happened, yet neither could really opt out. The grievances of one were eventually given utterance through the civil rights movement; the uncertainties of the other were most visibly evident in an attitude of genuine and widespread nervousness about change and an urgent defence of the status quo – a traditional return to what some would see as the 'siege mentality'. In the 1968 confrontation, both sides were to suffer, though some would argue that the greatest damage was only beginning for the Protestant majority. The treatment, intense and sophisticated, was applied to both communities, though the aim and the nature of the cure was obscure. Many of those who came to pass judgement or offer advice were professional in their interest. But there were inevitably many well-meaning though ill-informed visitors who came to the bedside with their minds already made up and their opinions formed, without really knowing what it was like to drive down that particular motorway. It wasn't that they were inexperienced motorway users. It was simply that their motorways passed through very different scenery. As time passed history alone would indicate how much of the advice was being listened to ...

Most historians find it difficult to decide at what point and in what way events led to a climax. Interpretation is by nature an individualistic exercise. So it was with the history of Northern Ireland prior to 1969. How far back into the mists of Irish history did one have to go to see the roots of that explosion of emotion and that climax of confrontation which was to mark the commencement of the current drama?

One side had little doubt. For the nationalist and Roman Catholic community the years leading to 1968 represented a period when their people felt alienated and marginalised from the common course of life in Northern Ireland. Their grievances over the discrimination in the allocation of work and houses, the denial of civil rights and the manipulation of electoral opportunities, resulting in a denial of any chance of a say in the government of their community, had resulted for them in almost universal community frustration. The degrees to which this frustration found expression depended to a large extent on individual effort. But the focal point would always remain the nature of the state itself. For most Catholics the partition of Ireland created an artificial entity in which they were subjected by the majority population to, at best, indifference, at worst, deliberate suppression. Many commentators have expressed amazement that such conditions could have prevailed as long as they did without a social and political explosion. Such a view fails to give sufficient recognition to the fact that, as history has frequently shown, social injustice, imagined or real, requires the coexistence of certain conditions before the frustration reaches a point of no-return. In Northern Ireland the build-up of frustration and claims of injustice required a moment in time when the world would listen and the methods used would have a reasonable hope of gaining sympathy rather than indifference. The civil rights march on 5 October 1968 was to mark the turn of the tide.

For Roman Catholics the civil rights issue was a new phase in their campaign of discontent. For perhaps the first time it was not nationalism *per se* which was the watchword. There was now a cry against that ultimate injustice which had for long festered just below the surface, but never far enough below to become a forlorn cry: second-class citizenship.

The basis for hoping that such a tactic would have a chance of success found its real *raison d'être* not in Northern Ireland but miles away in the activities of students on the streets of Paris and in the example of Martin Luther King in the southern states of the USA. It was the new era of community protest in the States and in Europe which was to provide the final encouragement, and to push civil rights issues in Northern Ireland over the brink.

Some years later during a visit to New Orleans, I had a lengthy conversation with the then Mayor of Atlanta, Andrew Young – a close colleague of King during the civil rights marches of the 60s. A remark he made has long remained in my mind: 'When the time is right and the idea has existed long enough there is no substitute for the voice of the streets.' The civil rights marchers of Montgomery, Alabama, and the thousands who had followed King to Washington to hear his 'I have a dream' speech fired the imagination of activists across the world. Quite suddenly people power was born. It was born out of vision, determination and endurance. It appealed to a sense of martyrdom and (significantly) it encouraged confrontation as a desirable plant for media attention and publicity. Peaceful protest may have been a feature of early 1968 but already the philosophy and the tactics were emerging which would call forth a reaction containing violence.

'It's not that we saw ourselves as leading a world revolution. There was a cause and how we did it developed as we went along,' explained Young. 'The most important thing was that people took notice – and there were enough who felt uneasy to be vulnerable in political terms.' Few people now doubt that this was close to the thinking behind the planning of the Northern Ireland Civil Rights Association.

The voices of Londonderry on 5 October 1968 may have appeared to lack the rhetoric of Martin Luther King's 'dream' in the great rally in Washington DC. We cannot now doubt that, in terms of the problems of Northern Ireland, the emotional timetable within the nationalist and Roman Catholic community was rapidly overtaking any logical timetable of reform.

The grievances of NICRA were crystalised in the phrase 'one man one vote'. While there was universal suffrage for parliamentary elections, only rate-payers had a vote in the local council elections. A key issue was that, in Londonderry, ward boundaries were aligned, so it was argued, to give a permanent advantage to unionists. The council controlled the allocation of public housing, and, given the nature and pattern of the council elections, the supporters of the Unionist Party were favoured. Thus a primary demand by the civil rights movement was for a points system which would reflect actual needs and priorities for families seeking houses. Discrimination in the allocation of houses was linked to claims of injustice in other areas of local administration and the call for the establishment of an ombudsman who would scrutinise public policy. The demands in the civil rights movement policy which were to prove crucial to Protestant and unionist reaction lay in their persistent call for an end to the Special Powers Act. This legislation had long existed as a pillar of the government's policy towards subversive terrorist activity. It included the power to arrest and detain people who were suspected of association and involvement in the IRA. But it was seen by the nationalist community as the opportunity to exercise further discrimination and to reinforce submission. To unionists, this call had more to do with the nationalist longing for an end to partition than the undoing of civil rights injustices.

It is impossible to over-emphasise the significance of this aspect of the civil rights scenario in relation to the long-term reaction of the unionist population to what was happening in 1968. It was impossible for many Protestants to distinguish between the demand for civil rights in the Roman Catholic community and what the Protestants perceived as a new attempt to raise a constitutional issue which attacked the very foundation of their stability as UK citizens. More than any other single issue, the grievances over the Special Powers Act and the way in which they were proclaimed by NICRA provided both the encouragement and the reason why many Protestants were openly antagonistic to the civil rights movement in 1968.

Outside the Province, reaction to the demands of the civil rights movement was generally sympathetic and supportive. In the United States there was widespread support among the Irish American population on the east coast and in such cities as Chicago. The apprehension in the unionist community in Northern Ireland was greatly increased by a vague and often ill-defined feeling that American public opinion was not aware of the unionist case on the constitutional issue. Leading American politicians responded to the purely civil rights dimensions of the movement in words which fuelled the view among the loyalist groupings in Northern Ireland that the overlap between what may be termed humanitarian questions and the question of the existence of the Province within the United Kingdom presented a real threat to their future. Not for the first time, suspicion of motives made its own unique contribution to the dominant fear that has dogged the footsteps of so many attempts to move the unionist community forward in its relations with its nationalist neighbours. In fairness, it must also be acknowledged that many unionists recognised the rightness of the demands. There was a feeling that the identification of wrongs in the Roman Catholic community, which stemmed from purely social issues, was inevitable. What made the process of reaction inevitable was the confusion over moves which were interpreted as a threat to the constitutional position of Northern Ireland, but which at the same time made people uncertain as to how far reforms could lead to changes which would themselves undermine what had for generations provided the dilemma of both the security and insecurity of the unionist position.

It is of particular interest in the light of what was to follow in later years that in 1968 churches of both the Protestant and Roman Catholic traditions began to adopt a public stance in favour of reform. Voices began to be heard from the majority community particularly, those of influential individuals in commerce and industry, urging the government to adopt measures which would meet some of the demands now being highlighted by the civil rights movement. The distinction between calls for reunification and calls for social reform was more plain in the utterances of official Protestant Church bodies than was the case in many of the public reactions of government. 'The authorities, on the other hand, could see no difference: this was the old wolf, even if it appeared to be wearing sheep's clothing.'[1]

However, the reaction of the Protestant community was a mixture of suspicious unease and shock. It was not that there was widespread denial that reform was necessary. It was more a consequence of the communal shock that demands had taken the form they did.

It is difficult to convey now, years later, the reasons for the reaction of so many Protestants to the civil rights challenge. To understand it completely is to assume an everyday acquaintance with people frightened by what they had come to perceive as years of effort to merge Northern Ireland into the Republic and into a future in which their principles and aspirations would be completely submerged in 'an alien culture'. The quest for reunification appears in Irish history time and again, not in terms of a constitutional development holding the possibility of a pluralistic state but, in the eyes of Northern Protestants, as a threat which would lead to the extinction of their ethos and culture. The very mention of any move which could result in a more favourable climate for this reunification is guaranteed to evoke passionate opposition among loyalists. Generations of Northern Protestants have come to regard all efforts to incorporate them into an all-Ireland republic with dismay. They have pointed to the perceived influence of the Roman Catholic Church, the largest denomination in the Republic, as evidence of what they most fear: the absorption of their beliefs and way of life into a state in which they would be greatly outnumbered and in which they claim to have seen little evidence that their ethos would be protected, despite protests which I have often heard from Southern Protestants that such is far from the case.

[1] Gallagher and Worrall, *Christians in Ulster* (1982), p. 40.

Frequently the decline of the Protestant population in the Republic is given as evidence of this danger. 'Republic rule is Rome rule' is a phrase which has emanated for years from loyalist platforms.

These uncertainties and fears have been easy fodder for those who most vehemently oppose Irish unity. Time and again opposition to reunification has made its own significant contribution to the suspicions of Northern unionists when faced with any approaches from the South. The call for a more pluralistic state, in which their identity would be safeguarded, has been in general confined to a more sophisticated approach. Outright opposition has marked the attitude of the majority. While it has fluctuated in intensity at times because of other more pressing demands, it has never been far from the thoughts of Protestants, whose fears too many from within their own ranks have been prepared to exploit. This has provided the history of the Irish people with chapter upon chapter of emotional rather than intellectual reactions, which have all too frequently resulted in violence.

So it was in 1968. On 5 October the world's media carried pictures and graphic accounts of the violence which erupted both during and following the civil rights march in Derry. The week of disturbances which followed in different parts of Northern Ireland brought extensive media attention to the situation. Marches by civil rights sympathisers were counteracted by similar demonstrations organised by the Reverend Ian Paisley and his followers; students were to form the People's Democracy; and the phenomenon of street confrontation became an almost daily occurrence.

In human history facts are sacred: in Irish history interpretation is if anything more significant. The events of 1968 have been carefully documented in countless studies of the story of Northern Ireland. Interpretations of their significance over the years since that time have varied between a condemnation of the reaction to normal and justified demands, to a condemnation of deliberate manipulation of a reform movement by people whose ultimate aims extend far beyond the redress of human rights.

It is ironic that the twenty years leading up to the dramatic events of 1968 had been a period of relative peace in Northern Ireland. Or perhaps it would be more accurate to describe the 50s and 60s as a time when there was an absence of outward conflict. In the immediate aftermath of the Second World War, the Northern Ireland government made concerted efforts to attract foreign investment in the form of industry and commerce which had been largely successful. This investment held out the hope of improved employment prospects for the Roman Catholic community – a hope of better things to come which were already reflected in the benefits of the welfare state for the poorer sections of society where there were relatively large numbers of Roman Catholics. Free secondary education introduced by the Education Act of 1947 soon resulted in an increase in the numbers of the minority community gaining university degrees. The seven-year IRA campaign, which came to an end in 1962 with a declaration that it would now concentrate on political activity, had gradually subsided through a falling off in support in traditional republican areas. There was also definite evidence that a growing number of Roman Catholics saw their future in a Northern context rather than in a united Ireland, although such a shift in opinion owed as much to some wishful thinking by unionists as it did to definite analysis. The change in traditional stances was further testified to by the loss of the two Sinn Fein seats at Westminster and the tentative suggestions that Roman Catholics might be welcomed within the Unionist Party. When Lord Brook-eborough retired in 1963, nationalists viewed the election of Captain Terence O'Neill, who had already spoken of his wish to build bridges between the two traditions, as a victory for the moderates. When O'Neill and the Irish Prime Minister Sean Lemass exchanged visits, despite vigorous protest by loyalist groups, the 60s seemed set fair for a new era of peace if not total reconciliation.

How far this period in fact represented new alignment and new approaches has been seriously questioned by many commentators.

> There were many warning signals, remembered in retrospect but under-rated in the exuberant optimism of the 1960s, that basic attitudes had not altered significantly. Moderate values in Ulster have their mythology, just as extremist values; and like all mythologies, they ignore those pointers which challenged the popular view of the tolerant sixties. The traditional Ulster values, which would have been threatened by reconciliation, may have been in temporary hiding, but they soon emerged with banners flying.[2]

Many who had seen in O'Neill the chance of a constitutional redress of their grievances were to be disappointed. Failure to deliver in any substantial manner soon led to a strong belief in many sections of the minority community that unionism would never, in the absence of pressure, allow changes. The possibility of parliamentary pressure from Westminster was given little credence: few people yet saw further than Stormont, the Northern Ireland parliament on the outskirts of Belfast, and at Stormont unionism prevailed.

As 1969 dawned, NICRA itself was facing its own internal problems. Following two marches the O'Neill administration agreed to replace the City Council of Londonderry with a Development Commission and to appoint an ombudsman. Such success, though limited, encouraged divisions within

---

[2] John Darby (ed.), *Northern Ireland: The Background to the Conflict* (1983), pp. 24–5.

the civil rights movement. Radicals, who now formed the People's Democracy, were convinced it would be wrong to abandon methods of protest which had already achieved something. Others felt more faith should be shown in the good intentions of O'Neill's government, through the voluntary suspension of marches. However, when the People's Democracy decided to march from Belfast to Londonderry in January 1969 there was a violent confrontation at Burntollet – and gone was the vision of non-violent protest.

The cumulative effect of the events of 1968 led to a steady and discernible rise in inter-community tension. Fear of attack from outsiders by both communities and the invasion of the nationalist Lower Falls area of Belfast by a mob which left 7 dead and 3,000 homeless, riots in Strabane, Londonderry and Belfast, police action in the Roman Catholic Bogside area of Derry which resulted in violent rioting, and nights of sectarian attack across the Province set the scene for direct intervention by Westminster. On 14 August 1969, convinced that public order had totally disintegrated and that the Royal Ulster Constabulary could no longer maintain law and order, the British government sent the army into Londonderry and the following day into Belfast.

Once more, for republicans the symbols of historic British oppression had returned to Ireland. At first, in those early days of our present troubles, the army was viewed by the Roman Catholic community as a protective force providing a shield in their areas from attacks by loyalists and the RUC. This view was widely held in areas such as the Bogside in Derry and the Falls in Belfast. Troops were greeted with tea, sandwiches and cakes. The barbed-wire barriers that were erected at the entrance to nationalist areas provided reassurance to those who had felt not only threatened by events but who were among the first to sense an emotion which would soon engulf both communities, but for different reasons: fear.

To some commentators there was a sense of *déjà vu* about it all. Within traditional loyalist areas such as the Shankill and east Belfast, there was a strange feeling that much was getting back to normal – there was even a sense in which people welcomed what they saw as a return to certainty. There had been much that grassroots Protestantism could not come to terms with when reform was in the air. It was, after all, 'us and them'. The warnings of right-wing politicians were being proved to be correct after all. Memories of the past were passed on by one generation to another – and a new generation was discovering that 'after all, nothing has changed.'

I recall a conversation with some teenagers in a coffee bar. They were somehow excited by the riots and had an unconcealed yet grudging admiration for those 'who are standing up for themselves at last'. One lad of about eighteen had little doubt about the future: 'It'll always be the same. If you give them an inch, they'll take a mile. It's either us or them – and it'll never change.' Such a fatalistic outlook had a familiar ring to it: the tragedy was that he wasn't alone in his opinion. For many loyalists the civil rights movement was only a cover, and moves for reform or unionist liberalism was merely appeasement. The words from a loyalist platform in Coleraine were gladly taken up: 'it's a rebellion we face.'

Sectarianism is one of the constant threads in the story of Northern Ireland. It is one to which we will have to return again. In those early days of 1969, it was visible not in collective actions by paramilitaries but in the fear and reality of mob violence. Motivated by rumour, fanned into life by individuals and small groups and manifested in mob and crowd instincts, it was a real and devastating fear. The petrol bomb, the brick and the homemade missile hurled at homes and shops; attacks on police patrols and individuals, all usually led to riot situations in many areas of Belfast and Londonderry. Behind the scenes, however, something much more sinister was happening.

Much of the tension was in particular areas. In east Belfast, which was predominantly Protestant and loyalist, the streets in the shadow of the shipyard along the Newtonards Road; in new housing estates on the outskirts of the city where many had moved to live away from those same streets, and particularly in areas where the two traditions faced each other in close proximity, events were being interpreted in only one way. This was the long-awaited republican attack which would eventually lead to a united Ireland. Civil rights demonstrations were one thing: no one was really taken in by them. There was a more important principle at issue.

Given the traditional instability, suspicion and fears in grassroots Prot-estantism it was predictable that unease would lead to action – and that action would be ripe for a particular sort of leadership. In community halls and pubs, in clubs and private homes there was one dominant thought – how can our area be defended? In many instances during the next few years makeshift barricades were erected at the entrance to housing estates and vigilante groups were set up to patrol at night. Defence was the watchword. Strange cars were watched, people's movements checked, and in the back-ground there were always those who were ready to suggest even more radical methods. People moved away from areas where they felt exposed or at special risk. Roman Catholics moved nearer their kith and kin; Protestants moved deeper into the heartland of loyalism.

Sectarianism and sectarian fears, uncovered by events which at times seemed out of real control, were the beginnings of the division of Northern Ireland into clearly defined tribal areas. The scene was set for the estab-lishment of organised paramilitary activity.

As a rector in a new estate on the outskirts of east Belfast I recall the night that, along with other clergy, I was invited to a community hall to meet those worried about defending themselves. A local community association which had concerned itself with the state of footpaths, street lighting and refuse collection, wanted to talk about other things. There were strangers; no one knew who they were. The case was plausible. 'We need to protect our young people and we need to make sure there is no trouble here – no matter what happens anywhere else.' The mood was ripe for action, although as yet untouched by organised paramilitary thinking.

Remembering that meeting now, years later, the depth and intensity of that fear remain vivid to me. When a local community has watched violence elsewhere portrayed in the media, and such visions are added to growing insecurity; when traditional threats re-emerge to enforce the 'I told you so' mentality; and when such ingredients come together in Northern Ireland with its history of sectarian instability, what can be considered in another age and from another perspective irrational takes on the appearance of the normal – or at least the inevitable. Questions which now seem obvious and reasonable – could it all have been stopped there and then? or, could no one see what was happening and do something? – are rarely asked in the heat of the moment.

On such an evening a frightened community was in fact encouraging something which seemed almost reasonable in the light of violence elsewhere. Stories were told of mob violence, stories which gained in horror and colour the more they were told.

In Protestant Belfast the Ulster Defence Association, the UDA, was being born.

In Roman Catholic enclaves fear was a reality. Attacks had begun and a fear of the unknown was preventing rational reaction. At one level, frustration at what were seen as deliberate attempts by loyalists to confront and overcome the calls for the redress of traditional grievances and the replaying of a scene all too familiar to the Roman Catholic community where promises of alleviation were unfulfilled, turned the glimmer of hope into a new sort of doubt about the future – and doubt led back to sectarian fear. Moderation was pushed to the side. Protection was the watchword here just as it was in Protestant ghettoes. But unlike the Protestant community, here there were precedents, there were structures, there were even more vivid memories to be stirred of what was done in other years by other people.

In January 1970 the Provisional IRA was formed. Not for the first or last time in the history of Northern Ireland, for Protestant and Roman Catholic, for loyalists and nationalists, there was the same thought. 'We've seen it all before.'

3
TERROR
UNLEASHED

The hourly news broadcast usually carries the news first. 'Reports are coming in of a shooting in County Armagh. There are no details yet. Security forces are at the scene.' Perhaps an hour later the phone rings.

This pattern has become very familiar and yet no two cases are the same. A son or father left home as usual to go to work in the factory, the shop or on the farm. There'd been nothing unusual about the parting. Perhaps he was a part-time member of one of the security forces. Alternatively, he may have had a job which could have been interpreted as supportive of the security forces or the government. He had become a target. They had waited for him because the homework had been done and his movements and habits were well known. The hail of bullets or the detonation of a bomb added one more statistic to the figures some government department would publish at the end of the year.

The story in the evening paper would have the details. Later, a statement would be phoned to someone in the media. He had been killed because his uniform or his work represented something which must not be allowed to stand in the way of the aims of a terrorist organisation. To take his life would bring headlines, and headlines are the oxygen on which such violence lives. No publicity is bad publicity, even if, just sometimes, it goes wrong. The wrong person is killed. A nun drives into a blast and is killed. A child is caught in cross-fire. The wrong home is attacked. Regret is expressed. It is the inevitable price of the armed struggle.

Behind the headlines there is news to be broken, relatives to be told. Shock and disbelief give way to sorrow and grief. Funerals take place. Condemnation fills the air. There are the inevitable calls for 'better security', for the reintroduction of internment or bringing back the death penalty. There are even sometimes questions at Westminster: reassurance that everything possible is being done to apprehend those responsible. Locally, there will be frustration and anger. There will be those who talk of retaliation, and at times the awesome spectre of tit-for-tat killing becomes a reality.

But nothing will replace the human life that has gone. One more statistic has been added to the list. One more widow has begun to pick up the pieces of her life and little children have begun to grow up without a father. It is virtually impossible to analyse the dimensions of human grief in such circumstances. The uselessness of such sacrifices should have brought a community to its knees after over twenty years. The fact that it has not, only makes the task of the sociologist and the commentator more difficult. There is no pattern here, they say. People are resilient and life goes on. There are indications of a new determination to keep life normal and to honour the sacrifice as they think best. But to detect an overall pattern is impossible.

Terrorism takes many forms. In Northern Ireland, where deep community division has its origins far back in history, paramilitary activity has found a natural stage when there is political vacuum. On the one hand, the various segments of the Provisional IRA made 'defence' of the Roman Catholic community their role in the late 50s, the 60s and early 70s. Gradually, justification for this began to pale as community life was reformed and many social grievances were removed. Added to this, the treatment of many Roman Catholics at the hands of the IRA in their own areas, and the growing disenchantment with atrocities which did not appear to be changing the overall situation were eroding support for the freedom fighters. More and more, the Roman Catholic community was itself becoming the victim of republican terrorism. There was increasing political condemnation of violence on the part of such parties as SDLP, which was to become one of the most significant political developments of recent years: the emergence of a constitutional Roman Catholic political party which was prepared to engage in and to succeed in local and parliamentary representation.

On the other side, various loyalist paramilitary organisations have been responsible for atrocities of horrific proportions. I recall those days in the late 60s when tension was high and in many Protestant housing estates the cry was 'defence'. Rumours were rife, and it was so easy to feel that in a short time IRA attacks would be launched against such communities. People were urged to be on their guard and vigilantes were a common sight on the streets of east Belfast, which the Ulster Defence Association and the Ulster Volunteer Force grew out of. It was only a matter of time before defence became attack. Sectarian murder of Roman Catholics, the atrocities of the notorious 'Shankill Butchers' and the parades of hooded figures in para-military dress may have been a reaction to events elsewhere, yet little could be done to minimise the natural fear such developments were to produce in the Roman Catholic community. There were those Protestant politicians who were only too ready to exploit fears and to encourage by word and action the belief that, if government was powerless to protect communities, then people had a moral right to defend themselves.

In Northern Ireland's violent story there is one dominant player – the Provisional Irish Republican Army, PIRA, the Provisionals. Earl Mountbatten, Airey Neave, Ian Gow, people attending a Remembrance Day service at Enniskillen, guests at a function in a suburban hotel, Conservative Party politicians in Brighton and hundreds of men, women and children have been their victims. Millions of pounds worth of damage have been done to buildings by explosion and fire-bomb. Condemned by many as terrorists, applauded by others as freedom fighters, they are champions of an ancient cause to some, instigators of terror and oppression to others. At once the object of fascination to commentators and of loathing to others, they have defied security policy moves, internment, trial without jury. They have claimed a degree of righteousness for their struggle which even many in the community from which they have come view as a blasphemy to the cause of Irish republicanism. They have at times held whole areas to ransom and they are capable of causing deep fear throughout a whole community. Their ability to deny courts the sort of evidence that is needed for convictions is a constant source of frustration to a police force which openly admits at times that 'we know who they are.'

The challenge PIRA poses to traditional thinking on what constitutes democracy, and how far a democracy can go to suppress terrorism without denying to the majority of people basic human rights, is only part of the dilemma to which we will have to return. There are many questions which we have not yet been able to answer. The brutality and atrocities perpetrated by PIRA, its ability to cause such suffering, its apparent refusal to listen to the condemnation which fills the air continually and its usual denial of calls to adopt political rather than violent methods have all led to the opinion which is expressed in so many ways and by so many people that they are 'mindless psychopaths', 'cowards' and 'thugs'.

Such reactions are entirely understandable, and stem as much from the frustration of a community endlessly victim to violence as from the normal human reaction to physical brutality. None the less, like it or not, PIRA is a part of the problem. Wish it though we do that they would simply cease to exist, the fact remains they are here, in our midst. Brutality and injustice accompany their actions, but I feel it is naïve to think for one moment that their actions are 'mindless'. The sophistication of world terrorism is accepted by experts in the security field. The hard core of dedicated activists are well trained and well briefed. The cell system now means that their internal security is extremely difficult to break down. Their ability to withstand interrogation is well known. Their methods have the hallmark of preparation and planning.

Much has been written on the significance and activities of the IRA. Their particular brand of terrorism is well documented and rarely fails to catch the world's headlines. To understand how they fit into the overall picture of Northern Ireland some indication is needed of how we have reached this point: a point at which much has changed since 1968, and yet a point at which so much tragically remains the same.

In Northern Ireland, on the British mainland and even in Europe, the Provisionals have brought suffering and devastation. The events of 1968-9 saw the emergence of Provo terrorism, and the emotions stirred within both communities at that time set the stage for violence. Yet few could then have imagined that two decades later this society would continue to be convulsed by a sophisticated and dedicated terrorist force.

In December 1969, the old IRA Army Council, by a majority of three to one, decided to turn its back on abstentionism and physical terrorism. Its decision to grant at least token recognition to the three parliaments most directly involved in the Irish scene, Westminster, Dublin and Stormont, was a break with traditional republican policy. Such a move brought to the surface the conflict between militancy and political activity. The militants then broke away to form PIRA, and the movement was split in two. The old IRA, the Officials, were by-passed by the new grouping which was to find it much easier to identify with the feelings of republican areas in Belfast and Derry, and in the fast-moving events of the summer of 1969 the IRA had lost much of its credibility in areas where it had drawn traditional support. The burning of homes and the attacks on parts of the Catholic community had failed to produce the anticipated, and indeed promised, reaction from the IRA: for many in those areas, the IRA had not provided the protection expected when the need was greatest. Later, the Scarman Commission, established to investigate the causes of the troubles in that early period, came to the conclusion that, while there had been IRA influence in the 1969 riots, the organisation had not in fact started the violence. But the perception remained that the IRA had failed to deliver. I remember seeing a slogan scrawled on a gable wall in the Lower Falls area of Belfast: 'IRA – I Ran Away.'

Contrasts were drawn between the readiness of the Derry Citizens' Defence Association, which included in its membership some active IRA personnel, to act, and the inactivity of the IRA in Belfast.

Opinion in the Unionist government was united in believing that there was strong IRA influence and involvement in the civil rights movement. It was even claimed that in the early summer of 1969, two-thirds of the actual control of all civil rights associations in Northern Ireland lay in the hands of members of the republican clubs. There was also a widespread belief that the citizens' defence committees which had grown up in urban republican areas throughout Northern Ireland were simply a front for the IRA.

The unease and uncertainty, helped by the fragmentation of the traditional republican movement, added to the influence of the Provisionals who could now recruit many young people alongside a sizeable proportion of older and more experienced survivors of former IRA campaigns. The command structures of the old IRA provided the basis for the Provisional organisation and arms shipped into Ireland from the Continent and Britain, supplemented by some supplied from the Republic, gave it the means to do what the old IRA had failed to do. By the summer of 1970, it was believed that PIRA had some 1,500 active members, and its growing strength of purpose contributed to the greatly increased level of violence in that year as compared with 1969.

During 1970, 23 civilians and 2 policemen were killed: of the 153 explosions in the Province it was estimated that all but 25 of these were caused by the Provisionals. Security sources believed that much of the increased street violence had also been incited by PIRA. By 1971 the level of activity had increased further and responsibility for the majority of the 304 explosions in the first half of that year was directly attributed to the Provisionals. Official security sources claimed that children were being used by PIRA to throw petrol bombs at the troops. During that same period the antagonism between the two arms of the IRA boiled over into a bitter and violent feud and there was much evidence of internal violence.

Demands for internment without trial for members of PIRA began to appear as early as 1969 within the loyalist community. This call gained in momentum, becoming most obvious when three young Scottish soldiers were murdered on the outskirts of Belfast in March 1971. Faced with a marked escalation in the violence by August, the government had 454 people taken into custody in a widespread security operation. 350 were eventually interned, in the belief that such a move would deprive PIRA of its most experienced activists and, consequently, reduce its ability to cause violence. It was argued that, only by taking out of society those known to be actively involved, and by doing so in one swift action, the situation would be sufficiently defused to enable the community to come to terms with what was happening on the larger reform canvas. By 1972 the number interned was to rise to 900, yet internment in 1971–2 was ineffective because many people were arrested who had little if any involvement in the terrorist campaign: arrests were based on insufficient intelligence.

Thus the consequences were catastrophic in community terms. A large section of the Catholic population lost any real hope of involvement in peaceful change. Violence increased as support grew rapidly for PIRA, world opinion moved in favour of a community that was seen as the victim of grave injustice, and any faith that security policies alone might end the conflict was undermined. From the introduction of internment on 8 August until 31 December 1971, 46 members of the security forces died, 97 civilians lost their lives, 1,437 shooting incidents were recorded and there were over 700 explosions in Northern Ireland. PIRA was credited with responsibility for all but one of the killings.

Anti-internment propaganda was now rampant in the Irish-American quarters of the States and at home PIRA had built up an arsenal of weapons and ammunition. The use of car-bombs, incendiary devices left in shops and public buildings and explosions detonated with growing expertise became a way of life for most of the people of Northern Ireland. The propaganda war in the States, fired by the mistakes of internment and the traditional anti-British feeling of many Irish immigrants, produced a steady flow of financial succour for PIRA. On a visit to America I was left in no doubt as to the depth of feeling in traditional Irish areas. For most, PIRA was the 'army of liberation'; money collected in the bars of Chicago, New York and San Francisco was 'for the support of IRA families and the dependants of those interned by the Brits', and the only solution to the problems of Ireland was the removal of all vestiges of British rule. This propaganda war was made full use of by the lobby system even on Capitol Hill, and many Irish-American politicians became active in support of 'the liberation movement'. It was to take years to convince many of the decision-makers in Washington that there was another side to the story. Once more, attitudes building upon traditional hostility had been ignited by contemporary action: internment became so quickly the ally of years of 'injustice' and terrorism the 'armed struggle against the imposition of colonialism'. The momentum of this propaganda war was intense and its success was to provide the basis for a feeling in the Protestant community which is still apparent today, that a majority of official American interest in the troubles has been over-influenced by 'one side of the story' only.

Anti-police feeling stemming from the events of 1968 and 1969 grew in republican areas in the aftermath of internment. The tragic events of Bloody Sunday in Derry when British troops killed thirteen people in riots after a demonstration gave PIRA added support.

During March 1972, Provisional Sinn Fein, the political wing of PIRA, demanded the abolition of Stormont and the declaration by Britain that it would withdraw from Northern Ireland together with a total amnesty for political prisoners. It proposed that four provincial parliaments should be established for Ireland. To support this demand PIRA called a three-day ceasefire which ended when there was no government response, but they repeated the exercise in June for a further thirteen days. During that second ceasefire a group of PIRA leaders was flown in secret to London for talks with William Whitelaw, Secretary of State for Northern Ireland. Despite the hopes of the British government that this meant a move from military to political activity, it came to nothing. In fact, the violence which followed was more intense and prolonged than anything which had gone before. During July 1972 74 civilians and 21 members of the security forces lost their lives: there were 2,800 shootings and some 200 explosions. To add to this upsurge, loyalist assassinations of Catholics increased dramatically despite the presence of so-called no-go areas. Such areas were carefully guarded by paramilitaries of both communities and eventually the government moved to destroy the barricades and open up such ghettoes to 'normal security cover'.

In 1973 the pattern of PIRA violence continued when 171 civilians and 79 members of the security forces were killed. On the one hand, PIRA attacked police and troops: on the other, loyalists stepped up their sectarian assassinations of Catholics. In February PIRA warned the main loyalist grouping, the Ulster Defence Association, UDA, that it was prepared to take serious action to prevent sectarian killing in the Catholic community, but no one was quite sure how far it was prepared to implement such threats.

In May 1973 government figures were issued which claimed that since 1969 123 PIRA members had been killed. Officially, PIRA admitted to losing 99 activists.

In 1974, a desire on the part of PIRA that loyalist opposition to the Sunningdale agreement and the possibility of power-sharing in local government should be allowed to bring its own special pressure on the British government caused a falling off in the general level of republican violence. In May the loyalist strike which paralysed Northern Ireland and caused the downfall of the power-sharing executive took public attention temporarily away from the Provisionals, who were experiencing serious internal difficulties after the arrests of key personnel and the 'leaking' of information on organisation and policies to the security forces. In a speech at Westminster, Prime Minister Harold Wilson disclosed that documentation seized by the security forces contained details of a 'specific and calculated' plan to take over certain key buildings in Belfast and to occupy loyalist areas of the city through the inciting of intersectarian hatred, chaos and violence. By the end of the year PIRA faced intense pressure from the increased anti-terrorist legislation at Westminster following the Birmingham bombings. Many saw the readiness of the PIRA leadership to hold a secret meeting with Protestant clergy at Feakle in the Republic as an indication of growing apprehension as much as a political ploy. The consequence of these Feakle talks was a burst of activity prior to Christmas. The Secretary of State, Merlyn Rees, listened to the clergymen's account of the talks and one of them met the chief of staff of the PIRA's army council in Dublin. All that Merlyn Rees would say in public was that the government would be willing to respond to any genuine cessation of violence. The immediate consequence of the Birmingham atrocities was to unify Westminster in support of the Prevention of Terrorism Act and to build up new degrees of anti-Irish feeling on the mainland of Britain. The Prevention of Terrorism legislation provided for the banning of PIRA in Great Britain, the detention of suspects without charge for up to seven days and for the expulsion of people considered to be a security risk to either Northern Ireland or the Republic.

In December PIRA announced a further ceasefire to allow the government time to consider the proposals put to the clergy at Feakle. Loyalist suspicion at what 'was going on' was rampant. But it was met by government assurances that there was no question of negotiation with the IRA. On 10 February the Provisionals extended the ceasefire into an open-ended truce as a recognition of what they claimed had been the result of discussions with British officials. An elaborate plan was set up to monitor the ceasefire through 'incident centres' in republican areas of Belfast and Derry. The original loyalist suspicions now became even more intense. There was talk of a 'sell-out' to the Provisionals and extremist loyalists mounted a campaign of anti-government propaganda. The SDLP became worried that too much credibility was being afforded to the Provos through these contacts with the government. Thus the ceasefire became more vulnerable and, when four soldiers lost their lives in south Armagh during July, the government began to question the ability of the Provisionals' leadership to control their members. The continuing assassination of Catholics was seen as the cause of the murder of fifty-seven Protestants in tit-for-tat actions. Loyalist opinion now identified what it believed to be a 'soft' policy by the security forces towards republicans in so far as only those activists against whom specific charges could be brought were being arrested. There was a widespread belief that PIRA had used the prolonged ceasefire to re-group and re-arm. In south Armagh (which Merlyn Rees described as 'bandit country') even during the ceasefire, six Protestants were murdered in a raid on an Orange Hall to bring to twenty-one the number of killings in that border area. In September no fewer than twenty-one explosions were recorded in one day in the Province and in November the government closed the incident centres. Before Christmas the last of those interned since 1971 were released.

Taken as a whole the toll of death in 1975 reflected the ceasefire period. Thirty members of the security forces had been killed, twenty fewer than in 1974: shootings dropped from 3,206 to 1,803 and explosions from 685 to

399. But 1976 was to see the murder of ten Protestant workers by PIRA in south Armagh following the deaths of five Catholics the day before. Catholic fear of revenge killings led to the arrival of the SAS in south Armagh. In February the death in prison in England of the IRA hunger-striker Frank Stagg finally marked the end of the ceasefire. Terrorism inspired by the Provisionals again became intense. By the autumn the new Northern Ireland Secretary, Roy Mason, claimed that 697 members of PIRA had been charged despite the fact that there were 297 murders attributed in the main to the Provisionals and the number of explosions was double that for 1975.

In 1977 there was some evidence that increased security activity was beginning to have its effect on PIRA. One result of this was widespread reorganisation of structures within the movement, new command lines of communication and an increase in 'punishment shootings' in republican areas as the organisation sought to strengthen its hold. In that year 29 soldiers were killed, but the total death toll had fallen to 112.

The fire-bomb attack on the La Mon House Hotel at the beginning of 1978 killed 12 people and badly injured a further 23. This atrocity shocked even PIRA's most ardent supporters. The 'dirty protest' by republican prisoners at the Maze Prison over the withdrawal of special category privileges took some attention away from terrorism on the streets. Attacks in Europe, the murder of a deputy prison governor and attacks on many towns and villages gave new credence to the government's belief that PIRA had manpower sufficient to sustain violence for five years. These same sources showed a new recognition for the 'professionalism' of the IRA. Its expertise and organisation had improved immensely. Gone were the expressions of 'mindless thugs' and in their place officialdom spoke of dedication, sophistication and international terrorist links. The intensity of attacks on premises in the first half of 1979 appeared to justify such estimates.

The murder of Earl Mountbatten in August 1979 and the massacre of 18 soldiers near Warrenpoint not only caused the cancellation of a visit by the Pope to Armagh but brought new pressure on the Irish government to toughen its policy towards IRA activity based in the Republic. When Pope John Paul II came to Ireland he issued a clear and unequivocal call to PIRA to stop its terrorism. His words of pleading to the men and women of violence reiterated the calls of churchmen – stop now and seek a different path. The response of PIRA was equally clear-cut. It could not 'in all conscience' do as he had asked.

The pattern of IRA violence in the 80s showed a definite change. From targets such as shops, offices, commercial plants, hotels and security bases, and attacks on security personnel and prison officers, a new propaganda war was to develop. The promotion of the hunger strike campaign, the encouragement of H-Block protests and Provisional Sinn Fein candidates at elections in the Republic in 1981–2 and the Northern Ireland Assembly election in 1982 marked a new attention to political activity. The demarcation between terrorist action and the role of Sinn Fein became more difficult to define. It appeared that increased attention to political activity had the backing of PIRA, and their ability to force the closure of shops and premises in republican areas in support of demonstrations and community-wide protests provided the most obvious sign of linkage. A new phenomenon appeared in the form of the 'supergrass', the informer who not only threatened the internal security of the movement but brought a new edge to the ability of the security forces to weaken the close-knit structure of PIRA. Informers such as Christopher Black, Robert Quigley and Raymond Gilmour led to the charging of many alleged PIRA members before the courts. Bringing cases before the courts in Northern Ireland in this way provoked widespread criticism within the nationalist community and official protests were made by the Irish government. The late Cardinal O'Fiaich coined the phrase 'internment under another name'. The fact that many convictions prompted by informers were successfully brought to the Appeal Court, and that several informers retracted their stories, eventually brought an end to the widespread use of the system.

The hunger strike in 1981 undoubtedly produced increased recruitment and sympathy, and while it was believed there were 500 hard-core terrorists operating in Northern Ireland in 1980 the deaths of 10 strikers produced a well of support from Irish republican sympathisers in the States and Europe. But by then damage had been done to the PIRA structure. Again within PIRA, leadership became divided between the influence of such opinion-makers as Gerry Adams, soon to become Sinn Fein's MP in west Belfast, who argued that republicanism required a greater political impetus, and of those determined to pursue the armed struggle. It was in 1981 that the first Northern Ireland MP was killed in the troubles, when the Official Unionist, the Reverend Robert Bradford, lost his life. Some 42 murders in 1982 were attributed directly to PIRA, an increase in security operations in the Republic posed difficulties of supply for the IRA and a consequent lull in activity ended with an attempt on the life of the Lord Chief Justice in Belfast.

In the winter of 1982 3 policemen were killed by a landmine explosion in County Armagh and a few weeks later 3 PIRA members were shot dead by the RUC on the outskirts of Lurgan. Immediately, accusations of a 'shoot to kill' policy filled the air. Questions were asked about the chances of arrest rather than shooting, and this controversy was to continue to surface from time to time. The existence of specialised anti-terrorist units within the police and army was admitted and such admissions added to the impression on the part of sympathisers that a policy of 'shoot first' and 'ask questions afterwards' was being adopted. Full use of the propaganda value of such accusations was made. Terms such as 'minimum force' and 'trigger action' became ready-made headlines and added to the propaganda effort throughout the world.

It was clear that PIRA felt it necessary to convince the public in mainland Britain that it was futile to maintain a 'British presence' in Northern Ireland. In 1984 a MORI poll indicated that some 50 per cent of the British public believed that any attempt to solve the Ulster question needed the cooperation of the IRA. Whatever encouragement the organisation received from such analyses, the need to convince British public opinion that life here was far removed from what was being portrayed as 'normal' by government sources became paramount. The attack on Margaret Thatcher and her government colleagues at Brighton brought world coverage and the inevitable increase in anti-terrorist measures throughout the British Isles. In 1985 9 RUC officers died in a mortar attack on their Newry base and attacks intensified on police stations in the border areas. Threats increased against civilian contractors who were working to repair security installations and further deaths to civilians followed. An increasing number of commercial interests announced that they had now ceased to supply the security forces as a result of threats. Evidence of international links between the IRA and sources of supply such as Libya helped to place PIRA in a world terrorist context. Despite atrocities such as Enniskillen where 11 civilians died in an explosion at the Remembrance Day ceremony, and incidents where 'deep regret' was expressed for the deaths of 'innocent people', there was little sign of a relaxation in the 'armed struggle'. But the cost to PIRA was mounting: 8 members were killed at Loughgall in 1987, 3 in Gibraltar and 3 more were killed in County Tyrone in 1988. However, their campaign against the security forces in the same period claimed 24 British personnel, 19 RUC officers and 18 members of the Ulster Defence Regiment. In the same year 3 off-duty RAF men died in Holland and a soldier was killed in Belgium.

An increased use of the car-bomb and landmines in county areas, a fresh assault on the centre of Belfast, a successful attack on a British helicopter in south Armagh, the murder of a senior judge and his wife and an attack on the home of the head of the Northern Ireland Civil Service kept up the level of death and injury.

Such were some of the landmarks in the development of republican inspired terrorism since the events of 1968. A catalogue of death and injury, damage to property and determined efforts to destabilise a community. The attacks have been prolonged and yet varied in their operation. While statistics tell their own story and it is possible to magnify efforts which on a world scale appear insignificant, when taken in relation to the size of the population of Northern Ireland they become massive.

To conclude that there is any straightforward philosophy or ideology behind the violence of the IRA would be to indulge in that degree of simplicity which has been a constant barrier to real progress in understanding Northern Ireland and is people. Their overall strategy may be conveniently designated as an end to 'British rule of the six counties'. But it is increasingly difficult to distinguish between individual acts and their purpose and longer periods of attrition and their goal. Republicanism gave birth to IRA terrorism: yet many believe, quite sincerely, that the activities of PIRA since 1969 have eroded the political or moral legitimacy of the republican philosophy. Agreement there may be on the evil of a British presence in Ireland, but the real difficulty for Irish republicanism is in deciding how that presence should be confronted. This was, after all, the real reason for the split within republicanism which made the birth of PIRA a reality. The PIRA adherence to 'national liberation' before 'national socialism' is in sharp contrast to the traditional view of the old IRA, that the real battle was for the hearts and minds of the working-class in both parts of Ireland before unification could become a priority.

If the emergence of the civil rights movement in the late 60s granted the IRA a new opportunity, that opportunity must be viewed in relation to the belief that a large proportion of the Catholic working-class lives in conditions of suppression and, indeed, repression. This condition is seen as a direct consequence of a sectarian state which owes its existence to the support of Britain. The existence of 'direct rule' from Westminster assists the republican apologist when he attempts to identify the nature of that 'British presence'. However, it must also be said that in the 1969 period the justification for military action on the part of PIRA owed more to the perceived need to protect Catholic ghettoes from attacks by loyalist mobs and the British army than it did to any philosophical dogma on the nature and meaning of that 'presence'.

It is quite easy to define the relationship between support for PIRA in traditional republican areas and the view of security force activity taken in such localities. Complaints of harassment or injustice on the part of police or army are closely related to the level of support for republican terrorism. It is a thin thread whose tension constantly changes. The actions of the security forces which arouse anger and resentment are a natural gift to the cause of PIRA recruitment and support. As one observer has expressed it:

Alienation from the state in Northern Ireland is bound to be exacerbated if those who purport to serve the state fall below its own proclaimed standards of impartiality. Such alienation is the life blood of PIRA recruitment.[3]

There have been examples of this throughout the troubles, not least during the internment period, the 'shoot-to-kill' controversies of the 80s and the periods of widescale searches of homes in south Armagh and Newry. The degree of alienation quite naturally increases in intensity when the authorities have been perceived to have turned a 'blind eye' to actions by the security forces, or when it is believed that demands for public inquiries into particular incidents are denied or at least ignored. We must remember that in the 60s a defensive role in republican areas was what their supporters demanded of the IRA. To move onto the offensive brought reaction from security forces in those areas where defence had been PIRA's primary justification. The success of recruitment and support has varied according to the republican perception of the consequences of PIRA action, but has not matched that of reaction to the actions of the security forces. Attacks on British army personnel help the 'troops out' movement and weaken the view that the army has any real role to play in Northern Ireland.

The ability of the IRA to sustain a campaign of violence over a long period has marked it out from many other world terrorist movements. As with all 'nationalist movements', a wide spectrum of individuals has identified with Irish republicanism, and this has bred an array of diverse ideologies. But the paramount consideration influencing the long-term resilience of the IRA has not been upsurges in support at particular periods, but the depth of passive support it has enjoyed. It has been argued that this is the very 'oxygen of terrorism'.

The presence of such support for individual acts of terrorist violence is doubtful. There is clear evidence of disenchantment within some republican ranks at particular excesses of IRA activity. After the Enniskillen Remembrance Day atrocity it was extremely difficult for republican apologists to offer any explanation for what had happened. Equally, when the La Mon restaurant was fire-bombed, or when civilians lost their lives because they happened 'to be in the wrong place at the wrong time', the only line which republican propaganda could take was that such unfortunate incidents 'are bound to occur in time of war'. Sinn Fein has found it difficult to give public support to the IRA in the wake of what are usually termed 'mistakes'. However, support for Active Service Units of PIRA is undoubtedly essential in the provision of 'safe houses', information and escape routes. And more

3. E. Moscon-Browne, 'Terrorism in Northern Ireland: the Case of the Provisional IRA', *Terrorism: A Challenge to the State*, ed. Juliette Lodge (1981), p. 153.

important is that passive support which contributes to the victory of Sinn Fein representatives at elections and the lack of opposition to the presence of known IRA activists in certain areas.

Sir Kenneth Bloomfield, former head of the Northern Ireland Civil Service, who retired after thirty years at the centre of government in Northern Ireland poses a question which is searching and significant: 'Is the Provisional IRA being defeated?' He continues: 'For only if it is and when it is, by a much wider range of measures than "law and order" alone, can people rule themselves – make the choices that appeal to them, un-influenced by force or the threat of force, as to how they are to be governed, where they are to live and work, whether indeed they are to live or die. In 1920 a British parliament, framing a new constitutional set-up, used classic words about "peace, order and good government". The third will never be possible without the first two.'[4]

The key to the ending of terrorism in Northern Ireland lies far beyond security policies. The key that one day must be turned lies in the creation of an atmosphere where terrorism has become irrelevant. While conditions remain in which the IRA and its supporters can argue that the only means of gaining a political objective is through violence, terrorism will continue. To turn tacit support into complete rejection must be the long-term vision. This will only be achieved when down-to-earth logic proves that there is another way to put forward long-term or short-term political objectives.

[4] Sir Kenneth Bloomfield, 'Who runs Northern Ireland?', *Fortnight Magazine* (November 1991), p. 17.

4
CIRCLE
COMPLETE

There is a widespread belief within the Protestant community of Northern Ireland that they are the real victims and casualties of the present situation, and there is a deeply-felt conviction that 'their case' has never been really understood by the outside world; that it has been misrepresented; that a grave injustice is being perpetrated when blame for the situation is laid entirely at their door. The degree to which they themselves are the victims of history or to which they as a community have contributed to their misrepresentation is of secondary importance to most of them. Their view is that the nationalist case has been accepted as the only real picture of the situation, and many Protestants continue to resent deeply the manner in which world opinion, particularly in the late 60s and early 70s, saw Protestants and loyalists as 'the voice of unreason, the voice of illogicality'.[1]

The picture portrayed in the late 60s of a strong and determined majority population suppressing all or most civil rights for the minority was apparently accepted by much of the outside world. It seemed that the world did not want to understand the loyalist position. In the United States the Irish-American lobby appeared to dominate attitudes towards Northern Ireland. At Westminster a majority of members seemed convinced that the unrest had sprung from the injustices inflicted by Protestants on Roman Catholics. The media, commentators, social and community researchers and public opinion in most of Europe appeared to Protestants to be interested in the minority alone. Protestants were seen as right-wing extremists with a traditional determination to maintain their supremacy at all costs.

Such was, and to a large extent remains, the Protestant perception of the beginnings of the present troubles. One cannot escape the conclusion that the loyalist case suffered as much in those early days from such perceptions as from a failure of presentation. Few people saw or heard a moderate or reasonable Protestant case; few if any could detect a moderate Protestant voice. There was a reasonableness about the nationalist position, a logic

[1] G. Bell, *The Protestants of Ulster* (1976), p. 21.

which history has always attached to the case of the apparent victims of circumstance.

Part of the recurring uncertainty and lack of confidence in themselves which has, I feel, plagued the Protestant community owes much to these perceptions, real or imaginary, of the late 60s and early 70s. In a way, Protestantism as a whole has never shaken off that experience, and the resentment it engendered.

What was happening to the majority community, and what was happening to its way of life, has a significance which has yet to be examined in real depth. It is the key to understanding the crisis of identity which is a primary source of the Northern Ireland problem. The effects of events on attitudes, emotions, perceptions and fears within Protestantism following the civil rights unrest of the late 60s have yet to be fully analysed.

> Since the late 1960s they have faced an upheaval that has been more mental than physical. While Catholics bore the brunt of physical suffering, their beliefs about themselves, their sense of identity, and their conviction that their demands were justified was more often strengthened than weakened by the events triggered by civil rights.[6]

The contrasts between republican-inspired violence and that which has stemmed from within the Protestant or loyalist community are significant. While world attention has most frequently concentrated on the activities of the IRA, loyalist paramilitary action has played its own devastating role in the conflict. Comparisons have often been drawn between the actions of the IRA and the 'reactions' of loyalist terrorists; the structural organisation of the IRA and the 'spasmodic' activities of the UDA or the UVF; the sophistication of the republican assassins and the 'amateurism' of the loyalist terrorist groupings; and the consistency of the IRA 'campaign' and the intervals between loyalist-inspired actions. Such distinctions are based on a comparison of the volume of paramilitary activity, and are usually linked to statistics of deaths 'claimed' by one side or the other. There are clear distinctions, yet beyond doubt the *threat* of loyalist violence has been just as central to the conflict as the occasions on which loyalist terrorists can be clearly identified as the perpetrators of death and destruction. If IRA terrorism has dictated many of the events in Northern Ireland since 1968, loyalist paramilitaries have provided the links which have made the circle of violence complete. It may be convenient to describe the activities of the main Protestant murder gangs as reactionary but there can be little doubt that a

---

[6.] Sarah Nelson, *Ulster's Uncertain Defenders* (1984), p. 11.

comparison of statistics indicates only a small part of their influence on happenings.

Retaliatory murders of Roman Catholics following an IRA atrocity have produced the real sectarian element of the troubles. If the typical loyalist terrorist reaction to the work of the IRA has been to kill at random anyone within a Catholic area, it is comparatively easy to speak in terms of reaction alone. The frequent appeals from Protestant pulpits at the funerals of IRA victims that no retaliation should take place are just one indication of the ever-present threat of loyalist terrorism. Archbishop Cahal Daly clearly identified this ingredient: 'Any Catholic, in their perverted mentality, is a suspect terrorist. Indeed, anyone encountered in a Catholic area is a presumptive "legitimate target" for assassination.'[7] Since 1968 over five hundred murders of members of the Roman Catholic community have been recorded in circumstances which can only be designated sectarian. Between 1972 and 1973 it is estimated that more than two hundred civilians were assassinated in Northern Ireland: the majority of them were victims of Protestant murder groups.

Any discussion of IRA violence will usually lead to an attempt to analyse the republican philosophy and to talk of an end to the British presence in Ulster, but it is even more difficult to find the mainspring of loyalist terrorism. As with the IRA, theories abound. Protestant-inspired sectarian killings are perpetrated by mindless psychopaths who will be found in any contemporary society but readily grasp the tribal labels of the divided society in Northern Ireland; their murders indicate the sectarian bigotry passed down to them by history and which religious/political tensions have encouraged; their work shows the real feelings which dominate the Protestant working-class areas; it was inevitable that a failure by government to deal with the IRA would prompt such responses; their actions indicate the deep fear and uncertainties of a population which feels unprotected in the face of non-stop republican assault. Yet the most popular theory, apart from the obvious identification of simple criminal behaviour patterns, is that loyalist violence stems from a widespread belief that without it their case will be ignored by a society which does not understand that 'the future of the Protestant community is at stake'.

Irrational, even unbelievable, this may seem to those who at a distance pause to consider such explanations for violence that have come from within a majority community, a community which should surely seek to maintain the moral high ground in the face of IRA terrorism, a community which frequently proclaims its adherence to law and order and which, in word at least, talks of religious freedom for all. Even if there is substance to their

---

[7] Archbishop Cahal Daly, *The Price of Peace* (1991), p. 76.

feelings of uncertainty about their constitutional future, why should the Protestant community manifest fears which have been addressed by successive British governments with the assurance that nothing can be changed in the constitutional position of Northern Ireland without the consent of this majority? How real, in other words, are those fears, and why should they find expression in naked sectarian killing?

There are other difficulties to be faced in the search for some lasting explanation for loyalist terrorism. If the root cause is anti-Catholic sectarianism, why does the level of Protestant paramilitary activity fluctuate in such a dramatic fashion? In the 70s, after the devastation of the IRA firebomb at the La Mon Restaurant, or the Enniskillen bomb, widespread retaliation in Catholic areas might have been expected. If the motivation for Protestant paramilitary action is purely political, involving 'the defence of the Protestant community' alone, it is not easy to understand the brutality of such episodes as that of the 'Shankill Butchers' when lengthy torture of victims took place before death mercifully ended their suffering. It is also difficult to reach easy conclusions when one considers the pattern of loyalist killings. The UVF was involved in a long catalogue of murders in 1975, yet appears to have remained on the perimeter of the violence during 1972 and 1973.

When community violence erupted in the late 60s, the emergence of Protestant paramilitary groupings in reaction to what was happening on the streets of Belfast and Londonderry could have been predicted. In many Protestant housing estates the UDA appeared first in the guise of a defensive organisation. They claimed to be the only means of organised defence in a community where the fear was growing that ordinary people were vulnerable to attack from without and that the normal forms of public security would be inadequate in providing that defence. But in one way it is hard to see the sectarian murder campaign against Catholics as a natural extension of that role: it is easier to see such actions as the reaction of a paramilitary organisation to organised and sustained attack by Provisionals on security forces which at convenient times could be designated as 'our security forces'.

Is it then possible to say how far such loyalist activities were linked to the prompting of politicians or community leaders? How far were traditional fears manipulated to the point where anti-Catholic feeling boiled over into sectarian murder? How far were such activities curtailed at particular periods because of the attitude of the Protestant community, as voiced by its political or religious leaders? Of all contacts I have had with those convicted and imprisoned for paramilitary activity one stands out in my memory. He was a man in his early twenties sentenced for life. He came from what could be described as a normal, working-class Protestant background. He had qualified in a trade and he had no previous criminal record. His offence was committed in the company of others and the victim was a Catholic. When I met him in prison he had served four years of his sentence. He was classified as a loyalist paramilitary. The strength of his connections with the organisation which claimed him was doubtful. His remarks said a good deal about how he and, he assured me, others felt: 'Those who told me we needed to do something aren't here with us now. They took us up to the top of the hill and left us. We were expendable ...' Such reflections were common to many loyalist prisoners imprisoned in the late seventies. They named names, referred to speeches and recruitment, felt betrayed. Nothing can possibly justify what they did, but it is not without significance that there were some community leaders who would not be welcome to visit them.

We cannot escape the conclusion that, in those early days of the troubles, paramilitary activity within the Protestant community owed a great deal to the party political. The lifestyle of many loyalist prisoners before the community erupted in the 60s was unexceptional. Anti-Catholic feeling may have been present in their localities, but they had no personal problem when they came into contact with Catholics at work or play. Something was added to their outlook and something was presented to them in forms they could not ignore to turn them into sectarian killers.

It is not in an attempt to justify or qualify Protestant paramilitaries that we must look again at the background to the events following 1968. It may be that there are other explanations which at other times people will accept for what happened on their side of the violent division. But for the present some explanation is needed to begin to understand some of the contradictions in the loyalist scene.

It is to that element of insecurity and fear which has recurred so frequently within the Protestant community that so much evidence points. The traditional idea that they were and are 'the British in Ireland' depended not alone on their religious and political outlook: it depended on the most 'outward' forms of that allegiance, the crown, Westminster, the British government, the attention of British politicians, 'the British way of life'. Their identification with those features of 'Britishness' was and is the outward sign of the inner aspiration. But this was as much a reason for suspicion as it was a basis for solidarity. If evidence appeared to the loyalist that the bond was in any way less than they imagined or wished it to be, suspicion could quickly turn to outright resentment and anger. Thus, during the early troubles, loyalty to Britain had its limits. If at any time British policy or British attitudes indicated any weakening of the resolve to maintain the constitutional link, Protestant confidence suffered. Once again the age-old enemy surfaced. The fear that British political policies were leading to the undermining of Partition was widespread. The establishment of a power-sharing executive in place of Stormont and the possibility of a Council of Ireland after the Sunningdale Conference were only two examples of what many in the loyalist community saw as a weakening of resolve, an erosion of traditional assurances. William Whitelaw's policy of releasing internees at a time when the IRA could claim that there were entire districts in the republican community where security forces could not go, and the security moves by the British army against loyalists themselves, together posed a dilemma for Protestant thinking which could not be easily resolved. In September 1972 in the loyalist heartland of the Shankill the army shot civilians in riot conditions. A year later loyalists were among those placed in internment. What, it was argued, did such events say about the cost of loyalty to Britain?

Not for the first time there was the belief that, if loyalists ever 'took on the British', Northern Ireland as Protestants viewed it would cease to exist. I remember so well the tensions, frustrations and anger within loyalist areas in the early 70s. On one occasion, the community held its breath as large numbers of loyalist paramilitaries confronted the army in Protestant areas. Eventually there was a general 'backing off', but the disbelief and the frustration remained. Loyalism had lost its way.

When the anger and frustration of loyalist communities have no obvious outlet, no identifiable target and no easy option, they turn on those who throughout their history have been the main cause of grievance, real or imagined. The victims come from the Roman Catholic community.

The fact that in those days many who made up the loyalist working-class population in Belfast and elsewhere refused to distinguish between the IRA and those people who had been born and brought up in the Catholic community only added to what was to follow. Voices were raised that found few to contradict them. IRA bombing was widespread. Visions of crippled lives and horrific injuries to shoppers and people 'going about their ordinary business' because of explosions in crowded shopping centres caused widespread anger. To the loyalist paramilitaries there was only one philosophy: if law and order could not be enforced by legitimate means, violence must be met by violence. The distinction between the IRA activist and the ordinary law-abiding Catholic was a luxury. Time was not on their side. Loyalism was being challenged on its own streets and in its own homes. How long must loyalists wait for 'firm action by the government' against those who were 'really responsible for what was happening'? Loyalist politicians helped swell the rising tide of emotion when they condemned the Catholic community as a whole, and some nationalist leaders added their contribution with calls for an ending of 'unionist domination'. The cycle of fear was almost complete.

There was a peculiar yet sinister symbolism in the emergence of the UDA on the streets of Belfast. The sight of hundreds of uniformed and often masked men and boys marching in military formation, manning road blocks, confronting troops and police and mounting street patrols produced a mixture of emotions. But for most who watched, not least in the Catholic areas, this was much more than an outpouring of loyalist reaction to IRA violence, this was the real face of the loyalist community. How, it was asked, could the tide be turned back? How could adequate and responsible control be exercised over such a mass movement which now adopted 'military' command structures, intimidated so many by its very existence and proclaimed a 'defensive role' but could not specify the precise nature of who or what it was defending or how it proposed to do this? For the government, here was what they had most feared: a confrontation on the streets with the Protestant community at a time when their security resources were facing such an onslaught from the IRA. For the Catholic community here was the emergence of what most had long believed: loyalists were only waiting for the right moment to attack them. Within the Protestant community there was a mixed reaction. In the traditional working-class areas of the Shankill and Sandy Row, and in the new Protestant estates on the outskirts of the cities, there was an identification with what the UDA 'had to say'; they had had enough and now 'there were those prepared to stand up and be counted'. But for many Protestants in the middle-class areas and in rural areas, there was growing consternation. What would happen next? Was this what they really wanted?

The paradox in Protestant thinking again focused on the constitutional question. How would Britain react to what could be seen as a challenge from within the community that had long claimed to uphold the British link? The unease of industrialists, trade unionists, moderate politicians and churchmen grew steadily. There were loyalist politicians who saw in the UDA the 'muscle' they needed to push home the message that there was a limit to what they were prepared to endure. IRA violence was one thing, but weakness on the part of Britain, when that weakness affected Ulster loyalism, was the real issue.

Recruitment to the UDA was extensive in the 70s. In certain Protestant areas young men were in plentiful supply. They had watched the army and the police engage the IRA, they had seen the action but had not had any part in it. When they were enrolled in the UDA they came under a military structure and the imagination and longing 'to do something' became reality in 'playing soldiers'. The excitement and the uniform, the orders and the 'authority' conveyed by those structures provided the motivation. Even though their role was largely confined to standing on street corners in uniform and carrying a stick, they had become 'someone' and that someone was now 'involved'.

Clergy working in such areas were in little doubt as to the danger. They could see the frustration and the manipulation of young lives which was going on. What concerned them most was what channels would be found to turn frustration into action.

There was no largescale invasion of Catholic areas by the UDA. This would have been impossible, given the level of the military and police presence. The police found themselves frequently confronting loyalist groups on the borders between Protestant and Catholic localities. But because such widespread geographical segregation had taken place after the riots of the early 70s, it was increasingly difficult to know what was actually taking place in areas 'on the other side'.

In these circumstances the sectarian attacks, when they began, were spasmodic, individualistic and random in nature. The killing of Catholics was explained in terms of retaliation for IRA murders, proving that loyalism was not weak and had 'taken enough', and that the victims were known to be members or at least supporters of the IRA. The sadism and the cruelty of these attacks sent shockwaves through the Protestant community. But such was the communal uncertainty and unease of the period that, tragically, there appeared to be an impotence, an inability to do anything more than protest that such actions 'do not represent all of us'.

It is virtually impossible to evaluate the pattern and real motives of those random loyalist squads of the 70s. It would be easy – far too easy – to understand what happened in terms of the waves of community emotion which swept huge areas of Northern Ireland. It was a community on both sides of the divide which was gripped by uncertainty and fear: fear of each other, but also fear of the 'enemy within'. What explanations there were within loyalist areas were confined to statements by paramilitary organisations or words spoken in court. On the one hand there was the obvious 'we have taken enough and we must hit back'; on the other, there was the more thoughtful explanation which indicated some degree of warped tactical planning: 'we must show the Catholics that the IRA doesn't really protect them and that what we are doing is because the IRA have attacked innocent Protestants.'

In east Belfast where I worked myself in the 70s recruitment for the UDA took place as it did further afield. One evening a group of new recruits fell into conversation with some people of their own age and background who had kept clear of the recruitment drive. The conversation turned to the sectarian killings of Catholics. The words of justification for what was happening were a chilling reminder of what was becoming the policy: 'We've got to show the Catholics what happens to them when they allow the IRA to kill us.'

Some loyalist politicians of that period carry an immense burden of responsibility for what was happening. Rhetoric and an abject failure to distance themselves from the emergence of the UDA and the splinter groups which sprang from it did much to encourage its existence. Few really counted the long-term cost of what was happening. A monster had emerged and there were relatively few people prepared to risk the cost of alienation from their community by denunciation or condemnation. Some did not understand. Some understood only too well. Few recognised the possibilities of a counter-reaction in Catholic areas in which the IRA would again become the real defenders. Some even held the view that Catholics could end the grip of the IRA if they really wanted to. Few seemed to recognise the mixture of complex problems, emotions and reactions in nationalist and republican areas which made such a renunciation from within extremely difficult. Even fewer were prepared to see that what was happening in loyalist areas was almost exactly what they had condemned 'on the other side': safe houses, refusal to give information, toleration of activities to the extent that they could continue.

The reaction within the areas from which many of the loyalist gangs operated was itself an indication of what was happening to Protestant thinking. Some people could not accept that loyalists were capable of such atrocities. Deep in the Protestant mind lies the recognition of law and order. Not always translated into practical application but lurking in the background, this has always characterised the Protestant ethic. Therefore, to recognise that people from within their community did such things was an affront to what Protestants had inherited in attitude and outlook. IRA atrocities told them what others stood for. To accept that similar atrocities could be committed by people who came from the same stable as themselves was almost impossible. In the 80s, this disbelief turned into a profound horror that Protestants were capable of such things. Sectarian murders continue but the kind of revulsion and condemnation which now wells up within the Protestant community when loyalists such as the so-called Protestant Action Force murder Catholics at random would have been the exception rather than the rule in those early years of the troubles.

The UDA claimed a membership of 50,000 in the 70s. It could be argued quite forcefully that the momentum was such that little could have been done by community leaders to turn the tide of events. Equivocation and a general ability to make excuses for what was being done in the name of loyalism led to an absence of any concerted effort to prevent support for sectarian killings. Hardliners in the loyalist movement backed away from open condemnation of such murders and it may be that a feeling of impotence was of less significance than the reluctance to exert influence which would erode the traditional party political platform and its constituency support. Moreover, it remains to this day doubtful if the UDA's own leadership could have brought about an end to sectarian murders. Soon internal divisions appeared, and feuds which were also visible on the other side in the IRA, indicated the frustration of a movement which had no united leadership. In time, the conflict between the activist and the political philosophy as much as disenchantment in the community, and police action against individual members, were to combine to bring about the demise of the UDA as a viable movement. Largescale racketeering and intimidation became more obvious, and the sectarian killings, while continuing to be a scourge of Northern Ireland, have become the responsibility of smaller and in consequence more sinister offshoots of the UDA.

Nor was the sectarian element in the activities of the UDA the only manifestation of the uncertainty and fears of the loyalist community in the 70s. As with the IRA in Catholic areas, 'punishments' were unleashed on their own people. Cruelty of a high order helped to support the grip on their own localities. The deterioration of relations between loyalists and the police and army, growing suspicion of the intentions of the government towards the loyalist population and a general breakdown in law and order provided the conditions in which violence could grow. Increased security attention greatly reduced the UDA's ability to operate on the streets in any degree of strength. More and more it is to the fragmented groupings of loyalist paramilitaries that the observer must look for those who continued sectarian assassinations. To place responsibility on one movement as opposed to another for the growth in such murders is extremely difficult. It was a period when many different pressures and emotions permitted the rapid and sinister growth of anti-Roman Catholic violence which will remain a devastating judgement on many more than those who donned uniforms and masks on the streets of Belfast in those days.

What resulted from that period of widespread sectarian intimidation contributed to the largest mass movement of people in Western Europe since the Second World War. Figures vary but it is thought some 10,000 families left their homes and moved to other areas: 40,000 people whose lives were altered by violence and the fear of what one community might do to the other is a devastating indictment of the point society had reached.

Sectarianism takes many forms. It is not restricted to any one section of this community. Random killings are the most obvious example but other examples will be given later. It is not easy to designate one terrorist action as sectarian and another as something else. There is a growing belief that the IRA is now engaging more in selected targets within the civilian population and that such attacks are sectarian. Recent bombs placed in mainly Protestant housing estates in Cookstown and Donaghcloney are being interpreted in this way. Not infrequently, it is concluded that such loyalist and IRA attacks aim at the community 'back lash'.

It is all too easy to allocate some sort of collective community responsibility for the actions of individuals. The vast majority of Protestants as well as Catholics disown what a minority has done 'in their name'. There is a new awareness of all that is negative for Protestants themselves when sectarian murders of Roman Catholics occur at the hands of those claiming to uphold the loyalist cause.

While sectarian terrorism continues in either community, reconciliation and better community relations will face many obstacles. Reaction to such atrocities has as much to say about the nature of that community as it has to say about hope for the future. Violent death has stalked this community for years. There is little difference, when it happens, between Protestant or Catholic grief and misery. No label, no flag of convenience, no so-called justification can remove the simple fact that murder is murder. To kill for 'a cause' may allow some instant recognition and provide the perpetrators with a warped sense of justification. But both communities are diminished by every life lost. To take a life because of a person's religion brings into play emotions of a special kind. It is the ultimate blasphemy.

5
THE HUNGER STRIKE

Two quite distinct events have brought into focus much of what actually divides the two communities in Northern Ireland, and have shown what each community thinks about itself and about the other. The first began on 1 March 1981.

In the Maze Prison some miles from Belfast a republican prisoner called Bobby Sands began a hunger strike. He was acting on behalf of some 360 fellow prisoners, who sought recognition as political prisoners and special status. For four years they had been making that claim. It began with the 'blanket protest' by men imprisoned for crimes which could be described as politically motivated. To distinguish between their status and that of others in the Maze they refused to wear prison clothing and instead covered themselves with blankets. This protest was to lead to the notorious 'dirty protest'. When their demands were denied, seven embarked on a hunger strike in October 1980 promising to fast to death unless the British government agreed to meet their five demands designed to designate and underline their imprisonment not as punishment for 'criminal offences' but for actions prompted and motivated by political aspiration. They wished to be prisoners of war.

They demanded the right to wear their own clothes, to refrain from ordinary prison work, to have freedom of association within the prison, to organise their own recreational facilities, to receive one letter, parcel and visit per week and to have lost remission time restored. They continued their fast for fifty-three days. A few days before Christmas 1980 they announced that the hunger strike was ending because they felt the government had met their demands.

It then appeared that the government had not in fact agreed. On 1 March Bobby Sands began to refuse food. He was joined by others and the demands were the same in each case: political status. Within a period of three months ten men had died. After each death another volunteer began a fast. It took sixty-six days for Bobby Sands, that twenty-seven year old man from Belfast, to die. During that time the media of the world invaded Belfast. Hotel space was at a premium. Cameras and crews from many nations walked the streets of Belfast – and waited. Northern Ireland was filled with foreboding. Predictions of widespread violence to accompany the death of one of the strikers appeared daily in the press. Tension rose in both communities and security forces moved to a state of readiness.

The hunger strike was to become much more than a demand for political status, much more than the individual drama of a group of young men fasting to their death. It was to become yet one more stage at which the deep frustrations and the even deeper fears of two communities came into frightening focus.

When Bobby Sands died his name and face appeared on TV screens and newspapers throughout the world. Reaction was swift. Padraig O'Malley captured some of the reasons for this attention:

> He was a hero, martyr, Bobby Sands, MP, lonely agitator. He had pitted his fragile psyche against the impersonal power of a government and he had won.[8]

Martyrdom had been accorded to Bobby Sands who had died for 'the cause'. Sympathetic treatment was accorded by much of the world's press. Anti-British feeling erupted in cities such as Athens, Milan and Chicago. In the States the powerful International Longshoreman's Union refused to deal with any ships entering an American port under a British flag. Irish-American opinion was almost unanimously in favour of the hunger strike. Bobby Sands had become the focal point for a wave of opposition to anything British – and particularly anything British with an Irish connection. But it was in Northern Ireland itself that the real effects of what was happening at the Maze were most clearly visible.

The hunger strikes drove wedges between the two communities in Northern Ireland. This was its most turbulent period since 1968. During the second strike sixty-four people died, thirty-four civilians and thirty members of the security forces. The reaction of Protestants and Catholics, unionists, republicans and nationalists, politicians and churchmen exposed much of the raw nerve of their respective communities and also how little common ground existed.

For Catholics the contrast between the activist and the moderate, the republican and the nationalist, the authority of the Church and the challenge of militancy – reopened wounds buried deep in Irish history. Martyrdom carried with it all the tragic pathos and bitterness of past generations in which the hopelessness of the great struggle to free a people from their bondage

---

[8.] Padraig O'Malley, *Biting at the Grave* (1990), p. 3.

and oppression, interwoven with the mythologies of past confrontation, brought fresh and urgent impetus to the hunger strike of 1981. Moreover, while memories of hunger strikes down through history were real – and had lost none of their emotional appeal with the passing of time – now there was a difference. Within the community not everyone saw the events in the Maze as inevitable, nor in terms of community support. There were other issues to be thought of. Support there was and support there was to build upon – but the community from which the young men came did not react with one voice and heart.

On the other side of the divide there was predictable resentment at the hunger strike: 'they want to die, let them, no one's forcing them to do it.' The hunger strike was a republican affair; it was tragic to see lives deliberately wasted, but they had chosen their own path. Their victims, their Protestant victims, had not been given any choice about dying or living. In the end, it was a republican matter – it had nothing to do with Protestants. The public statements of the loyalist politicians nearly always emphasised the idea of 'choice'. There was no real consideration of the human tragedy of young lives wasting away. They were 'committing suicide' – and suicide was wrong.

Behind such resentment there was a deep sense of foreboding about how the IRA would react to the deaths and hatred and suspicion of republicanism easily merged into that other prejudice which was never far from the surface, suspicion of Catholicism. The issues of the hunger strike were more than a claim for political status. To Protestants the claim had been obliterated by the greater debate – a debate which was not just about the right to die, but about what the world was making of the strike. How could such sympathy be marshalled in such a short time for a cause so immoral, unjust and clearly a manipulation of young lives by those who always seemed to win the propaganda war? Allied to this was the on-going watchfulness of Britain. Would Thatcher give in, would her Ministers talk to the strikers and grant the requests in the hope of bringing an end to the tensions?

In the Roman Catholic Church in Ireland there was deep concern about what was happening. A pastoral approach to the strikers and their families and a refusal to talk in terms of suicides stood in contrast with their co-religionists across the Irish Sea. Bishops as well as prison chaplains became involved in ministry to those who were refusing food. There was much talk in media interviews and from Catholic pulpits of injustice, tragedy and the need to show compassion for those whose ideals were on such trial. For many Protestants this degree of identification fitted in neatly to their inherited view of the political rather than the religious role of the Roman Catholic Church in Ireland. Niceties of degree did not matter: pastoral care for those within the same community may have been the aim, but for many loyalists it was simply support for the men behind the wire. Again the ambiguities of what one community saw as right and wrong, and how those perceptions became blurred across the divide, played the inevitable role in controlling the reaction of one to the other. How, demanded the hardline loyalist voice, could you ever trust a Church which is openly aligned with republican hunger strikers? Did what was happening now not prove 'they' had been right all along?

For almost everyone in the Protestant community it had become impossible to place the hunger strike in a purely moral context. The issues and the pressures of the time and the build-up of world reaction made the Protestant community feel even more isolated than before. Why should world sympathy flood in for suicide attempts, and be sidetracked from the numerous victims of the IRA terrorist? What had gone wrong?

The truth was that neither community really knew how to handle the effects of the hunger strike. The injured pride and tragic events of the past, and above all their apparent futility when viewed by a new generation, only helped to increase the depth and bitterness which each felt, but for different reasons: the sense of being again prisoners of the past which many Catholics had as they watched the strikers die, and the complete failure on the part of Protestants to understand why they wanted to choose martyrdom.

Given the emotions of the moment and the bitterness which had resulted from years of IRA violence, there was little incentive for Protestants to see anything of the significance of the hunger strike. If they had allowed themselves, or been allowed, the luxury of a calmer look at the scene, they might have noted the qualities of endurance and sacrifice which have long walked hand-in-hand with militant republicanism in Ireland. Fasting is a part of Irish Celtic mysticism and, although the hunger strike only became a real vehicle of political pressure in Ireland after the 1916 Rising, its methods and its motivation could easily be recognised within a Roman Catholicism where fasting and self-denial have a deeply spiritual significance.

For the hunger strike united several different aspects of the republican ethos: the sense of injustice, of being the constant victims of Irish history for reasons which had nothing to do with Ireland, the dependence on the community allegiance and 'the cause', but chiefly the re-application of a mythology which glorified self-sacrifice. The strike involved physical pain and it spread out tentacles of identity in which families, communities, religious beliefs, political aspirations and a self-justification for the pain and misery already caused to the victims of the IRA campaign became a sort of unity. The redemption of the cause and the redemption of those who, like the strikers, were involved in the IRA, could become a greater possibility if and when the hunger strike was seen to be accomplished. For Protestants the inevitability of the success of the hunger strike, of course, remained a burning issue. Would the hunger strikers see it through, or would their Church, their movement, their people, find a convenient way of getting them off the hook before it was too late? The role of the mothers of the hunger strikers was important. Could they persuade their sons to stop?

The solidarity of the hunger strikers within the Maze prison was complete. As time passed, and it became apparent that there was not going to be a change in the attitude of the government, the continuation of the protest rather than the achievement of its avowed ends became the priority. Fatalism set in, but it would not erode the hunger strike. Long forgotten by both Protestants and Catholics were the five demands. The machinery of a protest which owed so much to history had taken over. The government had not capitulated, but already there was talk of 'victory' at the Maze. In a sense, the hunger strikers had achieved their special status.

For Protestants it had all become a totally useless exercise carried out for propaganda purposes. But they were also a very angry community, their anger stemming from circumstances they could not quite understand. This failure to understand had little to do with Bobby Sands or the five demands and said much more about what they believed was right and wrong – and how you put forward what was right and wrong. There was a grudging admiration of the determination of those who were starving to death with their 'no surrender' attitude. Significantly, it was from within the loyalist rather than the republican community that the question was first raised: why can't the IRA order them to stop before it's too late?

Amongst the Catholics came a rising tide of resentment, not at the failure of the IRA to 'call it all off' but at the refusal of the British authorities to listen to the appeals of churchmen and politicians for negotiation to take place. A deep sense of powerlessness emerged, and a feeling that this was an echo of so much that had happened before, generations before. New questions were being asked – asked by Catholics of themselves as much as of others. What did they have to do before they were really listened to? Had anything really changed or was it just the same as it had always been: a powerless community, prisoners of their past, and still being judged for and by it.

Militant loyalism found it easy to confuse the hunger strikers with the crimes of the IRA as a whole. The hunger strikers were simply one part of the republican terrorist machine; they were as much a part of that machine as those who comprised the active service units beyond the prison walls in the community. Their part in the campaign was simply to fast to death, to attract world attention and generate sympathy. As the editorial in a loyalist newspaper put it, the hunger strikers were now of more use to the republican movement dead than alive.

The extent to which the Catholic community thought about reactions among Protestants is difficult to assess. It has been argued that the hunger strike provoked sufficient internal difficulty for the Catholic community to distract it from worrying about what was happening elsewhere. There were divisions within the nationalist and republican areas. But it seems likely that Catholics saw the Protestant community would not separate the hunger strike from their natural collective reaction to years of IRA terrorism. There were many Roman Catholics who sought to express just such a view in the correspondence columns of newspapers and on radio discussion programmes. They countered what they saw as the Protestant tendency to generalise about them by stressing that for many nationalists and 'armchair' republicans there was now the unenviable sensation of being dragged by different forces in different directions at the same time. The 'cause' could be given approval but the methods were repugnant. The amount of time between deaths, an inevitable and calculated part of the propaganda exercise, was also increasing the pressures within the community from which Bobby Sands and his colleagues came. It was also permitting the emergence of a growing number of Catholic voices who, while exercising immense care, were tending to ask if it was necessary for the whole community to be 'put on the rack' by the strike.

For the deeply-committed republican there was, however, no dilemma. Had they not known all along that 'Britain' would never do anything to meet the demands of the hunger strikers? How far they equated such a stance with the views of their Protestant neighbours is difficult to decide. Within those same areas there were many Catholics who were prisoners of the situation for other reasons. Their feeling of impotence stemmed from the simple declaration: 'if you aren't for them you must be against them.' Intimidation was widespread in nationalist and republican areas. The appearance of black flags on lamp posts to mark the death of each hunger striker was only one sign of a much deeper current. Not to be supportive and to be seen to be on the side of the hunger strikers was to be without doubt against them. To be less than enthusiastic about the avalanche of criticism directed against the British government for a failure to meet the strikers' demands was to be supportive of Margaret Thatcher. But finally, and probably of most social significance, was the fact that it was not enough to support the reason for the strike – it was equally necessary to support the method being used. Death itself had become more than a propaganda ploy: it had become the essence of the cause itself. In practical everyday terms the dilemma for the Catholic population was to find ways of being supportive of the long-term political aspiration without seeming to be supporting the methods at present being used.

This dilemma was itself far from being unique in community terms in Northern Ireland. For Protestants the political aspiration to maintenance of the union with Great Britain lies at the root of much of their thinking. But for the vast majority there has been an unrelieved disgust at Protestant or loyalist-inspired terrorism. Random sectarian killing of Catholics simply because they were Catholics was repudiated – 'they have no right to use our name.' But when loyalist murder gangs spoke of justification in terms of preventing the IRA working towards a united Ireland there were those who had difficulty in joining the widespread condemnation. In both communities, 'Moderation fell silent, sullenness became a substitute for passiveness.'[9]

Widespread violence within the Catholic communities was as much a measure of the frustration of a people who could not see a way out of the prison of the mind and heart which was symbolised by what was happening in the Maze. That frustration may have been linked with the dying of Bobby Sands and with what they saw as the refusal of the authorities to find 'a way out', but it spoke clearly also of generations of episodes in which Catholics saw their community as objects of discrimination. The thousands who walked behind the coffins of the hunger strikers had a common identity with other funerals, other martyrs, other faces and voices which had in their time seen powerlessness in the face of 'oppression'. This heritage again became a reality at the graveside of Sands, Hughes, McCresh, O'Hara, McDonnell and the others. The funerals strengthened to new degrees the links between the IRA and the communities from which it came.

Many loyalists saw the failure of Catholic community leaders and the Roman Catholic Church to influence the hunger strikers to end their protest and to save their lives not as evidence of the refusal to accede to their Church but as proof of the unity of the protesters, community and Church. The traditional view that the 'Catholic Church calls the tune' was so strong in Protestant thinking that few imagined, or were willing to accept, that the Roman Catholic Church was in fact making great efforts to ease the situation. Its failure to bring about an end to the strike was as much a sign of the allegiance and influence of the institutional Church in nationalist or republican areas as it was of the connection between loyalist activities and the various branches of the Protestant Church. For many Protestants it was difficult to separate the outward appearance of the hunger strike protest and the policy of the Church to which the strikers belonged. For generations loyalists had seen the Church and the Catholic community as indivisible, and the hunger

---

9. Padraig O'Malley, *op. cit.*, p. 155.

strike funerals cemented this perception. The niceties of distinguishing between pastoral care of one's people and outward support for political aspiration were largely lost on a community which had already suffered so much from the IRA. Had not the leading protester, Bobby Sands, been elected to parliament by his people? What did this say about the real loyalty of the Catholic community? Time and again the contrast between the freedom of the hunger strikers to choose their destiny was compared with the lot of those Protestants, mostly members of the security forces, who had been given no choice of life or death at the hands of the IRA murder gangs. The degree of media attention to the plight of the prisoners on hunger strike was deeply resented by the loyalist community. It was a resentment which was to drive deep into the attitudes of many Protestants in Northern Ireland: a resentment which lingers even today. Once more Protestants felt alone: the world did not understand their position, the world did not want to listen to the other side of the story, the world was paying scant attention to the real victims of the Northern Ireland conflict, the hundreds of innocent victims of terrorism and their families. As reaction grew across the world, and that reaction was seen to be based on a substantial degree of sympathy for the hunger strikers, Protestant attitudes already conditioned to the 'siege mentality' by years of republican terrorism, allied to what politicians so frequently referred to as 'government weakness in dealing with it', became even more anti-nationalist, anti-republican and, inevitably, anti-Catholic.

One of the first members of the security forces to be killed following Bobby Sands's death, RUC constable Philip Ellis, was a member of my diocese. It was a time of high emotion within the Protestant community. Calls for restraint and calm were easily interpreted by the extreme wings of the unionist community as 'more weakness'. The address I gave at the funeral was not an easy one to write. It did not seem to me that many people would be widely enthusiastic about the Christian message of forgiveness or reconciliation. What was happening to the price of human life, to human values and standards had confused many people whose sense of right and wrong appeared to be being turned upside down. All I could say then to a community which was so susceptible to the voices of division and retaliation was a plea for 'common sense' and a continued denial of the widescale Protestant 'backlash' so favoured in media parlance, but which had never become a community-wide reaction:

> Anger, frustration, resentment and bewilderment – these are not the feelings of extremists or people who constantly take a decision of life or death into their own hands. These are the continual, deeply personal, intensely felt reactions of those who have watched attempts to turn upside down the community's sense of values.

During the period of the hunger strike sixty-four people's lives were ended by violence, in addition to the ten deaths at the Maze. It does not take much imagination now to understand something of the long-term effect these statistics had on the Protestant community, especially when they are added to the traditional loyalist feeling that 'nobody understands us' in the outside world.

Far inside the trauma of the Protestant reaction to the hunger strike lay the view many Protestants held of the Roman Catholic Church. In the highly emotional atmosphere of that period many Protestant conclusions were given a new and sinister interpretation. Although the basis of this reaction lay in conflicting views on the morality, or lack of it, of suicide, many Protestants did not see, nor wish to see, anything but a Catholic Church which was ambivalent towards the aims of the hunger strikers. It seemed that those aims had by now nothing to do with five demands for prison facilities – those demands were only a means to further the real aim of a united Ireland gained by violence. Age-old suspicions of the Catholic Church and its people came to the surface in new and frightening ways. The fundamental differences between the two communities on many issues appeared to crystallise afresh as the hunger strikers died. From many Protestant pulpits questions were asked about teaching on what was right and what was wrong. A new examination of community morality became the order of the day. If Protestants saw something of the dilemma facing the Irish Roman Catholic Church it was not obvious in much of what was said. The fact that attitudes towards self-inflicted death on the part of English Roman Catholics appeared to differ from those expressed in Northern Ireland gave fresh impetus to unease about the Irish Roman Catholic Church in particular. This was to become a significant aspect of the sectarianism expressed in denominational terms. Frequently references appeared in Protestant articles and speeches to the 'ambiguities' of Catholic statements on the situation surrounding the hunger strikers. It seemed to many Protestants that there was always 'a twist in the tail'. Not for the first time in this conflict, language and the ways people used it became a tool of division.

Within Protestantism in Northern Ireland there is a very strong and at times all-pervading puritanism. The Protestant work ethic is but one example of how traditional adherence to a keen sense of right and wrong, just reward, recognisable and logical consequences, can be accepted only in a structure of absolutes. In theory, at least, the difference between right and wrong is clear. It is a rigid process as well as a rigid principle. But it is all too easy to permit such a premise to become a reason for rejecting the motives and actions of others who do not accept the same definition of right and wrong.

For Protestants, the hunger strikers had chosen to die. That was their choice. Attempts to dissuade them or to suggest any meeting of demands would mean becoming part of the process they had instigated: indeed, any such compassion would do scant justice to the feelings of the families who had already lost loved-ones through IRA violence. To make efforts to persuade Bobby Sands to call off his fast and yet to refuse to use the label 'suicide' was to blur the real issue of the situation – an issue which was all about morality. If the morality of the hunger strike was accepted then it was only a matter of time before the actions which had placed the strikers in prison could be subjected to similar treatment. The next step would be, it appeared to many Protestants, to accept the morality of 'the cause'.

The hunger strike brought Northern Ireland to a new brink. The world's media anticipated widespread community violence. Talk of the long expected 'civil war' filled many columns in the national and international press. There was an upsurge in violence, but the extensive 'backlash' did not materialise. What did in fact happen was more a testimony to the underlying seeds of the conflict. The religious aspects of the divisions, the different meanings of moral principles and the differences between theological dogma and the practical interpretations of that dogma by those caught up in real life terrorism came to the surface. How far the reactions to the hunger strikes exposed a failure by Protestants to really understand the emotions of Roman Catholics and, given the identities of the strikers, the failure of Catholics to understand what makes Northern Ireland Protestants what they are, is a matter of conjecture. None the less, the real significance of those events in 1981 for both communities lies not in matters of doctrinal interpretation. It lies in the apparent cementing of perceived notions each community already had of the other. It lies in the addition of another link to a chain that has to be broken, some day.

6

THE ANGLO-IRISH AGREEMENT

If the hunger strike was a period of intense heart-searching for the nationalist community in Northern Ireland, little can compare with the traumatic effect of the Anglo-Irish Agreement on their unionist neighbours.

The Sinn Fein vote in the Westminster election in the early summer of 1983 was to have a dramatic effect on all those involved in the Northern Ireland story. In Dublin, London and Belfast the message was direct and distinct. For the loyalist population it conveyed a challenge which it could not ignore – for the extremist it was the confirmation he had hoped for. 43 per cent of the vote in the nationalist community and the election of an MP to Westminster gave Sinn Fein not just a place of significance in the political expression of the Catholic community, it posed serious questions throughout Protestant Ulster. For those Protestants who had watched the emergence of the SDLP as a constitutional expression of the nationalist people with satisfaction that here was a face with whom they could 'do business', the impact of a Sinn Fein vote of 15 per cent of the nationalist vote came as a shock. Now the political voice of the organisation which had inflicted so much suffering on their community was emerging as a major political entity, only 3 per cent behind the SDLP in the overall Roman Catholic vote.

What, so many Protestants asked, did this imply about the Catholic community? What had it to say about moderation – what signal was it sending out to the Protestant people? But also, and of even greater significance, what did it mean within the Catholic community? For the Irish Prime Minister, Garett Fitzgerald, and for Margaret Thatcher, a political innovation which would end the Catholic isolation was an urgent necessity. The possibility of Sinn Fein becoming the majority party in the Catholic community was now real. The need to act was now urgent and essential if constitutional political activity was to be saved. On 15 November 1985, the Anglo-Irish Agreement was signed at Hillsborough Castle.

Britain and the Irish Republic established an inter-governmental conference, jointly chaired by the Secretary of State for Northern Ireland and a representative of the Irish government, the Minister for Foreign Affairs, which would concern itself with affairs in Northern Ireland and the relationship between the two parts of Ireland. The Agreement promised that 'determined efforts shall be made through the Conference to resolve any differences' between the two governments. A 'devolved' administration which would have 'widespread acceptance throughout the community' was given the support of both governments and the overall aim was expressed in terms of 'reconciliation' between Northern Ireland's two communities. Only a decision by the majority of people in Northern Ireland to change their constitutional status would involve an end to the link with Britain.

From a unionist perspective, the signing of the Anglo-Irish Agreement provided them with what they saw as dramatic evidence of how easily their traditional pillar of union with Britain could be threatened. There was a sense of disbelief, which was twisted by extremists into the claim: 'we told you so all along.' It was said that unionists had been told by reliable sources only twelve months before that Mrs Thatcher was 'solid on the Union'. In 1982 she had pointed out that no commitment existed for the British government to consult the Irish government on matters involving Northern Ireland. There had been at that time confidence felt in her stance by the Official Unionist Party. The Democratic Unionists of Ian Paisley were less certain.

The thinking of both governments was based on the hope that Protestants would find the concept of power-sharing with constitutional nationalists more palatable. But the longer they resisted the more certain would be the involvement of the Republic in the affairs of Northern Ireland.

Behind the Agreement was also the belief that a set of words, a political formula, would be sufficient to erode support for republicanism in its most militant form, but for loyalists no words and no formulae could remove the deeply-held fears of a united Ireland and of all that that would mean to their future and to their survival. Both governments hoped that nationalists would embrace the Agreement as proof that constitutional political activity could bring them added security through the involvement of Dublin. It was hoped that, once and for all, the Irish identity and vision of the Catholic community would gain respectability equal to the Protestant and loyalist wish to maintain their British link.

The Agreement provided the opportunity for the British and Irish governments to work much more closely on Northern Ireland affairs than ever before. Registered at the United Nations and given the official backing of both governments, it was a document which to its architects was a realistic attempt to end nationalist alienation, offer reassurance to unionists and thus provide a recognisable basis for inter-governmental cooperation. In the presentation of the Agreement it was stressed that it was designed to promote stability and peace in the North, reconciliation of the two main traditions in

Ireland, the birth of a new atmosphere of friendship and cooperation in the defeat of terrorism. Undoubtedly, the most radical innovation was the establishment of the joint ministerial conference of British and Irish Ministers. There was a secretariat to monitor political, security, legal and other social issues of concern to the nationalist community. The first meeting of the Anglo-Irish Conference was held on 11 December 1985 and the new role of the Irish government in this structure, together with the commitment that 'determined efforts shall be made' to reconcile real differences between the two governments, led to the widespread belief, not restricted to unionists, that more was involved than consultation.

To loyalists it seemed that the Agreement had effectively changed the political axis from London/Belfast to London/Dublin. But it was again the constitutional question that provoked their most vehement reaction. They perceived that the constitutional status of Northern Ireland had been changed. They felt marginalised. It would be accurate to say that in a sense they felt the first pangs of the alienation which, for other reasons and in other ways, their nationalist neighbours had complained of for years. The thrust of the document was to unionist eyes the inclusion of the SDLP at the heart of things and the virtual exclusion of unionism. At a stroke the unionist veto on political movement had been abolished and an SDLP one imposed in its place. 'The iron lady has listened to the SDLP and Dublin – and she's deaf to the unionists,' one writer complained. Overnight, loyalist opinion recognised what many had long feared: Britain would do a deal with people whose overall intentions they, the unionists, had never doubted. Northern Ireland, which they had always striven to keep in the United Kingdom, was a disposable commodity.

All the traditional fears of the loyalist community rose to the surface. Not for them the reassurance of Article 1 of the Agreement, that any change could only occur in the status of the Province with the consent of a majority of its people. Not for them the declared recognition in the same Article that there was no such majority wish at present. Did the Article not go on to say that, if such a swing of opinion occurred in the future, legislation would be produced to give effect to it? Behind the words lay the real threat – and they did not like it. But more important even than thoughts for the future were the deep feelings of mistrust within unionism about what the consequences would be of the Irish government now having 'a say in the internal affairs of Northern Ireland'? To their eyes the British government had been guilty of complicity in a deliberate weakening, even breaking, of their constitutional status within the United Kingdom.

Voices were raised in anger. The Agreement was denounced as a 'sell-out'. Frustration that they had been 'left out of the consultation process' brought loyalists out on the streets in their thousands. Moderation within the unionist family was swept to one side. Many points of disagreement between the two wings of unionism were forgotten. The Anglo-Irish Agreement had united unionists – and it had united them against it. Fifteen Unionist MPs resigned from Westminster and the consequent by-elections produced 418,230 votes against the Agreement. Violent loyalist protests, outside the location of the new permanent secretariat and their aggressive reaction at local council level signalled the first steps in what was a relatively new aspect of their thinking – the withdrawal of consent to the government. Protestantism had seen this weapon used before – by the nationalists. On those occasions it had been ridiculed by the majority population. Now through circumstances over which they felt they had lost control, similar thinking and action was to come from the loyalist community.

While the outward sign was of a Protestant population angered and dismayed by the Agreement, and the voices of opposition were loudest, there was also deep thinking going on from an early stage as to its significance for the future. Protestant moderates were not entirely silenced. There were those who resented the way the Agreement had been produced but who saw the dangers of an entirely negative reaction, one which saw nothing good in what had been agreed. The cross community Alliance Party, claiming the allegiance of both Protestants and Catholics, pleaded for time to think out the implications of the accord. Moderate unionists were unhappy with a totally negative reaction. As has so often been the case in Northern Ireland's history, the loudest voices were to be heard first. They had one message – no to the Agreement and no to what they saw it involved.

Protestant perception of the Agreement did not move much further beyond what was seen to be direct involvement and influence in Northern Irish affairs by the Dublin government. Had not Dublin's intention in the past for their future been, time and again, an all-Ireland republic, and did not this new Agreement advance this process further? Was this not an attempt in which Britain had a definite hand, to overrule any objections, to ignore any of their heart-felt views and aspirations and to push one million people against their will into an alien state and an alien environment? They were to argue, as they had so often in the past, that it was not any particular government's right to undermine the constitutional status of the United Kingdom, of which Northern Ireland was an integral part.

Thus James Molyneaux of the Official Unionists and Ian Paisley of the Democratic Unionists became allies in their opposition to the 'diktat' and in their opposition to the success of the SDLP in gaining such recognition from two sovereign parliaments. They were also united in their belief that 'Ulster says no' was the priority, reflecting a sense of unease which in those early days could be felt throughout the Protestant community. In their eyes the Anglo-Irish Agreement was a completely anti-unionist document. Instead of affirming and underwriting the constitutional position, the references about 'change in the status of Northern Ireland' meant expulsion from the United Kingdom, which was unacceptable to them. Could they ever again trust those guilty of what was for them political treachery?

In the heat of loyalist reaction little attention was given to the philosophy behind the Agreement, which for both governments was clear. If a way could be found to end nationalist alienation, if nationalists could be offered an opportunity to share in the government of Northern Ireland and the institutions of the land, then surely support for violence and those who perpetuated it would diminish. If unionists could be persuaded that the nationalist population really wanted this new involvement, power-sharing was a strong possibility. The opportunity was offered to nationalists to make a new beginning. The opportunity was offered to loyalists to open new doors. The possibilities on offer would take time to materialise, but a start had been made. It was the beginning of a process. The real difficulty was in communicating such aspirations to a sharply divided community where suspicion of words and the intentions behind words had become part of their everyday culture, a community which had reached a point of suspecting the motive behind virtually any political change.

The depth of feeling among Protestants at that time, if measured by the thousands who attended anti-Agreement rallies or filled the correspondence columns of newspapers, was intense. There was little or no attempt to analyse the document as a whole and any efforts to encourage a measured response were apparently swept aside by the weight of emotional feeling. People were judged not on their attitude to the 'small print' but on whether they were for or against the Agreement. Grievance with almost any part of public policy identified the Agreement as the source of that problem. As someone said, 'unionists can even blame the weather on the Hillsborough signing.'

If those who signed the Anglo-Irish Agreement wanted to encourage the Protestants to believe that the minority community would become less alienated from mainstream life, they failed. For Protestants its terms gave Dublin a definite foothold in their affairs without in any way encouraging a reciprocal role for Belfast in the Republic. The impression that not only had they been left out in the cold as the Agreement was being prepared but the fact that they lost the ability to govern themselves when the Secretary of State became their representative in all matters of concern to their community, as envisaged by Article 5(c), added further fuel to the fire. How could they be expected to accept such a position when no Secretary of State had an electoral mandate from the unionist constituency?

Soon the opposition to the Agreement adopted a different tactic. The figures produced by the by-elections, and presented to the world by unionists as a referendum on Hillsborough, were quoted to justify opposition. Words such as undemocratic, unrepresentative, unjust became terms as comfortable for Protestants as they had been useful for generations of Catholics. It was argued that the Agreement had not been offered but imposed in an undemocratic way. The very people for whom it was designed were in fact those who resolutely opposed it. In the by-elections the unionist anti-Agreement vote represented some 71.5 per cent of the total poll. The Agreement was supported by only the SDLP, representing 13 per cent of the Province's electorate. Of perhaps more significance, though perhaps only marginally, the SDLP had the pleasure of seeing the Provisional Sinn Fein vote drop by 5.4 per cent and their own rise by 6 per cent, temporary proof that the Agreement was working.

Despite the united protests, the British government appeared determined to let the Agreement remain as it was. The extent to which the British government underestimated the depth of traditional unionist fears of Dublin during the planning stages of the Hillsborough Agreement is debatable. In private some of those involved in that process expressed surprise at the level of the unionist opposition. As time passed it was possible to discern a subtle change in opposition tactics. At first there was a relentless refusal to accept, let alone to discuss the spirit of what had been signed. But there was growing criticism that unionism was depending too much on the power of its traditional size rather than on reasoned argument. Westminster's consistent refusal to move, the support of much of the outside world for what had been agreed and a gradual weariness with unproductive protest began to take its toll. British Ministers at Stormont, while at first expressing genuine surprise at the strength of unionist opposition and boycotted by locally elected representatives, began to talk of the effect of the Agreement as not being as bad as unionists had at first imagined. Surely, they argued, it was to the advantage of unionism that through the Anglo-Irish Conference the Republic's government could be made to be more involved in security issues and that it was in the interest of the Northern majority that Catholics could feel themselves to be more a part of decision-taking, thus eroding support for the IRA? When the UDA document 'Common Sense' was published, there was a new breadth to the arguments of the unionist case which, coming from such an unlikely source, reflected a change in the atmosphere. Now there was talk of movement which, while not representing any fundamental change on the main constitutional issue, brought to the surface degrees of compromise hitherto unheard of within the loyalist camp. A task force report, jointly produced by a group from both wings of the unionist parties, suggested more positive strategy for the future. Such was the gradual change in thinking that unionist leaders were at pains to point out that nothing had changed in the real opposition to the Agreement: it was simply 'a change of tack'.

Events in the Republic, which stood to gain a great deal from the Agreement, initially gave welcome encouragement to unionism. There in a national referendum in 1986, 63.5 per cent of the population rejected the concept of divorce: where now, argued the loyalists, was the evidence of any eagerness to produce a pluralist state south of the border? In 1990, a ruling in the High Court in Dublin effectively concluded that there is not just an aspiration but a legal imperative on the Irish government to actively pursue their territorial claims on the North. How did this fit in to the spirit of the Anglo-Irish Agreement? To loyalists it appeared that the basis of the Hillsborough Agreement was being eroded in that events in the South questioned the spirit of cooperation of the 'new relationship' proclaimed at the signing. Much was made of this in speeches from the unionist leadership. At the grassroots level it appeared that what was emerging was far from any obvious mood in the Republic to see a fresh picture of reconciliation between the two jurisdictions. What now, unionists asked, of that new vision – had anything really changed? Those who had vocally opposed the Agreement questioned the intention of their Southern neighbours to create a new atmosphere.

Attendances at protest meetings in Northern Ireland diminished. There was a perceptible falling-off in enthusiasm for street protests. More and more the emphasis now fell on speeches and claims that the Agreement was without substance. It was increasingly convenient to point to developments in the Republic as evidence that the Agreement was in fact only geared to give Dublin a precarious foothold in the North – that there was no evidence of better relationships with the South. Claims that the security situation had improved because of increased cooperation across the border fell largely on deaf ears. Unionists got the impression that each time the inter-governmental meetings took place agendas were dominated by complaints about the administration of justice in the North or accusations levelled at the activities of the British security forces. Criticisms of the Agreement's irrelevance superseded outward protests, in spite of continuing evidence that the opposition of loyalists was undiminished. British Ministers were denied access to meetings, outward contacts with them continued to be refused and much publicity accompanied a refusal by the Belfast City Council to allow any Ministers to attend the annual Remembrance Day service at the Belfast City Hall.

A leading British civil servant remarked in my hearing that, even if the unionists had been a part of the early discussions, it would have made no difference to the outcome. After all, he said, their veto had to be faced up to – and he would not have envisaged any change of heart at that stage. I was left with the clear impression that whether or not consultation had taken place (a fact consistently denied by unionist spokesmen) those involved in the preparation of the Agreement saw no point in engaging in any such discussions in depth.

Loyalists had no doubt: Dublin was the obstacle; it was the problem; it was the barrier which loyalism could not see beyond. Events in more recent times, during Peter Brooke's attempts to get inter-party discussions under way, have again highlighted the opposition unionism has long harboured towards the Republic. But the effect of the Anglo-Irish Agreement within the unionist family went much deeper than the re-emergence of traditional antagonism towards the South's political intentions. Many people have argued that it produced a new realism in unionist thinking. No longer could problems in Northern Ireland be addressed in isolation: unionists had been compelled to think of relationships outside their immediate community. And this thinking was long overdue.

Certainly, a new urgency of response to wider issues has been evident. But it is the nature of those responses rather than their detail which is significant. Traditional unionist philosophy stemming from its insistence on the constitutional issue has been supported by a basic conviction at the grassroots level that, ultimately, a united Ireland with a million Protestants compelled to accept some form of incorporation into a state which they cannot accept, is the aim. Extremist loyalist opinion has depended on this fear for generations. Fear of the influence of the Catholic Church in the Republic has been quoted *ad nauseam* to prove that absorption would be for them much more than a political problem. True pluralism in the Republic, in which Protestantism would have a lasting future, is said to be non-existent – and such developments as the referendum on divorce and the opposition of members of the Catholic hierarchy to the sale of contraceptives in the South provide further evidence of a state which has little to offer Northern unionists. It is claimed that the success of the IRA campaign in the North depends on there being a 'safe haven' for terrorists across the border in the South. But underneath any specific reasons for opposition to the Republic remains the corrosive general fear of the unknown amongst the majority of loyalists.

It was now no longer only the nationalist community in Northern Ireland which felt alienated. The uneasy relationship of loyalists with Westminster had taken a new turn – and for them it was not a turn for the better. The shock experienced at the Agreement was not only to the unionist system – it went straight to the individual thinking of many who now faced the reality of what they had been led to believe for generations. They were on their own.

In the immediate aftermath of Hillsborough, there was an awareness that limits had to be placed on the process of opposition. If they wanted to remain in the Union, non-constitutional means could not be employed in any protest. At all costs the Union could not be further weakened. The limit of British government toleration could not be defined accurately, but it was recognised as a reality. The danger of widespread protest leading to violence such as had occurred during the loyalist strike was very real in 1985. A massive anti-Agreement demonstration in the centre of Belfast was peaceful. What would loyalist paramilitaries do? The community watched and waited with varying degrees of concern. But history was not to repeat itself in that regard. Had attitudes so changed that the threat was now removed?

For years the two branches of unionism had coexisted but their relationship was far from easy. As a consequence of the 1985 Agreement, unionists came together in mutual opposition. The United Unionist Pact appeared to remove much of the former competition. To the nationalists it was ironic that the Anglo-Irish Agreement had succeeded in achieving what events in the late 60s and early 70s had manifestly failed to do: unionism united. Economic questions, even that of employment, faded into second place. All attention now focused on the one basic constitutional issue – the sovereignty of Northern Ireland.

When loyalists confronted the reform programme of Terence O'Neill and the power-sharing executive of Brian Faulkner in the years following the trauma of 1969, they had done so in different ways and under different banners. Traditional unionism had involved itself in rhetoric and unease over betrayal of traditional principles. Radical unionism took to the streets and pushed loyalism to the limits. By 1985 no such outward difference was visible. There were fears that extremists might push the moderates into actions which, while foreign to the moderate position, might become inevitable. Many of the older school felt uneasy about an alliance which brought them under the same auspices as their more extreme colleagues – but such was the depth of feeling they found they could 'live with it'.

What could not have been envisaged at that early stage, however, was another phase in the Protestant reaction. The apparently continuous opposition to the Agreement at every opportunity took its toll. Protestantism discovered a limit it had not come to before. Were there not other avenues along which to pursue its cause? Was it expedient to present an endless opposition based on the negative 'Ulster says no'? As in the nationalist community's reactions to IRA violence, within unionism frustration gave way to doubt. Disruption to normal life and, in particular, the disadvantages of continued opposition in the face of consistent British government support for the Agreement, in particular for the commercial and business community, began to emerge.

It is difficult to assess precisely this process of disenchantment. It could of course be argued that opposition was perceived as going nowhere, failing to impress Westminster that what was viewed by unionists as a disastrous mistake had been made. The British parliament spoke in an almost united voice in support of the Agreement. World opinion welcomed 'movement at last' in Ireland, and was critical of the negative stance taken by loyalists which was 'what we would have expected'. Loyalists were told two things: the Agreement has the backing of two sovereign parliaments and it won't be as detrimental to your position as you imagine. Unionists all had the same response: we have seen it all before, and look where it has got us.

The perception was that the outside world was once again receiving and accepting only one version of the Northern Ireland story which was certainly not a unionist version. All such emotions and reactions, allied to the uncertainty of where their future lay, contributed to a period of shocked disbelief that what loyalists feared most had now happened. It was no longer a possibility. It was a reality. Who were their real friends? Where was their true home?

For the majority of Protestants the Agreement altered in a fundamental way their relationship and their attitude to the government at Westminster. Two underlying fears surfaced in a new and dramatic fashion. In the first place Dublin had gained a foothold in the affairs of a Province loyalism had guarded and protected for generations, and, secondly, there was genuine uncertainty as to the precise nature of what many regarded as betrayal by Britain.

We have seen that feelings of insecurity have long determined the Protestant approach to political arrangements and relationships. Fears of the consequences if the 1800 Act of Union should ever be overthrown were succeeded by the uncertainties of Home Rule. Once Partition became a reality and the emergence of an independent state south of the border, the fear was that the Northern Protestants would be 'sold down the river' by those they claimed as their allies – the British themselves. The link with Britain was vital to them. Yet the paradox was and is for Protestantism: do the British really want us? For generations loyalists have been prepared to fight for the maintenance of the British link. The realisation the Agreement brought them was that they might be fighting for a link the other partner no longer saw as inevitable or even desirable: the realisation dramatically altered Protestant feelings of fear.

Their despair was much more than the dismay of a people who had had to face unpopular decisions. They had moved closer to the very thing they had so vigorously opposed in the aims of the IRA, a united Ireland. Their despair was made complete by the fact that the 'protectors' of the identity they had fought for, the British government, had been a major player in their deception. So they were driven back into the arms of protest. They were driven back to the mental state they recognised most easily – a feeling of siege. They felt betrayed. The clock had been put back. Their attitude to the British and Irish governments hardened. Their reading of history took a new turn. Their attitude to their closest neighbours, the Catholic nationalist and the Catholic republican population, became even more one of resentment. On the surface there was little evidence of what history will surely one day recognise, that within Protestant Ulster changes were taking place which would have a profound and extensive effect. It was to take time for the Protestants to realise that the tide of events was no longer going to wait for them, for their traditional ways of expressing their historic aspirations. New ways had to be found.

Much is made in the story of Northern Ireland of what is usually called the Irish dimension – that is, the degree to which attitudes, decisions and policies South of the border can, ought to or indeed do, affect the situation in Northern Ireland. There are people who see the Irish dimension as near the root of the problem. There are people who see it as the vital and necessary dimension to a solution, a dimension which not only places efforts at solution in proper perspective, but which holds the key to any real hope that their grievances, their fears and their frustrations can be met. For many it became a reality through the Anglo-Irish Agreement.

To many observers outside the Province it appears clear that there is an Irish dimension to the process of change and ultimate peace in the North. Ireland is a small island on the edge of Europe. Why, they ponder, cannot its people come together to find their own solution? Immediately, the nationalist sees hope, the loyalist further threat and danger.

When travelling through Ireland, North and South, I always encounter a range of attitudes to the 'Irish dimension'. In the heart of the Republic there is bewilderment that the troubles are continuing. People express their horror but of late also genuine frustration amounting to boredom (not that such boredom represents antagonism or anything like it). It is a boredom born of almost total incomprehension. So many people wish the problem of Northern Ireland would simply go away, disappear somehow. Any sign of hope is greeted with enthusiasm, but not with a great deal of certainty that it will achieve anything. In the North among loyalists there nearly always surfaces the belief that: 'anything from that source will mean interference – it can't be good news.'

For a long time I have held the view that an immense amount of good, positive and constructive progress towards solutions in Northern Ireland can flow from events and attitudes in the Republic. I believe that sensitivity to the genuine feelings of unionists and nationalists in the North can be a major step forward to better relations within Northern Ireland. Such sensitivity will always depend on real knowledge rather than impressions formed far away from the troubles or on the basis of propaganda from within the Province. It is in the long-term interest of Ireland as a whole that peace and stable relations prevail between the peoples of Northern Ireland. In the new Europe which is fast emerging there will be little patience with purely regional and internal differences: real though such problems are for the Irish people, the truth is that Europe will be moving on in the years ahead. Moreover, given the close identities of the nationalist outlook and the influence of the Republic, there will always be that Irish dimension to the problems of Northern Ireland.

However, what appears to me to be of more importance than the dimension itself is the way it is expressed. Thus, first: does the existence of Articles in the Republic's constitution which refer to the jurisdiction over Northern Ireland actually further the legitimate philosophies of Irish nationalism? Does their existence really further the process of reconciliation in Northern Ireland? Is there genuine basis for doubting the claim made in the Republic that any future united Ireland can become a reality only with the existence of such constitutional provisions?

Nationalism and republicanism like unionism are perfectly legitimate political aspirations. The tragedy is that each has had periods of destructive attitudes and actions when their legitimacy has suffered. Too often their legitimacy has been hi-jacked by extremism.

The Irish dimension is a reality in the eyes of many people who reflect on Northern Ireland's problems. There can be no substitute for good neighbourliness in Ireland. Yet there are indications that what is more important for the immediate present than an Irish dimension which is linked solely to the idea of national unity is peace, justice and reconciliation for the communities of the North.

Thus, secondly; a remark made to me by a politician in Dublin a few months ago seems to me to place the Irish dimension in perspective: 'Loyalists will never agree to Irish reunification, not for generations. What we have got to see is justice and fairness now for all the people of the North. The other question will have to wait ...'

One's response to such a remark will again depend on one's particular political philosophy. Certainly, there seems little possibility at present of a majority of people in Northern Ireland seeking the removal of the border. This is the reality of the situation. Thirdly, the 'British-Irish' identity crisis is as significant as the 'Irish Irish' – and this must always be placed alongside the question of any 'Irish dimension'.

Speaking of a recent declaration from a republican source that the only really lasting peace for Northern Ireland lay in the removal of 'the British presence', a Protestant said to me: 'Well, what do they intend to do with me? I'm just as Irish as they are – but I'm British. Does the removal of a British presence mean me too?'

Any glib use of the phrase 'British presence' means far more to unionists than troops on the streets or British Ministers at Stormont: it covers a way of life for a majority of people in the North, their very identity, however indefinable.

7
SOCIETY'S
RETRIBUTION

The most obvious casualties of the Northern Ireland conflict are those people who will carry in their hearts, minds and bodies for the remainder of their lives the consequences of terrorism.

The marks run deep: fathers, sons and brothers whose lives have been cut down by bomb or bullet; women and children killed or maimed because they were in the wrong place at the wrong time. Both communities have buried their dead. The scars of years of violence have been etched on so many families and in so many homes.

It is difficult to find a single family in this close-knit community which has not been affected in some way by the loss of life violence has brought. Coming to terms with this tragic toll has been the experience of both Protestant and Catholic families. The re-adjustment in human terms has been as costly as it has been emotional. But the statistics of terrorism tell only one part of the real story. When I listen to official spokesmen talk of the number of dead and injured, I find it increasingly difficult to imagine the real extent of the circle which has gone on widening around each of those statistics.

For statistics can be comforting. When you talk about figures and facts you do not have to stretch your imagination too far. The reality is somewhat different. There are other facts and figures which tell of another aspect of this tragic story. Those other figures, those other statistics are just as real and, in their own way, just as tragic for those involved.

Many will argue that those other people are part of the cause of the suffering. It was their action or lack of it which brought all those other tragedies into being. If they had not set out to kill or destroy we would not be thinking in terms of the human consequences of violence. They are now paying the price for what they did. No one can argue against the linkage of cause and effect. Yet they are also part of the tragedy. They too have their feelings. They too are human beings with families who care and are parts of the jigsaw which must be solved if real peace and stability is to come.

There is a strange feeling of community satisfaction when a terrorist is tried and convicted. That conviction will never bring back his victims, but some people see the conviction as one less terrorist free to carry out more atrocities. For others the sentence of a court will mean a case has been solved, more statistics can be completed. In all the divisions and pain, the removal from society of such a person will produce proof, if proof is desired, that crime does not pay and that terrorism is being met by a judicial process which is society's real safeguard in the long run. Detection and the burden of proof required for such convictions are themselves significant in a violent society, being central to the way any democratic society faces the challenge of lawlessness.

The gulf between perception and reality has been a recurring theme of the Northern Ireland story. This distortion has been at its most dramatic when one considers public attitudes to the ways the judicial system has faced up to the administration of justice under the pressures terrorism imposes in a community which has also to attempt the maintenance of fairness, objectivity and honesty where a major consequence of the divisions is widely differing estimates of right and wrong: one man's terrorist is another's freedom fighter; one man's paramilitary activist is another victim of circumstance; one man's convicted criminal is another's martyr.

A prison visit is at the best of times a sobering experience. To visit those held in a Northern Ireland prison because of paramilitary activity is to see at first hand one of the real tragedies of our conflict. Men imprisoned for many years, some as a consequence of horrendous murders and attacks, living out the most useful years of their lives behind bars, present any visitor with a glimpse of the results of what has happened in the outside community. Men who succumbed to the fears and tensions of a divided community, caught up in the net of violence, perpetrators of death and misery, members of paramilitary organisations who have obeyed the orders of some who still walk free: men destined to spend long years paying for the sectarian divisions of their community.

They come from different parts of the Province and they come from different backgrounds. On some faces are the distinctive marks of 'the cause'; they are 'prisoners of war' living out each day with a routine and a philosophy which reflects their version of Colditz or the prison camps of Singapore generations ago. They were 'unlucky' and they take their incarceration as an inevitable part of what they tried to achieve 'outside the wire'. They respond to the influence of their superiors and they do so in ways which make the ordinary routine of the prison of secondary importance to the demands of the cause they still support. There are others whose expressions are different.

Many prisoners were caught up in something they could not understand or control. Where they lived dictated physical and emotional responses to suggestions or fiery oratory; when they lived presented them with little alternative than to be fodder in the hands of others who had great ideas of what 'needed to be done'. The sectarianism and the fears of the 60s and 70s which knew no distinction between Protestant and Catholic ghettoes swept them up: the revolver or the explosive was easily available, as were those who knew how to use them. Now, years later, they are changed men. Those years have made them different. The resentment is no longer directed at 'them' but at those who led them or encouraged them. Membership of a paramilitary movement has been rejected. Not all would claim to be disciples of peace and reconciliation, just waiting to change the world once they are released; most of them are disillusioned, still bewildered by it all, yet no longer those who want to die for the cause.

The culture of Northern Ireland's prisoners of the troubles is remarkable. They have created a community within a community. It has spawned its own mythology, and heroes are not just those who have died on the hunger strike, but those who were as defiant in the dock of a court as they were on the fateful day or night of the murder or the explosion. The emotions of those men who live out sentences in the Crumlin Road or the Maze, the aspirations of those in the ultra-modern Maghaberry, the opinions of prisoners on the shores of Lough Foyle at Magilligan have an influence over events beyond the walls which is significant and vital to any understanding of Northern Ireland. At times, such as the drama of the hunger strikes, that influence has been unbelievable. At others, the length of sentence, the pleas of innocence and the claims of 'a change of heart' have become political footballs contributing to reaction and counter-reaction in the prisoners' communities.

Since those early days of 1968 crime and punishment have become questions of prime concern for Ireland as a whole. Society has been confronted with intense and emotive issues. The decisions of courts, their method of operation and the sentences passed have also influenced the conflict. They are the object of passionate and divisive debate far beyond these shores: questions about the nature of a society's revenge or retribution, the consequences of a communal abhorrence of paramilitary activity and the levels of forbearance in society during a period of violence.

When a community faces the intensity of community violence that Northern Ireland faced in the 70s, followed by a prolonged period of terrorism, careful consideration of principles can become a luxury. Crime and punishment, the nature of punishment and its relationship to the rehabilitation of offenders, prison conditions and long-term planning so vital to the character of a free society can be subject to reactionary policies. Basic issues become of secondary importance to the needs of the moment, needs which frequently manifest themselves in terms of removing from society those people whose actions are considered detrimental to the well-being of the community at large. Attempts by politicians to meet the upsurge of violence with significant facts and figures of convictions become a priority. There have been occasions during the past twenty odd years when one wonders if crime and punishment in Northern Ireland has been pushed to the back of the community conscience.

In the years following 1968, the web of violence encompassed not only those people who fired the shots or set off an explosion. Those who planned terrorism, provided support or cover, failed to provide information or aided and abetted in a multitude of ways have all helped to boost the prison population here. Many were convicted in their teens or early twenties and their sentences were for life or at least indeterminate, and the ways in which these sentences are reviewed have provoked passionate public controversy. Their offences and the influence still exerted over the prisoners from beyond the prison means that security has become a priority in prison policy. It is remarkable, given the level of 'high risk' prisoners in the Northern Ireland system, that anything approaching genuine moves towards rehabilitation are even contemplated, yet over recent years there have been great improvements in the conditions under which long-term sentences are served. Although the strain on prison authorities has been immense, in the vast majority of cases, prison officials have achieved a great deal under the extremely difficult conditions where the organisation and discipline imposed by paramilitary organisations, and most noticeably by what are termed 'godfathers', have led to a highly organised and sophisticated system of communication on both sides of prison walls. Reprisals against prison officers or their families and the ability of paramilitary organisations to influence attitudes inside a prison have posed difficult and dangerous problems for prison authorities.

But above and beyond the facts of prison life there are fundamental questions which a violent society must not be alone in asking. Is imprisonment the only way of eliminating terrorism? Are the figures of those serving long sentences for crimes of a paramilitary nature in fact a judgement on society's failure to create situations in which such violence can be avoided? In short, is the paramilitary prison population a measure of a community's ills?

To take away a person's liberty is devastating. This is obvious. In the face of widespread terror and atrocities, calls for conviction and punishment are urgent. The fact of conviction and the fact of a long sentence lead to a sort of quietening of the community conscience. Protection of society demands the removal from its circulation of those who have murdered and maimed, for whatever reason. But have we engaged in sufficient genuine research into what such policies mean in the long term? Sociologists have frequently spoken of the connection between social deprivation and crime. Unemployment is often quoted as the most significant social ill contributing to young people turning to violent crime. But do such considerations change when the tensions of political divisions in Northern Ireland became a source of encouragement for politically motivated crimes? 'Murder is murder', no matter what the excuse given. The connection between crime and punishment in an area of politically motivated terrorism differs little from the debate in 'normal society'. However, if we are talking about peaceful change in the community, we cannot separate issues of crime and punishment from the sort of society we are seeking to create in the future. In Northern Ireland it is accepted that we have had the highest proportion of prisoners per capita in Western Europe. A society which seeks to move forward to a just peace can never afford to ignore the demands of a prison philosophy which will make its own significant contribution to its future. Prisons are a reflection of what a society regards as wrong-doing, crime and guilt. When a society has to respond to prolonged terrorism they can so easily become 'the easy way out' for a community which has not been granted the time or the opportunity to know precisely what it is about.

I have often been approached by members of a prisoner's family because of domestic and emotional concerns consequent to a long sentence. The strain on a family in such circumstances cannot be overestimated, nor can the effect on attitudes outside a prison be overstated in the category of those cases unique to the Northern Ireland situation which fall under the Secretary of State's pleasure. In many of the cases brought to my attention a prisoner will have been sentenced at an early age, often as a result of crimes committed in the early years of the troubles. The court decided that he should be detained for an indefinite period. Periodic reviews of the sentence are carried out, but the practice of not informing a prisoner or a family of the likely length of a sentence can be demoralising and negative, something which it is impossible to justify save on grounds of security or prison discipline. I have been aware in recent years of welcome changes in this policy. Punishment, particularly when many years have been served and in several cases periods longer than the 'life sentence' in other parts of the Western world, can be meted out humanely even in a violent society. A regular review of every indeterminate sentence should surely be the norm. In fact, it should be possible for a prisoner in such a category to be given clear indication of the length of that sentence.

In Northern Ireland life imprisonment is the mandatory sentence for murder and is imposed for a range of other serious offences. A sentence of detention at the 'pleasure of the Secretary of State' is mandatory for murder committed by a person who was below eighteen years of age at the time of the offence. The procedures for reviewing both categories are the same except that those prisoners held at the Secretary of State's pleasure (SOSPs) have their cases considered at an earlier stage of the sentence itself. Thus it is now customary that SOSPs have their cases reviewed as a matter of normal procedure for the first time by the Life Sentence Review Board after eight years have passed. This is two years earlier than life sentence cases which are not normally reviewed until ten years have been served.

The overall prison population here is very different from other parts of the United Kingdom. In November 1991 24 per cent of the sentenced community were serving indeterminate periods of imprisonment and of these 88 per cent had been convicted of terrorist-related offences. The vast majority of the 408 prisoners serving indeterminate sentences had been convicted of murder. These prisoners came from both communities and the majority had links with either republican or loyalist paramilitary organisations.

The percentage of prisoners in this category who have been released has increased in the past few years. In 1985 62 inmates fell within this category. By March 1990 there were 25 prisoners of whom 8 had been given release dates and the judiciary had been consulted about the release on licence of another 2 prisoners.

The dilemma for a society which sees crime and punishment as a vital issue is how far it can distance itself from responsibility for those conditions that permitted or even encouraged a person to become involved in terrorism or violence. It can be argued that many inmates in Northern Ireland prisons, there as a result of politically inspired violence, are in fact the victims of circumstance. A community cannot help to create the conditions which encourage or permit paramilitary activity to flourish and then, having condemned and sentenced a person, often a young person, for such crimes, ignore the conditions under which such punishment is administered.

Criminal actions can be clothed in many garments. Justification for such deeds come under many headings. Reasons can be, at heart, merely excuses. Nothing can justify or excuse murder. To argue that a young person is so caught up in turbulent times and is merely a victim of circumstances beyond his control forcing him to commit a criminal act is often a plausible way of explaining the inexplicable. It is not only during periods of prolonged terrorism that convenient explanations, which have more to do with what is in fact happening in society, can be put forward to help to explain why some people commit certain offences. Too often such reasoning becomes a warped means of justifying those deeds. It is therefore wrong to explain all that has happened in Northern Ireland since 1968 as inevitable because of 'the circumstances'. Special pleading is common when no other explanation appears feasible. I have listened to and read comments which indicate an ambivalence about the fact that sheer criminality has been the *raison d'être* for many offences committed here during the troubles.

Undoubtedly there have been many instances where pressures, intimidation, blackmail and the atmosphere of communal hatred or prejudice have encouraged attacks and assassinations. It is when society reaches the point where it can no longer distinguish between the politically motivated crime and the crime which is no more than that – a crime – that the corrosive effects of terrorism have begun to be felt. 'Murder is murder' is a phrase all too familiar in the Northern Ireland story. Such thinking can equally be applied to many other less serious crimes. How far violence is justified, when it is the result of a political philosophy or aspiration, will long remain a subject of heated argument. History has shown that the line between cause and consequence is not always easy to draw.

On those many occasions when I have been introduced to a home which has been brought to its knees by the murder of a much loved father or son, consideration of crime and punishment seems light years away from the anguish and suffering of that family. Inevitably, appeals are made to the local community to assist in the conviction of those responsible. In the middle of such a tragedy few people want to think further than the removal from society of those who have caused such sorrow.

Yet there is always the human side to the relationship of those who have lost loved ones at the hands of terrorists and those who are ultimately convicted of the crime. It is a relationship which is often unspoken, undefined. There is a sense of relief that someone has been made accountable, a sense that while nothing can 'undo' what has happened at least they have been 'caught'. Just occasionally, there is another element. Its presence is neither a judgement of those cases where it is absent, nor a particular attribute when it occurs – unless, of course, it is what I believe it to be, a powerful example of the goodness and strength of spirit which can break through in human relationships. It comes to the surface when a relative of someone murdered wishes to contact the perpetrator of the crime. There are many reasons for this. Chief among them must be what I can only describe as the deepest and most personal of Christian virtues: a mixture of human compassion and even forgiveness which is remarkable.

> I simply want to say something and I don't know what it is. But I can't get him back, he's gone. Yet I can't go on living without trying to understand why – and I'll never understand until I talk to that man and he hears how I feel. I want to forgive, but I know it'll take time.

These are the words of one person whom society can classify as a victim because she lost a husband, but also the words of someone who was already seeing something more beyond the suffering and sorrow. Statistics do tell only a part of the story.

In a tragic way both families, and terrorists who find themselves behind bars, are victims of a situation in which the price of life is cheap. However deep the distress and however difficult it is to evaluate punishment objectively, society will be diminished if insufficient attention is given to the ways in which punishment is administered.

Attention to the humanitarian aspects of prison conditions is not always popular in a divided society. Northern Ireland has seen more than its fair quota of community revenge. Retaliation for paramilitary activity by 'the other side' is frequent. Equally, the society which suffers a prolonged period of terrorism tends to be influenced by the level of public revulsion at the nature of the crime committed, and this is always a dilemma for a court. There have been many voices that have warned Northern Ireland that it should not 'go soft' on prisoners who have committed some of the most dastardly crimes imaginable. Often such demands have been at the centre of debate. Cooler heads and cooler judgement must never ignore the wider implications and consider that, while providing adequate protection for society, the urgency of lengthy periods of violence must not blot out what punishment means for the nature of society itself.

It is very easy to be accused of weakness in a violent society when one talks of rehabilitation or reform in relation to prisoners. No one can possibly doubt the necessity to imprison, and thereby remove from a position in which they can inflict great suffering on others, terrorists who, regardless of public opinion, murder and attack apparently at will. Punishment in this sense is seen by all right-thinking people to be not just imprisonment and the loss of freedom, but the removal of a threat. No consideration of what a prison stands for or what constitutes rehabilitation can possibly affect such thinking. But, equally, nothing should prevent the humane society striving to understand the nature of imprisonment, what it involves for the prisoner and what it should seek to achieve in the long term.

Society can itself be diminished if its reaction is to think of punishment alone. Nothing but sympathy can be felt for those who have to make hard decisions on the evidence before them in cases of atrocities and murder. Nothing but sympathy can be expressed for those charged with the responsibility of guarding society from people determined to murder and maim for whatever reason. But the point must surely be made that long and hard thinking is essential if the policies of punishment are not to be confused with those of prevention, the aims of rehabilitation are not to be dominated by punishment in terms of years behind bars and the long-term effects on society of reaction to violence are not to be geared to considerations of that punishment alone.

Cardinal Cahal Daly has written recently of the importance of the connection between punishment and the ideals of a society seeking social change:

> Our society is desperately in need of a change of heart. A change of heart cannot be forced but it can be evoked. Only mercy can evoke mercy. Compassion cannot be compelled by force or fear; it can only be shown. By being shown, it justifies itself and indeed justifies justice. Clemency and mercy are not simply Christian virtues. They can also be forces for political change and social transformation.[10]

Any society has a duty to protect itself from danger to its people. There are those who should and must be removed from society: those who show no sign that they have any intention of relenting from lives committed to some of the most serious crimes recorded in recent times. Punishment is an essential part of a community's statement of what it believes about itself. But the nature of that punishment and the conditions under which it is administered must always be at the heart of the conscience of a just society. Too often a society which allows the mere fact of conviction and punishment to be its reaction to wrong has succumbed to the subtle aims (the erosion of principles) of any movement which uses violence as a means of political pressure.

I have, to be honest, seen cases where allegiance to a cause has never diminished through years of imprisonment. I have also seen what I am satisfied to be a genuine change of heart, where more would be gained by a return to society sooner rather than later. Memories of conversations with convicted paramilitaries in which the intensity and determination of the prisoner to maintain loyalty to the cause dominated every word spoken are vivid. No matter what length of sentence was imposed it was hard to imagine any change of heart. Equally, I have listened to those who believed that they could be a powerful influence for good if on release they could persuade others to opt out of the paramilitary stranglehold, to persuade others that from their own experience they have learned that 'violence was not the way.' I realise there is widespread cynicism abroad about 'prison conversions'. In a society which has suffered so much this is understandable. The greatest possible caution is essential in any approach to those who, having destroyed lives or threatened society through violence, begin to talk about a change of heart. Yet I am convinced from my experiences that in some cases such attitudes are genuine. I have seen the powerful influence some ex-prisoners

---

[10.] Archbishop Cahal Daly, *op. cit.*, p. 109.

can exert on release when they have the courage to disown paramilitary organisations.

As the full force of community violence swept this Province some years ago the legal system was swamped with cases which the courts were unable to deal with at any great speed. The gathering of evidence and the essential preparation took time. The consequence was a rapid growth in the numbers of accused awaiting trial in custody. This situation presented prison authorities with urgent problems, not least the question of adequate accommodation. Over-crowding with all its attendant social and psychological problems often reached crisis proportions, and the strain on prison staff was intense. Prison chaplains encountered many cases where the attitudes of those remanded in custody and their families became extremely difficult to deal with. The system quite simply was being stretched to breaking point. Again in recent years there has been an improvement in the situation. But one cannot help feeling that no effort should be spared to minimise the period between the first appearances in court and the main trial and decision.

Overall, looking back now in the 90s to the years when the prison population of Northern Ireland was swollen so dramatically as a consequence of orchestrated violence, one is conscious of immense change. Many of those who entered prison in the early 70s are back in society. A remarkable proportion of those released have remained free of paramilitary involvement, though there have been notable exceptions. Prison conditions have been vastly improved. Facilities for rehabilitation are among the best anywhere in the world. Examples abound of prisoners following university courses and obtaining degrees, of prisoners receiving training in trades which is equal to anything expected in the outside world, of ex-prisoners being received back into a society which has itself to a considerable degree moved on from those traumatic days of the early troubles. But events behind bars can still exert great influence on community reaction in Northern Ireland. The days of the hunger strikes remain a vivid reminder of how quickly and how intensely events outside can be generated from 'within'.

The booklet, *The Report on the Work of the Northern Ireland Prison Service 1989–90*, makes a clear point about the changes in prisons:

> The photographs which appear later in this report are grouped under three headings – 'The Past', 'The Present' and 'The Future'. This is designed to make the simple point that the present in Northern Ireland's prisons is better than the past and that the future could be even better. The Prison Service is intent on maintaining this momentum despite the efforts of paramilitary organisations to turn back the clock.

When I talk to prison chaplains and official visitors to the prisons of Northern Ireland I am given a clear and lasting impression of the efforts which are being made to see that prisoners are given every possible opportunity to grasp the chance to face up to their future lives in a responsible way. The whole range of professions geared to maintaining the welfare of prisoners and their families has become acutely aware of the special problems and opportunities of the Northern Ireland situation. Pastoral care of inmates and the needs of their families are a priority for clergy, staff, social workers and probation officers. Too often insufficient credit is afforded to those involved in this on-going work. They face many obstacles which have little to do with prison life itself: the home environment, the prevailing situation in areas greatly affected by paramilitarism and the chronic unemployment situation – all have a distinct bearing on policy and practice. And comparing the atmosphere I found on visits to prisons ten years ago with what I encounter now the change is vast. Despite many comments and attitudes, often generated for party political or purely sectarian reasons outside prisons, on the regime and conditions, no objective observer can fail to be impressed by the overall improvement in the living conditions of a large number of prisoners. The attempts by paramilitary organisations to have inmates convicted of terrorist-related crimes segregated inside the prison continues to produce tensions and at times actual violence, and the policy of refusing to encourage such segregation, and instead of integrating the prison population to reflect the sort of community many outside seek for the future, has become a priority for government. Many of the lessons of the past have been learned.

However, the point must be made again. Terrorism will have succeeded and violence will have won if punishment or the removal of a terrorist-linked offender from freedom are the only features of prison policy. The balance between the protection of society, the punishment of a convicted prisoner and the return of that person when conditions are conducive to his release is much more than the guiding principle of a prison system. It is also a clear indication of what any community really thinks about progress. Among the lessons of Ulster few possess greater urgency than the importance of adequate planning and research into the nature of the relationship between crime and punishment.

The true nature of what from pulpit or sanctuary can be equated with evil will long provoke philosophical and theological debate. There have been times when the people of Northern Ireland have seen what can only be described as the face of evil.

The events of the last twenty odd years have produced a new definition of the casualties of terrorism. A society which forgets the needs of those who have lost most at the hands of the terrorist, indeed a society which at times has seemed to forget that such people have to go on living with the scars of such losses, will be further diminished if it allows the demands of the moment to blind it to the way it deals with those who caused those same scars in the first place.

8
WHO ARE WE?

Political problems demand political solutions.

To the outside world the Northern Ireland problem is simply a matter of religion: it is about Catholics and Protestants who cannot agree on how to share a small piece of earth: it is about the violent means they use to impose their aspirations on each other. To live and work in Northern Ireland is to experience the tragic consequences of such oversimplification.

The situation here brings into focus other issues, in particular issues of power and influence: the power to make things happen and to have influence over the results; of employment and the opportunities for employment; of security and what security means. At the heart of these is 'the constitutional issue', that traditional Ulster phrase. Commentators have tended to distinguish between the nature of institutions and the parameters of the constitutional. Yet such niceties of definition do not inherently follow from the way the two main groupings in Northern Ireland view the conflict. For Protestants and unionists, as for Catholics and nationalists, the nature of institutions and 'the constitutional question' are interwoven. This attitude naturally affects the form the confrontation takes and also determines the limits of any movement of one towards the other. The opinion of either side of the main constitutional issue, the shape of Northern Ireland, its form and future, has a definite bearing on how that side regards any change on domestic institutional questions.

In recent years unionist opinion has greatly resented the presence of Sinn Fein on the local councils of Northern Ireland. This resentment has shown something of the depth of feeling in the Protestant community *vis-à-vis* the political voice of the IRA. But, for a unionist, the battle against Sinn Fein on the floor of the councils of Northern Ireland is much more than opposition to the political face of IRA terrorism. They see this as a confrontation between those who wish to safeguard the constitutional future of Northern Ireland within the United Kingdom and those who seek to erode the very local structures and institutions created to maintain the United Kingdom identity, in using them. The often combative exchanges between unionist and republican councillors in those council chambers stem from the resentment felt by unionists at threats to the overall constitutional position, and their perception that the other side is determined to oppose such stability at every level of institutional life. When observers speak of a lack of 'normal political activity' in Northern Ireland, they frequently use a shorthand for what is a more complex issue: the correlation of institutionalism and constitutional perspective.

I have often been told in England that unionists and Protestants would find it much easier to justify concessions to the minority population of nationalists and Catholics if they could limit their demands for change to institutional matters. Such suggestions imply that nationalist thinking fails to distinguish between the two levels while the other makes a clear distinction between the two. I cannot accept this conclusion because of what I have experienced of attitudes within the two main communities. Time and again unionist politicians have spoken to me of the lessons to be learned from the way republicans have used their positions in local councils and area boards. They have spoken with genuine earnestness of what they see as attempts by their opponents to 'undermine the position of Northern Ireland' by making the Province 'ungovernable' at the institutional or local level. The consequence of this has often been that something which to loyalist thinking would be seen as a compromise is most certainly not accepted as such by others.

Since 1968 there have been distinctly different perceptions of what constitutes the unionist position. Many unionists speak of reforms in housing distribution, location of industry and allocation of employment as being more than generous concessions to those appeals for change which were the hallmark of civil rights demands in the 60s. It has been said frequently within the unionist and Protestant community that 'enough is enough': they have gone far enough and now is the time for much greater compromise by them. The failure to perceive any movement on the part of the nationalist community or its representatives is generally accepted by unionists as further evidence of their determination that Northern Ireland must not be allowed to work or succeed. On the other hand, for many Catholics and nationalists their discontent is aimed at a basic refusal by unionists or Protestants to contemplate real equality of opportunity and citizenship – in other words, progress or the lack of it.

Since 1968 there has been little clearer indication of this situation than the implementation of the Anglo-Irish Agreement and its aftermath. Deeply resented by unionists, welcomed by nationalists and the cause of so much conflict of opinion and attitude since its signing by the governments of the United Kingdom and the Republic of Ireland in 1985, this agreement crystallised the differing perceptions of the two communities – as have, in 1991, the efforts of Mr Peter Brooke, the Secretary of State for Northern Ireland, to bring the political parties around a conference table to discuss the future government of the Province. Appeals for compromise have produced the inevitable nationalist response that unionists will only make concessions when forced to do so. A new agreement superseding the older one and based on trust of the unionist community alone is not possible, they argue, because pressure alone compels unionist movement. Unionist generosity which would, in the eyes of the outside world, be a tangible move towards greater community stability, is made impossible by their inability to see beyond the institutional and constitutional questions. Any movement on the one is linked entirely in Protestant thinking to the other. Such a link lies deep in the Ulster Protestant outlook. It is a fact that is not always appreciated by those outside the Protestant community. The failure to understand this and the reasons for it have had, at best, negative results and, at worst, led to tragic mis-understanding.

The consequences of such Protestant views have become a recurring theme in the current situation in Northern Ireland. From their perspective, the events of 1922 and the birth of Northern Ireland seem acceptable and totally justified. To be told that the state of Northern Ireland has failed as a political entity is a complete anathema to Protestant thinking. Have unionists not as much right to self-determination as nationalists? Do not unionists have the right to those institutional structures within the Province which make this self-determination a reality? Surely, unionists would argue, if the structure of the state is legitimate, a nationalist cannot be expected to find easy integration into Northern Ireland. Why should a majority population be expected to facilitate a minority viewpoint if such reforms have more to do with the overall constitutional position than local reform? As far back as 1968 the unionist reaction to calls for reform by the civil rights movement gave an indication of much that was to follow. The suspicion that much more was involved than meeting a community call for legitimate reform gave rise to the resentment which extremists were able to exploit within Protestant areas. It follows that unionist thinking believes that the majority of nationalist grievances have been met over the past quarter century and those which remain will be addressed as and when overall constitutional stability becomes a reality.

It is in this context that an explanation can be offered for what is seen outside Northern Ireland as one of the real mysteries of unionist thinking. On the one hand loyalists demand a future which is cemented within the United Kingdom: unionists speak of rights that should be shared willingly with their neighbours but in the British framework. Yet there is more to the nationalist case for equality between the two communities. The crisis became obvious when the unionist community had to confront the 'Britishness' of the thinking implied by the Anglo-Irish Agreement. Here was a dilemma matched only by the frustration and bewilderment felt by unionists as they faced the evolving British policy towards Northern Ireland under direct rule, when British politicians spoke of 'British standards' consequent to 'British loyalty'. Often reference was made to the injustice of Northern Ireland receiving treatment at Westminster which was more geared to the government of a colonial empire than to a loyal and involved part of the United Kingdom. Legislation controlling life in Northern Ireland, frequently put before parliament as an order in council, late at night and before a poorly attended House of Commons, became the focus of deep unionist resentment. But it was when policies which appeared to be based on what had been designed for the 'mainland', rather than the 'special conditions of Northern Ireland', were 'imposed' on the Province that the depth of the unionist dilemma became apparent. The Protestants felt that their loyalty to the 'British way of life' gave them the same rights as their fellow citizens on the mainland: it did not always appear to others to justify the degree of opposition by Ulster unionists to British policies.

Again, the consequences of these constitutional aspirations and their effect on policies of reform throw some light on the dilemma facing unionist political leadership. Even if major concessions towards a nationalist standpoint were considered desirable, a major problem would arise when the leadership sought to convince a constituency which for generations has been confident of the inter-relationship between the major question of the constitutional future of Northern Ireland and local institutional developments. As one unionist politician once put it to me: 'To go too far ahead of the troops without first assuring them that the constitutional issue is safe could be suicide.'

Of primary importance in this context, the question of the sharing of power in a local assembly or chamber is an extremely emotive one for many in the unionist family. While many Protestants seek developed government allied to majority rule, there is an inherent opposition to executive power-sharing. It is argued that while compromise or movement may be desirable, it is both asking and expecting too much to share executive local power with anyone who cannot accept the constitutional position of the Province. Even unionist politicians who favour some degree of power-sharing argue strongly for a clear formula clarifying and securing the position of the majority. Power-sharing for them would be a concession – not a basic political right.

A report by the Unionist Task Force left no doubt that power-sharing at the constitutional level would depend on the acceptance by nationalists of the constitutional future of Northern Ireland as unionists see it and the forfeiting of the role of the government of the Irish Republic as custodians of the nationalist interest. For a unionist, any role for the Irish government in the affairs of Northern Ireland can only be considered if there is a corresponding acceptance by Ireland of the legitimacy of the state of Northern Ireland. The claim of Articles 2 and 3 of the Irish constitution regarding the future of Northern Ireland have long irritated unionist opinion. Any intervention in the internal affairs of the North by the Irish government, and in particular the role afforded to it by the Anglo-Irish Agreement, is to a unionist totally unacceptable.

Opportunities for employment have also long been a sensitive issue between the communities. Fair employment legislation introduced during the period of direct rule has had a mixed reception from unionists. While their attitude to this legislation is perhaps less intimately connected with the constitutional issue and more to the economic well-being of those they represent, at least one commentator has seen a connection between 'their general attitudes to reform and their resistance to strong fair-employment legislation. In both cases, formal equality of opportunity is offered while substantive equality of the traditions is resisted.'[11]

It is on the question of security that so much of the dilemma between constitutional and institutional issues becomes most obvious in unionist thinking. There are repeated and consistent calls by unionist politicians for a stronger security policy on the part of the British government. These calls inevitably follow any upsurge in IRA activity. Unionist thinking mainly accommodates only one solution to the IRA threat – military defeat. Attacks on the security forces are attacks on the legitimate means of the state to defend itself. There can be no compromise on this issue, for such attacks are a threat to the people they have been elected to represent. Prison reforms which tend to give any special treatment to convicted IRA members are bitterly opposed, and the possibility of a reintroduction of internment is not only legitimate for many unionists but essential. IRA terrorism takes unionist philosophy no further than a return to the constitutional question – and in so far as attacks on the security forces are an attack on the legitimacy of Northern Ireland, stronger policy to defeat terrorism is a constant call.

It has been long argued that unionists only consider reforms at a constitutional level when they are compelled to do so. All discussion on power-sharing from the nationalist perspective stems from the wording of the Anglo-Irish Agreement. Without that, they argue, unionists would never have even discussed the possibility. Such a conclusion is debatable for I detect a

---

[11] Sarah Barber and Myrtle Hill (eds), *Aspects of Irish Studies* (1990), p. 5.

change in some unionist thinking on the issue. In the current debate on the future of the North there are unionist voices which talk of a new start, a fresh beginning. How far such thinking would have emerged without pressure from without is, like so much else in this situation, a matter of conjecture for future generations. Would unionist opinion as a whole ever countenance the construction of a new state rather than the piecemeal reform of the old? Would such a possibility ever let them move on from their fears on the constitutional issue? Would that mean that nationalists would be presented with proposals they could find impossible to reject? Such possibilities in the present climate seem far in the future.

When we turn to look at the Catholic or nationalist stand on constitutional and institutional issues we find processes of reasoning similar to those present in the unionist community, because of the prominence of the constitutional issue itself. Republican thinking is based on the belief that when Ireland was partitioned a system of relationships came into being in the North which removed once and for all the possibility of fragmentary reform. To such thinking, tampering with institutional structures will fall far short of equality for Catholics. For constitutional nationalists however the picture is different: for them there is always the possibility of an institutional settlement in Northern Ireland in the short term, although in the long term they still aspire to a united Ireland.

The SDLP which represents the majority of Catholics in Northern Ireland was founded on 21 August 1970 and absorbed most of the members of the old Nationalist Party, National Democratic Party and Republican Labour Party. It is a member of Socialist International and the Confederation of Socialist Parties of the European Community. It was presented to the public as a radical, left-of-centre party, seeking civil rights for all and a just distribution of wealth. It professed to promote friendship and understanding between the two parts of Ireland with re-unification to be based on the consent of the majority.

The Party's first major move was to withdraw from the old Northern Ireland parliament at Stormont on the grounds that it was withdrawing its consent from the institutions of government. When internment was introduced in August 1971 the SDLP sponsored a civil disobedience campaign through the withholding of rents and rates. When direct rule was introduced in 1972 following the suspension of Stormont the SDLP took the opportunity to suggest new forms of government. Its document 'Towards a New Ireland' proposed that Britain and the Republic of Ireland should exercise joint sovereignty over the North. When the Anglo-Irish Agreement was signed it was a moment of triumph for the party: here at last was the recognition that representation of nationalist and Catholic grievances could be reinforced by the backing of the Irish government. The Agreement was for the Party a framework where nationalists have as much say as unionists. Partition may be accepted as an unavoidable though unpleasant fact, but it cannot grant the unionist majority unquestioned rights over the nationalist or Catholic minority. The Party represents itself in Northern Ireland as the rational and moderate face of nationalism. This moderation has been maintained even when refusing what many unionists would view as genuine attempts at compromise. But within the Catholic community the SDLP faces criticism from the Workers' Party that it is immovable in its nationalism, and the Sinn Fein view is that it has lost any real desire for ultimate Irish unity.

The SDLP has never put forward Irish unity as the only priority. There has been a recognition that, if nationalists have a right to be Irish, so unionists have an equal right to be British. But the identity crisis which is so much a part of the Irish problem generates its own dilemmas for the Party as it seeks to be the representative of constitutional nationalism. By allowing for the possibility of an institutional settlement, without denying the equal possibility of Irish unity, it permits differing strands of nationalism to find a resting place within its ranks. The crucial issue is as noted, equal rights. From this perspective, the real need is a radical change in state structures to allow both unionist and nationalist a fresh, equitable start.

By Northern Ireland standards this position is radical. To accept the existence of Northern Ireland is not to accept the dominance of unionist authority within it, or that unionism should ever have a final veto on reform.

On the question of security policy, nationalists take the view that the defeat of the IRA can only be achieved through political means and do not consider that security policy can ever be separated from other reforms such as those affecting the legal and political systems. Speaking at the annual Party Conference in 1988, John Hume emphasised that security considerations cannot be pursued as though there already existed agreement on the legitimacy of the state itself.

Talk of a final settlement is premature while unionists fail to see the aspirations of a united Ireland to be as valid as claims to the British connection. For the SDLP there is always the risk that unionists will return to the old manifestations of majority rule if pressure is relaxed. The nationalists believe they have already made significant changes in their views, involving definite concessions to the loyalist philosophy. Indeed unionists and nationalists both believe that they have already made compromises, that they have both moved towards agreement. Looked at from their own political perspectives, both traditions have come a long way since 1968.

*   *   *

Thus at the bottom of the conflicting views on the matter of political institutions in Northern Ireland there exist divergent views on the legitimacy of the state, and in this each community has a very different understanding of what constitutes compromise in political terms. For both unionist and nationalist the crucial issue of the legitimacy of Northern Ireland remains paramount. To the unionist, if the legitimacy of the state with its 'British identity' were to be lost, then so would the argument for the maintenance of the union with Britain. This would be to acknowledge that Protestantism did not possess an unconditional right to self-determination. To nationalists an unconditional acceptance of the legitimacy of Northern Ireland would be the end of an aspiration to a united Ireland at some future date. It would also mean an end to their argument for full equality in all aspects of life in the recognition of the two traditions in Northern Ireland. Should devolved government become a reality and should it include some form of power-sharing, until the argument over constitutional legitimacy is resolved, serious and significant differences will appear over the issues of authority, power and security.

Sadly, until a formula is found to place the real issues on some agenda where discussion can flow freely and unhampered by Irish political history, it will remain unclear how political accommodation can be attained. Given the history of Northern Ireland it will also remain unclear how political accommodation can be maintained.

These then, not in party political terms alone, but in terms of how both communities view their cultural, political and religious future, were the problems which faced Peter Brooke when in 1989 he first indicated that a new effort might be possible to bring the political parties to the conference table. He saw that the leaders of the constitutional parties might be prepared to allow actual political power, authority and responsibility to be given to locally elected representatives in the Province. In short, devolved government limited by areas of mutual agreement, involving relationships between the various sides in Northern Ireland and between Northern Ireland and her neighbours was a possibility. For the unionists this was the opportunity to find a replacement for the Anglo-Irish Agreement. For nationalists it was the opportunity to find a place in some structures of devolved government secure in the knowledge that, if all failed, the Anglo-Irish Agreement remained. On 7 September 1990, speaking to the current affairs society of St Louis Grammar School, Ballymena, Mr Brooke voiced his views following discussions with the parties:

Since politics is the art of the possible, my role has been to explore with the parties the extent to which they would find it possible to accommodate each others' views and interests without any sacrifice of principle or of their own essential interests. I have been impressed and encouraged by the readiness of those with whom I have been talking to acknowledge others' positions and to adjust their own position in the interests of finding a way forward.

He saw a new readiness to engage in party political dialogue. Was there now such a radical, even dramatic shift in opinion that a new beginning was in sight even given the fundamental differences which existed on the ultimate issue – the constitutional question? Real issues should be examined:

In any event I hope all will explore with me the substantive issues they believe need to be covered, and how they would fit into the overall framework established so far. I venture to suggest that many of those issues will not be new: how can we address the concerns of the minority community that its voice too can continue to be heard at the highest level of decision-making, for instance, or the concerns of the majority community about Articles 2 and 3 of the Irish constitution?

He hoped there was a 'mutually acceptable path through the various party positions to arrive at a basis that safeguards everyone's essential interests'.

Such an achievement would undoubtedly have a significant effect on the Anglo-Irish Agreement itself – a fact that both the Irish and British governments were prepared to admit. In Peter Brooke's words: 'We face a challenge and an opportunity which will not last for ever: we must seize it.' The continuing terrorism and the belief that such dialogue would mean more than an exchange of views which would lead to political accommodation – that it would lead to the end of terrorism – was sufficient grounds for a weary and wary people to wish his initiative well.

In the Roman Catholic community the divide between the republican viewpoint, with Sinn Fein absent from the table, and the nationalists was again visible. The SDLP welcomed the opportunity and John Hume in his opening speech spoke of the urgent need to face traditional differences with openness and honesty:

If we are to succeed in resolving our differences then we must face those differences honestly and directly. There is little point in either of us saying to the other: 'we cannot change, so you must.' Neither of us can change what we are. What we can, and must, change are our attitudes, our intolerance of difference, our repeated pushing of difference to the point of division. We must begin by accepting each other for what we are, accepting that we each have an absolute right to be what we are and that we cannot, either of us, change what we are.

Sinn Fein, from the sidelines, saw the talks as doomed to failure because not only was their voice unheard at the table, but the structures for the talks could not be truly representative of the Irish people.

For the unionists the division between the integrationist and the devolutionist approach was evident, but they were united in their resolve to see the talks as successful only if 'the constitutional link with Great Britain was copper-fastened'. There was obvious unease as they contemplated the point when the Irish government would enter the scene, but equally there was a willingness to talk of the 'totality of relationships' in these islands and an equal assurance that they would meet Dublin face to face once, and only once the first part of the procedure had been successful. So far as good relations with the Republic were concerned, there was also the significant statement that a settlement within Northern Ireland, which strengthened its place in the United Kingdom, could produce such a relationship.

Meanwhile, the leader of the Alliance Party, John Alderdice, spoke of the opportunity for all sections of the community to participate fully and with real power in how they were governed, the need to protect the rights of minorities and the absolute necessity to have confidence in the law and those who administer it. He too spoke of diversity:

> The task to be shouldered by the participants in the talks is to find structures which express the richness of our diverse aspirations and aptitudes – and afterwards to stand by those structures, nourish them and make peace endemic in Northern Ireland life.[12]

The original timetable for the Brooke initiative was to be ten weeks. The aim was an ending to over twenty years of stalemate between the constitutional parties in Northern Ireland. The purpose was progress in political terms.

> There are many issues which remain to be resolved within the various camps, even as negotiations commence, and then an equitable solution must result. The Anglo-Irish Agreement has been shown not to work and was basically unstable because it excluded 22 per cent of the Irish race – Northern unionists – from the process. The opportunity exists to bring in a real agreement which encompasses all, offers the potential for peace and stability and ends the spiral of sectarian violence. The alternative is a continuation of *ersatz* politics and another decade of violence – a prospect too horrible to contemplate.[13]

[12] John Alderdice, *Fortnight Magazine* (May 1991), p. 11.
[13] Christopher McGimpsey, *Fortnight Magazine* (May 1991), p. 13.

While no one imagined violence would be ended overnight, few failed to recognise that the symbolism of what was being attempted was a powerful and significant milestone in the Northern Ireland story.

> It may be that the process of talks which begins today in Belfast will not lead to a new settlement within the North and between the peoples of these islands. On the face of it, as seasoned commentators have observed, those who sit down together will come to the table with mutually irreconcilable agendas. Yet there is an overall objective in common, one which transcends individual party aims: to put an end to violence and to achieve conditions in which the two communities can live at peace with each other ... Those who sit down today to begin this process have the chance to shape the destiny of their country.[14]

One vital piece of the jigsaw, genuine dialogue between political leaders who were themselves just as much prisoners of history as the communities they represented, provided the hope that something could emerge to give hope to a tired people. The communities were to learn a little more about each other as they came to recognise more about themselves.

[14] *Irish Times* editorial (30 April 1991).

9

THE RELIGIOUS DIMENSION

A story which circulated widely in the mid-6os, had an element of truth to it. It was said that an Israeli reporter was confronted by paramilitaries in north Belfast with the question: 'What religion are you?'

He replied, 'I'm a Jew.'

The immediate reaction was: 'But are you a Protestant or a Catholic Jew?'

It has been convenient and popular, the further you are from the events of Ulster, to discuss the troubles as a consequence of religious division. I have lost count of the times I have been faced with the question: 'It's all about religion, isn't it?' – with its presupposition. For the international media Ireland has stood for only one thing: religious bigotry and division. It is a war between Protestants and Roman Catholics. The intensity of religious allegiance in Northern Ireland is a phenomenon which is almost impossible to explain to those who have come to accept secularism. At best it must appear strange – at worst naïve. I remember an American correspondent asking me if those involved in a riot the night before had been throwing stones because of their disagreement on Papal infallibility.

The truth is that Northern Ireland is a religious community. Frequent census returns and reports of religious denominations have indicated a ready willingness among the large majority of people to claim religious affiliation. Something like 80 per cent of the population readily admits to church membership. In England the figure is closer to 13 per cent. However, when such figures are analysed by church bodies in relation to active membership, the picture changes dramatically. The convenient labels of denominational allegiance on a census form bear little resemblance to the attendance at a place of worship on a Sunday.

The Saturday evening *Belfast Telegraph* devotes an entire page to the list of church services to be held the following day. Churchmen continue to be asked for opinions on current affairs on the assumption that religion is a vital part of the life of the community, and religious education is one of the most sensitive parts of the school curriculum. But active everyday involvement in church life is subordinate for many to a desire to be identified by one or other of the main religious labels, which are comforting, traditional and have a significance greater than religious faith alone.

A recent survey in the Church of Ireland claimed that in a strongly loyalist part of Belfast church attendance by the 90s had dropped to a mere 13 per cent. For the clergy this has slowly but relentlessly become a challenge, which is not confined to the various Protestant denominations. I recall the late Cardinal O'Fiaich, Roman Catholic Archbishop of Armagh, pondering the declining attendances at Mass in Ireland. I had remarked on the results of the surveys within my own church on Sunday attendance. His response was surprising to me, having become accustomed to seeing the large numbers attending services in Roman Catholic churches: 'Everywhere I go I find priests talking about fewer taking their religious obligations seriously.'

Beyond the problem of church allegiance being, from one perspective, a comforting label, there is the problem that church allegiance remains central in many people's lives. In Northern Ireland allegiance to one church has often tragically meant opposition to the other.

Protestantism in Northern Ireland is divided. Apart from the main denominations of Presbyterian, Methodist and Church of Ireland there are numerous sects and groups which are strongly evangelical. This fragmentation of the Protestant tribal community has added to the difficulties of seeking a clear picture of religious influence. It also helps to explain part, but only part, of the suspicion felt by many Protestants of the Roman Catholic community. For, in contrast to the fragmentation of Protestantism, the Roman Catholic church has the appearance of a united and highly disciplined entity. The church, the school, the priest and the rapid growth of so many 'community' organisations within Roman Catholic neighbourhoods have led to the view among many working-class Protestants that this is a Church which commands and receives total loyalty. For them the religious practice and political dogma are inseparable. When a Roman Catholic bishop or an SDLP or Sinn Fein politician speaks, it appears to them to be the 'voice of Rome'. Theological differences, the subtleties of emphasis, and divisions similar to their own within the Roman Catholic community are hidden from those who still cling to the expression 'Rome rule'. These 'current' divisions, so to speak, run hand in hand, of course, with the divisions of history. Battles fought centuries ago continue to have an impact. The Battle of the Boyne in 1690 is seen as a decisive victory of Protestantism over Catholicism. Even now, on its three-hundredth anniversary, there are few signs that its result has lost any real significance for a population polarised by 'victory' and 'defeat'. Triumphalism continues to be a vital quality in the ethos of much of the Protestant population, which shows only periodic willingness to grasp pluralism as the way forward.

Time and again the corrosive effects of fear and its fellow traveller, uncertainty, have influenced events and dictated reactions by entire communities. At a personal level, violence and intimidation have brought genuine fear to individual lives and homes. Fear of consequences or public reaction has made many a reluctant captive. Fear has made its own unique and entirely negative contribution to that other ever-present element of this story – sectarianism.

Sectarianism has taken many forms in the history of the Province. It has sprung from many sources. It has had many consequences. There has been party political sectarianism which has prevented any real political dialogue for many years. Unchallenged use of political power has gone hand-in-hand with structured sectarianism. Social sectarianism has been endemic because of the closeness of this community and as a consequence of the earlier commercial and industrial power being concentrated in relatively few hands. But the most obvious sectarianism, lying at the root of so many of our problems, has been religious.

Religious sectarianism has itself taken different forms, always with disastrous consequences: tensions between Protestants and Roman Catholics, mutual suspicion of each other's religious/political identity, ignorance of each other's practices or beliefs, attitudes of religious apartheid which are only gradually beginning to disappear, and open hostility to anything ecumenical. Frequent references are made to the allocation of employment or the promotion of employees on purely religious grounds. In the early days of the civil rights movement attention was focused on the accusation that housing allocation was dictated by sectarian considerations and that these were entirely of a religious nature. The 'one man one vote' call had as much to do with divisions on grounds of religious identity as it was connected to electoral reform. Ultimately the paramilitary campaigns were to produce the most fundamental blasphemy: sectarian killing.

I recall a visit to the southern states of America at the time of the racial riots and the start of the Martin Luther King era. So much I witnessed and listened to bore similarities to the Irish situation. Here there was also distrust and suspicion, boiling over into violence, and there were visionaries and a long history of self-perpetuating community uncertainties. I learned one lesson from both: reconciliation cannot be achieved by legislation alone. People need to want to be reconciled.

If religious intolerance is the outward and visible sign of a sickness in this community, one must ask about its causes as well as its consequences from a religious point of view. If it is a recurring feature of daily life it presents a challenge to the churches: it prompts questions about the relevance of the churches and their influence, about the nature of their teaching and the integrity of the example they have set, about the ways in which Christianity has been portrayed through the generations, about power and control. For the churches the questions are numerous. As more than one commentator has concluded: the churches in Northern Ireland are on trial.

In 1980 the Role of the Church Committee of the Church of Ireland had little doubt as to the way forward. Recognising the existence of religious sectarianism in Northern Ireland, it concluded:

> It is essential that this be acknowledged by all the Churches, and that we do all in our power to combat prejudice and remove bigotry where it exists in our own membership or within the community as a whole.[15]

Such wording in a church report will seem laudable and worthy of support by many. But several questions arise. Do the Irish churches actually acknowledge the existence of religious bigotry and intolerance based on religious beliefs? Are the churches willing to examine in depth their responsibility for in any way encouraging their attitudes? To what extent are the churches prepared to actively oppose sectarianism in Irish society, and to actually make changes in their structures to help in its eradication?

These questions go to the sensitive root of a great deal of the churches' activities and even of their witness. To acknowledge the existence of sectarianism and sectarian attitudes is one thing: to acknowledge that we may have had a part in their development is less comfortable. Yet I believe the time has come to not only ask those questions, but to attempt to answer them. The 'us' and 'them' mentality is undeniably present in the life of Northern Ireland today, and religion has a role in this. But in many instances what constitutes religion has become an inclusive label for attitudes and actions which are anything but Christian. Both communities have played their part in this process. Sectarianism is not the prerogative of one tradition only.

It is all too easy to cite examples of how 'the other side' has fostered negative attitudes towards their neighbours. Extreme Protestantism has been accused of encouraging anti-Romanism, but one must ask is the extremist alone among Protestants in seeing the Roman Catholic tradition in purely negative terms? From the extremes of the anti-Roman Catholic sermons, writings and statements which question the very identity of the Roman Catholic faith as 'Christian', to the more moderate view that tends to dwell on the association of their Church with nationalistic or republican philosophies, the thrust is the same. It differs only in matters of degree.

---

[15] *The Journal of the General Synod of the Church of Ireland* (1980), p. 115.

Equally, within the Roman Catholic tradition one has come across a questioning of the willingness of the Protestant Church to speak of justice, equality and truth. Such examples may be infrequent, but they do exist. The late Roman Catholic Primate of All Ireland, Cardinal O'Fiaich, once remarked that there was bigotry in both traditions, but that while Roman Catholic opposition to Protestants was influenced by the political situation, in the case of Protestants prejudice towards Catholics was religious in nature.

It is extremely difficult, having acknowledged the existence of sectarianism, to 'get to the bottom' of what causes it. The antagonism felt by some Protestants towards Roman Catholics is often classified as distrust of 'the power' of the Roman Catholic Church. Northern Protestants will cite the falling numbers of their co-religionists in the Republic as evidence of what happens when a state is dominated by Catholics. They will talk about the effects of 'mixed' or inter-church marriages where rules about the upbringing of children are seen to close the door on any continuing Protestant religious allegiance. They will warn that the rising Roman Catholic birthrate will eventually lead to a total demographic change. Above all, they will express suspicions about the political aspirations of 'Catholics in general', aspirations which they see enhanced and encouraged by the public statements of Roman Catholic Churchmen. All too frequently I hear remarks about 'the failure of Catholics to support the Northern Ireland state', their reluctance to support 'the security forces' and their 'constant recital of imagined injustice'. It is debatable to what extent practical ignorance of Roman Catholics has grown out of the pattern of separate communities, living by themselves, working with those who are co-religionists and to a large extent taking part in recreational activities which are not 'mixed' in membership, to say nothing of their children being educated in schools which are largely segregated – not by design but by custom – has made such attitudes inevitable. Undoubtedly, these are highly significant factors.

As I have said before, Protestantism, for historical reasons, is a fragmented body. Denominationalism is important for Irish Protestants. While at times, particularly in a party political sense, it is possible to generalise about Protestant attitudes to a particular issue, it is not always possible to talk of a united 'religious' opinion. In some Protestant churches membership of inter-church bodies is impossible. Reasons given for such attitudes vary, but undoubtedly a common denominator is at best a reluctance and at worst open opposition to involvement with the Roman Catholic Church.

When Roman Catholics have looked towards their Protestant neighbours it is undoubtedly true that their political/religious alignments are what they see first and foremost. Their memories of discrimination, the ascendancy and power of Protestants come into play, as well as the determination of the

Orange Order to parade with 'triumphalism' through Catholic areas. When such parades end in a church service the feeling of insult deepens. For many Catholics Protestant extremism *is* Protestantism and moderate Protestantism is not as easily recognised.

Removal of fear must be the key to dismantling religious sectarianism. Fear of the unknown, of what people will say or do, of how they will react, of what goes to make up the institutional life of another religious denomination or church is born out of ignorance. Knowledge must take the place of ignorance. Where institutions fail individuals often succeed. Human contact in which people are people and find out that they have roughly the same problems, the same fears and the same hopes can and does destroy barriers.

I remember a vivid example of two communities, the one completely Roman Catholic and nationalist, the other composed of convinced Protestant unionists. An agreed 'no man's land' stretched between them. Contact was minimal. Occasionally, teenagers would throw stones across the divide at each other. Outsiders would have been content to conclude 'never the twain shall meet'. In both communities there was a high proportion of elderly, house-bound people, largely dependent on others for the necessities of life.

Quite suddenly, adverse weather brought severe flooding to both localities. Homes were flooded, furniture and personal belongings destroyed, some people had to be rescued by inflatable boats. Before the waters subsided human feeling had overcome traditional enmity. The hands that lifted elderly people to safety, the arms that held little children, lost their traditional identity. 'The no man's land', for a few days at least, didn't count. The flood was the same for Protestant and Catholic, unionist and nationalist.

Such a simple episode can be dismissed as insignificant. But many other similar stories could be told. When there is a common problem people find there are other priorities, other issues more pressing and more uniting than traditional suspicion. When the Belfast shipyard faced economic hardship there was no problem in unionist and nationalist leaders combining to put the case to government. When farming faced particular difficulties because of developments in the EEC, party leaders did not hesitate to combine resources. When employment possibilities depended on American invest-ment, delegations from across the divide were successfully formed. When famine disaster struck Africa, appeals for aid produced many combined efforts in both communities in Northern Ireland. Overseas visits by children from schools or youth clubs in both traditions have become a common occurrence. Cultural and educational projects have spanned sectarian differ-ences in a remarkable way. All such successes, spasmodic though they be, have in common people meeting people with shared concerns.

Another area where much progress has been made is on the question of mixed marriages. A joint working party composed of representatives of both traditions have faced the difficulties and, while certain problems remain in particular areas, the concept of joint pastoral care has become a reality. Integrated schooling has received the support of government and, while the Roman Catholic Church has still difficulties with the idea, it has survived the first painful moments of growth. A school programme for the mutual understanding of different traditions has begun, introduced as part of an education reform programme.

Yet reconciliation is probably the most overused word in our vocabulary. It is also one of the most convenient targets for those who wish to foster and feed division. Reconciliation is not a fact, it is a process. Too many see it as something that will be achieved as a consequence of one emphatic gesture, but it is a process, the cumulative effect of changing attitudes by individuals and institutions, the removal of the more obvious causes of injustice in either community and a willingness to see social wrongs in another locality as quickly as one can identify them in one's own.

The churches have consistently condemned violence on both sides of the divide. There can be little doubt that the majority of people in all denominations want an end to violence. They will disagree over the causes and on the ways society should counter violence, but more people than ever long for an end to it. Is it possible for churches, given their passionate pleas and prayers for reconciliation, to reduce community separation or alienation, without an erosion of deeply held denominational principles? What can the main Protestant churches do to meet the pressures exerted by the more extreme wings of their traditions; to find ways of moving towards greater understanding of the Roman Catholic ethos; to begin to analyse the effects of extremist views on their long-term futures? Within Roman Catholicism can there be a greater sense of urgency in examining the apprehensions and fears of Protestants which attach to the implementation of those rules on inter-church marriages, the baptism and upbringing of children? Within individual church teaching what priorities can the denominations give, and what priorities ought they to give to the impact of teaching doctrines or dogma not essential to their principles but which are divisive in our current situation?

If denominational adherence has helped to cement communal separation, surely the churches have a moral obligation to face up to and to acknowledge the fact of such division? There are still too many Christians in Northern Ireland who see reconciliation between the churches as a sign of weakness. For many of both main traditions there must be a surrender of principle if reconciliation is involved. How can the message be spelt out that reconciliation does not mean surrender but understanding, cooperation and, above all, learning to live with difference in peace? In the end, the real crisis for the Irish churches must lie in the threat that religious sectarianism provides to the very credibility of the Christian faith.

In the years leading up to the events of 1968 there was an absence of really concerted inter-church effort to address the social or community conditions in Northern Ireland. It seems that what is usually termed the social implications of the Christian Gospel received only a spasmodic and definitely a denominational response. Once the violence erupted in the late 60s and early 70s the churches were largely unprepared to meet the needs of the community at anything other than a largely superficial level. As someone has put it, the churches 'were at first a social ambulance service'. Violence on the scale experienced in those early years of the current troubles posed issues for which the thinking of all the Ulster churches was unprepared. Statements of condemnation, though a natural reaction, were no substitute for an understanding of the implications of what was happening. The pressure to 'say the right thing' came from many sources. Party politicians, facing the same frustrations as society at large, turned to the churches and appealed for calm and supportive statements. Was this an early acknowledgement that the religious dimension to the troubles could be addressed by the churches alone, or was it the more significant admission that they themselves were incapable of controlling the monster which had been unleashed?

In the polarised atmosphere of Northern Ireland the amount of practical pastoral work at the parish or local level which has been faithfully accomplished cannot be overestimated. Many a situation of potential trouble has been defused by the unheralded leadership, caring and example of clergy and devoted people. But ministry to the needs of people, essential though it is, can never be a substitute for the prophetic voice of integrity, courage and truth. The removal of fear remains the chief duty of the churches. That fear is the real 'enemy within' for the religious communities of Northern Ireland.

If it is accepted that organised religion has a role in a divided society, it follows that its purpose must be much more than providing spiritual guidance for the adherents of the various denominations. Pastoral care of its members has long been the main thrust of Irish church life. Visitors to our shores have frequently remarked on the close identity clergy in Ireland enjoy with their people. Generations of church members have come to accept this closeness without question. The 'home-going' priest or minister is an integral part of the parish and congregational scene. But the danger remains that this can lead to over-identification with the fears and aspirations of one's flock to the detriment of objective Christian teaching which, at times, requires words and leadership neither immediately popular nor easily understood.

Churches are based on certain theological values, and those values are enshrined in the doctrines which translate the eternal truths each denomination holds dear. But the principles at the root of such positions must be translated into the language of the everyday lives of people. The challenge to the church is to so influence people's lives that the basic truths will be seen to have a practical, on-going application. Spirituality is not something to be practised solely in church, but in everyday real-life situations when people relate to each other. In Northern Ireland the absolute necessity for this is obvious.

> Even among those who do not go to church, the language of religious identity is not very distant ... Indeed, religious tradition remains the most consistent guide to political outlook.[16]

Indeed, the religious label of people in Northern Ireland is a reliable guide to their political outlook. For most people, whether actively involved in church life or not, religion is more vital than doctrine. As I have said previously, the links between Protestantism and the various strands of unionism, and between Roman Catholicism and nationalism and republicanism, are as significant a feature of how people perceive one another today as they have been throughout the history of this Province.

Time and again church leaders have commented upon political matters. Calls for change in political attitudes have been frequent over the years. The question to which we must return is simple to express, but complicated in detail. How far are the churches justified in urging that political changes be made in a divided community to end violence and sectarianism if the churches themselves have not resolved their own differences? How far is there a real willingness within the churches to practise in their own arena that which they demand of others? Many people believe that the churches have as much to do in their relationships with each other as political parties have in theirs: '... the churches as a whole have tended merely to mirror their followers' opinions rather than lead them toward each other.'[17]

The dilemma for the churches in this field is not merely academic. The fear and unease so many people express about ecumenical activity is more indicative of people's attitudes than of theological or doctrinal debate. Ecumenism is often equated with a form of surrender or appeasement. In some areas of Northern Ireland the churches are the sole source of inter-community activity, but the fear that cross-community or inter-church activity could promote division, and unwelcome and uncomfortable controversy means

---

[16.] Duncan Morrow, *The Churches and Inter-Community Relations* (1991), p. 3.
[17.] *Belfast Telegraph* editorial (8 May 1991).

that the soft option of inactivity is attractive to many people with normally good intentions. The risks involved are often parochial in character. Misunderstanding of motives and ignorance of what is involved in the long term supersede any immediate or local advantage. This is not an imaginary factor. It is a real and relevant part of the fear syndrome which has dogged our footsteps in this generation as much as in the turbulent past.

With the importance of the local parish and congregation to community affairs in Northern Ireland, no greater task faces the churches than to be active in easing the fears amongst the people of Northern Ireland. To identify the role of the church is one thing. It is perhaps the easiest part of the process. To understand what is involved in becoming real agencies for greater understanding is a very pressing need. The church cannot condemn others for leaving undone what they ought to be doing themselves.

10

THE INNOCENT VICTIMS

The appearance of children in the midst of the tragedy adds its own immediacy and poignancy to the troubles of Northern Ireland.

They have walked behind coffins at funerals clutching the hand of a widowed mother; they have hurled stones at troops or police; they were the pale faces in the crowd surrounding someone being interviewed on TV after an incident. They were and are the children of the conflict.

Since 1968 several generations have grown up, not knowing what passes for normality in most communities beyond these shores. Many of them have paid a special price for being born in this part of the world and during these particular years.

As in so many instances, it is possible and dangerous to generalise. As before, a great deal depends on the family circumstances in which they live, the area from which they come, the school they attend – and, yet again, the religion into which they were born. Approximately half a million young people under the age of seventeen live in Northern Ireland. All have grown up during what for generations has been the longest period of concentrated civil disturbance in the Western world.

In certain areas they have been used – used to prove a point or provide a significant dimension to a protest. In certain places they have been a part of the scene which has varied from street confrontation to sullen protest. In other areas of comparative affluence they have grown through the most precious years of their lives conscious of the uneasy background of conflict taking place elsewhere, but conditioned by attitudes at home. They have had to accept conditions, not because they chose them, but because they have never known anything else. Their hopes and visions of the future have depended entirely on their surroundings.

Many saw in the lives of a father or an elder brother the inheritance of unemployment and the tedium of having nothing to do. The tension of living in cramped homes which in the early years of the troubles were common in areas of riots, or through endless home-searches, did not really have the effect sociologists might expect: they had never known anything better. The influence of a father or elder brother who had no work to do and who was 'always about the place' was reflected in a general feeling of 'this is the way it is'. A few miles away young people of the same age, though more privileged, still knew what inconveniences the troubles could mean for daily life: disruption of travel and transport, road blocks delaying traffic, conversations about 'us and them', parents involved in business or public service worried about personal safety, restrictions on where it was safe to spend one's free time and where it would be dangerous to go, and the constant media coverage of violence elsewhere. What was the future of these children to be? For many it was an education or job opportunities outside Northern Ireland. Was there any point thinking of a career near home? Many of them became our most precious export – young lives of ability and promise.

Prior to 1968, children in this country were of little interest to the outside world. The media coverage of the troubles changed this overnight. Suddenly, Ulster's children became useful topics for headlines and popular subjects of pictures. Since those early years and some 2,000 deaths later, the world continues to show an interest in what has happened to those young people. The level of interest may have diminished as the children of Romania and Albania play out their own tragedy. But social scientists, educationalists and religious writers have contributed to a mass of analysis and commentaries on their situation and lifestyle.

> It would be untrue, therefore, to say that violence has only made life worse for young people in Northern Ireland, without bringing any benefits at all in its wake. The one benefit young people have derived from the conflict is that, at the very least, it has served to focus attention on them and on issues long neglected in the past.[18]

Violence may be the most obvious topic in any discussion of the conflict in Northern Ireland, but it is only one cause of deprivation in the experience of many young people. This society has been one of the least affluent regions of the British Isles and recent EEC reports have recognised that poverty here can be traced back to the 1930s and even before. Growing up in large families, in houses where there was gross overcrowding with few of the basic amenities, and with corrosive adult unemployment, was an everyday experience for over 30 per cent of children who in 1975 were described as coming from 'low-income' families.

I recall talking in 1969 to a school teacher who had spent her entire professional life in an area of social deprivation in the northwest of Belfast. The background of so many of her pupils affected her deeply. Her words

[18]. Ed Cairns, *Caught in the Crossfire: Children and the Northern Ireland Conflict* (1987), p. 12.

were much more expressive than many academic analyses in those years: 'I get the feeling I'm only educating them for a life of unemployment – and none of them will ever escape from it.' In 1982, of school leavers seeking employment in such areas, 75 per cent became unemployed. It must be obvious that such statistics contributed to the formation of the social outlook of so many young people in those years. These figures for unemployment also help to explain the excitement and status offered by paramilitary activity in certain areas.

This is a community of close-knit families and traditions. Not all areas of Northern Ireland have experienced the same social needs or conditions in a uniform manner. Nor at any one time. The truth is that when we talk about the children of the troubles we need to specify which children we are talking about and from which area they come. One generation of young people in the Bogside of Londonderry will have had a very different impression of conditions from a similar group in County Down. One age group will have found its only contact with violence as nothing more than the inconveniences of security operations, while others of the same period will have lived and breathed guerrilla warfare for weeks on end. Young people in west Belfast during 1970 fell asleep at their desks in school because riots had raged throughout the previous night. Today the picture has changed, with armed action involving only a few people and lasting for a few moments. Since the 70s the violence is more often limited to paramilitaries confronting the security forces in an ambush situation. However, although the conditions may have changed for many of the children of the troubles knowledge of what violence is and what it does, knowledge of what happens when terrorism is promoted as an attractive cause worth supporting, and violence which takes away a father or brother have been a tragic part of their formative years. Most commentators agree that the real numbers of children who have suffered actual physical injury because of the violence are unknown. Figures such as 150 deaths in the under-fourteen age group have been mentioned for the period 1968–87. It is virtually impossible to go further and assess mental disorders or the psychological effects of the situation on children.

For years they have been exposed to potential sources of stress although, again, the degree and nature of such exposure have varied considerably. In the late 60s gun battles in the streets outside their own homes, or the mass movement of families from area to area in the 70s led to disruption and pressures which we can only imagine. For children who lost a close relative, often in horrific circumstances, the consequences are equally unimaginable. For children whose exposure to violence was restricted to the endless television coverage of atrocities in other ares, the effects were more subtle but no less significant.

Few of us will forget the words of the little child who, having just witnessed the murder of his father, phoned his grandmother: 'Can you come down to look after us? Bad men have just killed my daddy.' Waiting for a parent to come home, seeing a father leave home in uniform to go on duty, hearing frequent conversations about someone who has been murdered or arrested, watching numerous TV news broadcasts – who can estimate the cumulative effect of such pressures on young minds?

As one who has all too frequently found himself in homes suddenly stricken by murder, I am haunted by vivid memories of young faces. They have varied from disbelief and total, yet understandable, incomprehension, to stark terror. Gathered up by relatives, taken to other homes to avoid the aftermath of tragedy, talked about and worried about – 'what will become of them' – huddled in corners staring blankly at other blank faces. The grief of adults is somehow predictable; the grief of little children is another matter entirely.

When I read elaborate accounts of the effects of stress in Northern Ireland on young people and I find that many experts conclude that probably only a relatively small proportion of children have suffered serious psychological consequences requiring definite medical attention, I must admit to what will appear to be an entirely subjective reaction. It may be that children are by nature adaptable and resilient, that children overcome when we least expect them to do so. I sometimes wonder, however, if it is too soon to draw such hard and definite conclusions. It is true that, contrary to what might have been anticipated, the vast majority of children have not become psychological casualties of the conflict. Such conclusions can be compared favourably with estimates in other world areas of conflict and violence. But I still wonder.

It is a well established fact that 'atmosphere' has a vital role to play in the reaction of a young person to tension or stress. Time and again I have noticed that the speed with which parents respond to the needs of a child in such circumstances has had a positive effect. It continues to amaze me how quickly a child has been the human catalyst in a return to everyday living again in a home plunged into tragic grief. 'We've got to get back to normal for the sake of the children, you know.'

What is probably even more significant than any discussion of initial stress and grief is the level at which a child can come to terms with what they have seen or experienced. After over twenty years of violence it becomes part of the scene. Reginald Maudling's often-quoted phrase 'an acceptable level of violence' continues to be provocative even now, years later. But, I ask myself, is there a degree of frightening truth about it so far as young people are concerned? Is it possible that several generations of Ulster's young people have simply come to accept something that has 'always been there' for as long as they can remember? Is it also possible that children come to cope with violence and all it involves by concluding that violence is not really as severe or significant a social experience as some people believe? But coming to terms with conditions over which one has apparently little or no control is no substitute for asking basic questions about it. I must admit that the possibility that children have grown up in a world where levels of violence and terrorism have become somehow socially acceptable is a horrifying prospect.

It might have been predicted that violence would have a negative impact on the behaviour patterns or moral practice of the majority of young people in what was by tradition mainly a rural, conservative and basically religious society. Yet family ties are very strong in Northern Ireland and in the vast majority of cases children are brought up in relatively secure homes. Parental example and discipline in Ulster have impressed many observers. Equally, sociologists are fairly unanimous in the view that the moral outlook of the children of the troubles has not undergone any dramatic revolution. Juvenile delinquency has tended to follow a pattern suggesting other causes than a prolonged period of violence and community conflict.

There are always stark examples which the media and others will highlight to support a contrary view. The misnamed practice of 'joy-riding' in west Belfast, which involves the stealing of cars by young people and driving them in the hope that they will be chased by police, often ending in tragic deaths, has been linked to what some writers call 'a breakdown in law and order'. The existence of protection rackets operated in certain areas by paramilitary organisations, we have been told, has led to a new set of values among large numbers of young people. While there is some justification for these conclusions, it is surely much more obvious that a lack of amenities, unemployment and general social deprivation in such areas are the real reason. Excitement and the craving for recognition and authority in ghetto areas clearly added to the impetus to be linked with paramilitary movements in the 70s. Today it is not so easy to draw the same conclusions.

It is common that a young person in Northern Ireland adopts and accepts the religious or political ethos of his or her parents. 'Unquestioning' acceptance of the parental outlook is often the norm. To be born into a Protestant family has generally meant inheriting a unionist outlook. To be born a Roman Catholic has involved inheriting the nationalist or republican philosophy. It is perhaps worth posing at this stage a question which requires more extensive discussion later. To what extent has the traditional process of accepting from an early stage in life the attitudes of another generation itself been a powerful encouragement in the long term for the perpetuation of historic divisions? Is the influence of the home so strong in Northern Ireland that the process of changing one's attitudes to those on 'the other side of the sectarian divide' involves changing something much more complex than what we so glibly refer to as 'community attitudes'? How far is the Ulster question dependent on attitudes conveyed at the cradle which will remain unchanged until the grave?

Whatever the reason, the majority of children in Northern Ireland are conditioned from an early age to think in terms of their religious identity. In the case of Protestants they will have attended a state school in which religious education is a part of the curriculum. That religious instruction will have been based to a large extent on the Bible. They will have been educated alongside other Protestants. The fragmentation of Protestants into Pres-byterians, Anglicans, Methodists, Baptists, or others, will have been sub-limated into a course of religious education which, Biblically based, is often thematic in reality. In the case of Roman Catholics the child will have attended a school where Church teaching predominates. The parish and the school have long been the traditional centres of learning in Roman Cath-olicism. Protestant Church schools ceased with the transfer during the twenty-year period beginning in 1930 to the state system. Only recently has the phenomenon of integrated schooling become a possibility in Northern Ireland. Government support for the few integrated schools now established in the Province, of which something has already been said, has given encouragement to the philosophy that educating children of the two traditions alongside each other will help to change long-term attitudes to each other, despite the traditional belief of both Roman Catholics and Protestants in the importance of having children educated with others of 'their own beliefs'. To what extent integrated education with substantial government support will come to play an increasingly important role in the future remains to be seen.

There has long been satisfaction in Northern Ireland educational circles that academic performance has exceeded that in other parts of the United Kingdom. Statistics over the years have supported this view. However, given the problems of the community, it is inevitable that questions are asked about the contribution of education to social awareness. Does the traditional structure of education in Northern Ireland contribute to community division or is it a powerful force in the process of reconciliation? The question leads to the conclusion that in Northern Ireland academic success is one thing; the process of citizenship in a divided community is quite different. The view that segregation commences during school days has been put forward frequently as a criticism of the current structures of Northern Ireland schools.

Those who accept this premise have taken hope from the emergence of integrated schools such as Lagan College in Belfast. But integrated education is still a tender plant on the Ulster scene. It is too early to draw real conclusions. Nor is it possible to conclude that certain divisive characteristics are attributable to present educational structures and are distinct from other considerations such as inherited family influence, religious allegiance or particular community ethos. In some cases those who find encouragement in the growth of integrated schools have to contend with the establishment of their own separate schools by sections on the edge of both communities. Some would argue that, while it is probable that segregated schooling does not discourage prejudice between religious groupings, it is less clear if it encourages inter-group friction.

Throughout the years of conflict schools in Northern Ireland have been an oasis of stability for children. No praise is too great for the efforts of teaching staff to maintain normality, often in areas and at times of acute community unrest. The influence of teachers has been vital in providing an atmosphere of 'business as usual' for young people. The fact that academic results have continued to flourish despite so many difficulties in the community at large is a testimony of note to the professionalism and dedication of teachers at every level in the Province.

In any divided community, education is a sensitive issue. In the history of Northern Ireland it has long been so. 'Touch our schools and you touch us' has been the political as well as the religious call. So when a new departure was introduced under direct rule recently to provide for a curriculum which encourages mutual understanding of differing traditions, the reaction was predictable. An elaborate and detailed syllabus which would allow children to study the histories of the other Irish communities as well their own was strongly opposed by those who drew security from traditional versions of the past.

This said, whatever the opposition, once more not everything has been predictably negative. Never before have schools catering for differing sides of the divide made more concentrated efforts to combine for various extra-curricular activities. Joint visits abroad by Protestant and Roman Catholic children, joint projects on community issues and collaboration between schools of each tradition have increased greatly. Cooperation between professional bodies historically linked to one side or the other is frequent and sustained. And of even greater current significance has been the achievement of plans for a common curriculum of religious education.

However, it is a sobering fact which is not restricted to education alone that society cannot legislate for reconciliation. Although integrated education seems an obvious forward step in any polarised community, if it is seen to be enforced opposition will become entrenched. Where agreement is possible between parents there is no doubt that integration can have a real role to play.

Children, we are often reminded, are the next generation. The future of any community lies in their hands. Given the problems of Northern Ireland, it is not surprising that attention frequently focuses on 'what they will inherit'.

What does the future hold for our most precious commodity? Predicting the future in the Province is a precarious exercise to say the least of it. Contrary to the general impression that little will change in attitudes during the next generation, I feel that there is a new breeze of understanding beginning to blow among many of the children of today. It is far from being a wind of change. But in my visits to schools on both sides of the divide, in my contacts with young people in clubs and elsewhere, I am conscious that some if not all of the lessons of the past are being learned. There is an anxiety to move forward, although the way to move forward is not yet clear. Youthful vision is an encouraging sign: not yet the need to face adult reality; not yet the need to relate vision to the hard facts of life. But what evidence there is suggests that a degree of realism exists among many teenagers in Northern Ireland which was not necessarily the case a generation ago. If this realism is to blossom the role of schools is of vital importance. That role may in the end be to encourage the awkward questions that should have been asked generations ago.

The real question is: can such hope be turned into adult reality? But there are other questions. Will society allow that new generation the liberty to grasp such a reality? Can this new generation ultimately bring about political change in this society in the future? If we consider that children are so conditioned by the political attitudes of their parents, and do not ask questions which will lead to independent judgement, what hope is there of any real change?

Are those people who predict that we will see not just a repetition of current attitudes but an intensification of them in the next generation correct? Is there real basis for such a pessimistic view? The fact that a percentage of our best educated young people are leaving the Province never to return supports such a claim. Large numbers of young people are not the fodder paramilitaries require: all that is needed is a small percentage of dedicated adherents.

No one really believes that the conflict will disappear overnight simply because today's young people will bring new ideas with them into adulthood. Life is not so simple: attitudes are inherited; prejudices remain; bigotry can grow from generation to generation. Something more than vision is needed.

Questions are needed as much as answers. The real hope for the future of the children of the troubles is that gradually new relationships will be possible – not because they are enforced but because people genuinely want them to happen. It is not just a case of adopting an attitude because 'it has always been the case.' But it depends on a new willingness to say, 'that's not what I want in my day.'

Will enough of today's children say when it counts: 'It doesn't have to be like this'? A recent experience here in Armagh threw these issues into stark relief. The Mall in the centre of this ancient city provides a pleasant green patch between Georgian buildings. From there, early one morning, the city was shaken by a bomb explosion which ripped through a car driven by a well-known and respected local businessman. He died instantly. The flames which engulfed the car made it impossible for anyone to approach it. A few hundred yards away, at the opposite end of the Mall, dozens of children were making their way to schools at the beginning of another day. Had that bomb been detonated close to them the result would have been catastrophic.

As the emergency services coped with the tragedy at one end of the Mall children paused and then continued towards their schools at the other: terrorist violence had claimed one more life; a short distance away a new generation resumed its daily routine. The two scenes were separated by a few hundred yards.

Too often we talk about children as 'the next generation'. In truth they are really a part of this generation already. They are a part of today. Their tomorrow is not in their hands alone.

11
THE MEDIA:
HOW THEY
TELL IT

Mass communication in a divided society is at once the servant and the master. The power and influence of the mass media in the history of the Northern Ireland conflict have been immense. The obsessive need to know what is happening and to comment upon it, the opportunity to use the media to influence a community, to persuade it or to manipulate its outlook, the chance to put forward political argument or spread propaganda, the means of expressing a cause, the preaching of dogma, words which incite or words which seek to speak peace, attempts to quell rumours or to spread them in the first place, advice and efforts to calm situations of tension, appeals for help – these are just some of the possibilities the media offers the troubled society.

In the early years of the present conflict the media had to come to grips with a situation largely unknown in the British Isles – a community torn apart by violence, by internal conflicts and loyalties, with questions about its nature posed with urgency and immediacy. Events were reported not only to the world far from the streets of Belfast or Londonderry but also to the people of Northern Ireland themselves. Reporting of facts and figures, interviews 'on the spot', eye-witness accounts of tragedy, the normal activities of the press in a free society – these found an inevitable corollary, comment. The interpretation of events and any assessment of their overall significance brought the predictable public response. Maintaining the fine distinction between fact and perception, reality and belief, soon became a daily and nightly dilemma for the professional journalist.

By the early 70s few if any homes did not possess a television set. Such is its power to inform and to form opinion, to influence how people react to events or personalities, television represented Northern Ireland to the world. It also became a focal point for a confused and shocked community. Radio coverage of events, comment and particularly photographs in newspapers, statements often on the spur of the moment by the key political or religious leaders, explanations of actions or policies by security experts or spokesmen, facts and figures, excuses or words of justification – these became food and drink to a people who listened to the hourly news broadcasts with a devotion and fascination born out of uncertainty.

The issues for the journalist covering events in a violent society cannot be examined in the isolation of his or her professional view of the task. What is shown or said has an influence out of all proportion to the time allocated for that coverage on the screen or printed page. A fact can in the very instant of its portrayal become comment. Comment in its turn will exaggerate or minimise the selective element involved in editorial policy. What is seen or heard can within hours totally influence public reaction. In a violent society the medium itself can easily become the message.

As the years since 1968 have passed, professional journalists have learned to live with the consequences of working in the Northern Irish environment. Northern Ireland for its part has learned that what is portrayed by the media can decisively influence the opinion the outside world has of the Province and its problems. As a people we have become very sophisticated and yet somewhat fatalistic in our understanding of that influence. The troubles have produced their own media culture. Personalities have become household names overnight as a result of the attention (or lack of it) they have received, and events have taken on a significance simply because they have caught the attention of the camera or the microphone. It has become clear – not only to social scientists – that people use and convey ideas long before they have learned to define them.

Undoubtedly, it has been the violence in this society more than any other factor which has caught the world's attention. From those early years of street protest and riots to the more spasmodic but equally devastating incidents of terrorism today news stories have often suggested that violence is the norm in Northern Ireland. The fact that so much else is happening which is positive and 'peaceful' is lost sight of, if the only news worth reporting to the world is one of violence. Such news sells programmes and newspapers. The media's accuracy in recounting dramatic events may be beyond reproach from the journalistic standpoint: its accuracy as an overview of what life is actually like for the majority of people here is a very different question. Allied to this is the growing recognition that Northern Ireland no longer commands the interest and sympathy of the outside world, which has moved from impatience to boredom as the conflict continues, endlessly it seems. 'No other current affairs subject induces such anaesthesia in mainland Britain – nor exerts more pressure on the BBC.'[9]

The degree to which media attention itself encourages an atmosphere of tension or adds an almost romantic appeal to the terrorist cause will be

[9] John Ware, *The Listener* (8 March 1990), p. 10.

debated as long as the world has to cope with terrorism. In Northern Ireland coverage of the activities of paramilitaries has provoked reactions which have themselves contributed to our judgement of our society. Seamus Heaney, the Ulster poet, has written of the 'high wire of the first wireless reports' of terrorist activity. How do the media tell people what is happening in a society such as this? Journalists largely depend on what people tell them is happening. They will collect different opinions, all of them deeply and sincerely held; they will be confronted by different versions of the truth. They are not always eye-witnesses of what has happened.

In 1974 the Ulster Workers' Strike brought this community to a virtual standstill. The key to the success of the strike lay in the provision of electricity for the Province, and pressure mounted on the workers in the power stations. Hour by hour we received reports not only on the level of supplies at those power stations but on the likely response of the workers there themselves. The media told the listening public what they saw happening, what was not happening, where important supplies could be obtained, and they made predictions as to the likely actions of the power workers. There was to be widescale criticism of the media influence on the outcome of the stoppage: it was alleged that it had underscored the reality of the strike and thereby helped to bring down the power-sharing government. No one can really assess today the validity of such comment, but it is a reminder that the media was not only broadcasting about a divided community – it was communicating to it.

When the hunger strike by republican prisoners in the Maze Prison brought the Northern Ireland troubles again onto the front pages of the world, the deteriorating physical condition of the men was directly connected with the level of violence in the community. Tension rose day by day. There was an atmosphere of foreboding. TV and radio crews descended in large numbers on Belfast. Hotel accommodation was booked up solidly for weeks by journalists sent to cover the impending explosion of republican wrath. Camera crews appeared daily on our streets. It was impossible to escape the conclusion that the media 'expected' a dramatic and devastating consequence to follow the deaths of those who refused all appeals to end the fast to death. Did such media attention contribute to the impending tragedy? In fact the predicted public reaction failed, largely, to materialise when the deaths occurred. But the opinion persisted for a long time that we had seen evidence of not only the effect of excessive media attention but also its potential influence on a society vulnerable to violence.

Sectarian murder has become more common of late. When the media reports such a tragic and dastardly act as an assassination, often a random killing, simply because of the religious identity of the victim, we have become used to hearing that a 'Catholic' or a 'Protestant' life has been taken. It can be argued that such identification encourages retaliation. I know that professional broadcasters have long agonised over this issue. I have been told that this is in fact what the listener wants to know. But others believe that, given the average person's knowledge of this close-knit community, identifying the religious or political allegiance of the victim would be easy anyway. It is, they argue, unnecessary and immensely emotive to mention such labels. My own view is that those bent on retribution do not depend on the niceties of broadcasting for their so-called justification. Yet in a peculiar way, the very need to mention a person's religion in such circumstances indicates yet another tragic dimension to the dilemmas of Northern Ireland. We want to know, but should we?

How far is it justified for a camera to intrude on human grief? What is acceptable, and how far has society a right to see what violence does to ordinary people? The question of what is acceptable reporting and what is not is guaranteed to raise the temperature. Do people want to see mutilated bodies after an explosion? Do people want to see the anguish and grief of a young widow and her children? Do people want to see a soldier engulfed in flames and frantically trying to beat them out? Do people sitting round a TV screen want to see a body lying beside a country road? Where should the line be drawn? I know of the on-going concern of reporters who witnessed what happened after the capture in March 1988 of two army corporals who had strayed into a republican funeral in west Belfast and were later murdered. Yet the pictures of the attack on their car will remain vivid for millions as long as the footage of film can be replayed in years to come.

Those who saw the carnage in July 1972 of what has been designated 'bloody Friday' in Belfast will never forget the pictures of bodies in plastic bags being removed from the scene of the explosion. Was it right to give the world such a horrific view of the atrocity? Was it right that the people of Northern Ireland should see in such detail what had happened in a bus station to innocent people?

I remember very clearly the moment when for me such questions ceased to be merely academic. When I and other clergy have to officiate at the funeral of a victim of the violence we see something at first hand of human grief. On one such occasion, despite precautions, a foreign TV crew managed to intrude into the church and before anyone could react had thrust the lens of a camera inches from the face of a twenty-year-old widow. Such an incident was exceptional, but in a dramatic way it did not matter at that moment that there were wider considerations to take on board: it did not seem to matter that there might be an obligation to inform. She had not asked for the world to see: it was all wrong ...

For quite some time in the early 70s it was rumoured that teenagers in a part of Belfast had been paid by TV crews to throw stones at the police. Such stories, like many others, seemed to gain credibility over time. Allegations of this nature were fodder for those who not only resented media coverage of particular incidents but welcomed, for various reasons, anything which would discredit the work of the press. Given the numbers of overseas reporters who have at times invaded Northern Ireland, it is possible that some may have indulged in questionable practices. I can only say that in my experience I have yet to meet anyone who gives that particular story credibility. The wider issue, however, remains. How much does the mere presence of a TV camera in an area of tension encourage reaction? Perhaps the events of one evening during the hunger strike drama in the early 80s may help to balance the situation. It was rumoured that there was to be widespread trouble in a part of west Belfast. Several crews were despatched to cover the story. After some hours, they returned with nothing to report. Later, a police announcement was issued to the effect that in that same period one thousand bombs had been thrown at the RUC in Belfast.

During the past twenty-three years the main actors in this story have become more and more expert in the use they can make of the media. Not long after 1968 it became obvious that television and radio interviews could be means of influencing viewers or listeners. Propaganda always plays a part in a divided community. The ready access, provided by a media prepared to devote much time and money to Northern Ireland, to people's homes and, through their homes to their minds and actions created possibilities a number of figures could not ignore.

Access to the media in any unstable situation is of prime importance for the paramilitary. It is not only a ready-made outlet for justification, explanation or even excuse: it is the most powerful means of attracting and maintaining attention. The straight interview or statement of policy can be transmitted to a population in ways which make the traditional party political platform largely irrelevant. Even the most grim coverage of an atrocity can be used to put over the rightness of a cause. The distinctions between a right to be heard, to be granted a platform for views acceptable only to some, and the need to protect a community from words or actions not acceptable to the majority exercises all those people responsible for the formation of public opinion. For propaganda can and does take many forms. Of course, debates about what the public should see or hear lie close to interpretations of what constitutes the 'free society', the democratic state or 'the just community'. To what extent should society be protected against itself?

Is it acceptable that an apologist for violence should be shown on TV within hours of an atrocity in which many have been injured and some killed?

Is it acceptable that the viewer should be confronted by those who support terrorism in the aftermath of an explosion which has jeopardised the jobs of ordinary people? Should people have to listen to what is termed a 'justification' for violence which to the majority is merely an 'excuse'? Yet a free society should be capable of listening to the voices of even those who, although a minority, represent a percentage of the population. Freedom of speech, so dearly maintained and protected in other circumstances, cannot really be compartmentalised.

Investigative journalism has come of age in the past few years. Some of the most significant developments in this field have emanated from the Northern Ireland situation or from circumstances linked to it. 'Death on the Rock', an investigative TV documentary into the actions of security forces in Gibraltar, programmes on the alleged shoot-to-kill policy of security forces in Northern Ireland and the famous Stalker affair have created opportunities for in-depth media investigation of controversial subjects. Journalists have vigorously defended their right (their duty even) to seek out the truth 'in the public interest', but the reactions from the public and government have been equally vigorous. In the wake of such controversy voices within the media have been raised in defence of the freedom of the press and the professional integrity of those involved:

> Of course journalists must be accountable, and I think the Broadcasting Complaints Commission can provide both a useful redress for the public and act as a sensible constraint on any excess, but ultimately journalists should be responsible to the facts, not to government.
>
> During the last eleven years I've worked with some outstanding television journalists, in front and behind the camera. They should not be crabbed and confined by a suspicious government or a nervous broadcasting establishment but set free. Trust the journalist and trust his audience.[20]

The appearance on TV of supporters of the IRA may be offensive to the majority of people, but it can be argued that, even in Northern Ireland, to suppress them or to deny them access to the media is certainly an erosion of the concept of a democracy, even if that democracy is precisely what they seek to undermine. What if, against the wishes of a majority on each side of the divide, they perpetuate a regime of terror – has society a right to protection? In fact, could it not be that society is defeating its own ends by exercising such censorship, is playing the game of the terrorist and thereby adding a degree of credibility to his or her case? This proposition can be

---

[20.] Roger Bolton, 'Fact and Friction', *The Listener* (3 August 1989).

countered by the argument that there are other means available apart from the media to make political points. If those other means, viz., the ballot box, were not available, then the issue would appear to some to be clearer. But this is not the case.

The arguments for and against were forcibly put when, in 1988, the government introduced legislation to ban Sinn Fein from the public media. Professional journalists not only faced a real dilemma; they felt almost universally that they were being denied the right to report fairly and objectively. Their argument not only highlighted the traditional issues but underlined what many felt was now the real ethical and moral problem of the conflict in Northern Ireland:

> Reporting Ulster in any depth is getting harder. It isn't just that more and more ordinary Catholics and Protestants with grievances about the excesses of the security forces or the brutality of the IRA fear to have them publicly aired. Nor are the government's broadcasting restrictions only to blame. It is, I believe, that after twenty years of stagnation, the Unionist and military establishment have adopted a kind of black-and-white view of the world. Broadcasters are either for or against terrorism. No longer is it credible to be revolted by the IRA and at the same time highlight the deficiencies in government policy or misconduct by the security forces. Criticism is itself seen as a kind of subversion bringing aid and comfort to the IRA.[21]

To speak as some did of a 'war' situation was to encourage much of the basic philosophy of such groups as the IRA. To speak of exceptional circumstances requiring exceptional policies came closer to government thinking. To unionists such a situation demanded not only a greater military and security effort to defeat terrorism; it demanded that society should not have to listen to or hear the philosophy of those regarded as the 'fellow travellers' of terror.

It has also been argued that a mature society can and does exercise its own judgement and censorship: it has the right and opportunity to 'turn off'. Let people, it is said, make their own judgement on what they see and hear: if they are secure in their views against terrorism, then nothing but positive good will come from exposing the voices of terror to rigorous cross-examination in full public view. Journalists argue in support of this view that society should trust their professional ability to exercise and be seen to exercise impartiality and fairness. A majority of the media argue that strong and active coverage of news is not only a pillar of democracy: it is vital to its continued existence. To advance their case they argue that guidelines for

---

[21] John Ware, *The Listener* (8 March 1990), p. 10.

interviews with supporters of terrorism already exist, and that they should be allowed the liberty to exercise professional integrity and responsibility. Against this view stand those who are utterly opposed to the opportunity to 'promote' terrorism in any form.

The debate continues to rage. Paramilitaries continue to attack. The media reports and comments. Northern Ireland remains divided on this question. History will decide.

The ways in which the media portrays terrorists, or perhaps the ways in which terrorists are permitted to portray themselves, is possibly of less concern to government than is the issue of media intrusion. In any democracy public perceptions of events will determine the limits of policies a government will feel able to pursue. If the public image of a terrorist is that of a 'freedom fighter' or 'liberator', this will have very different consequences for policy than would the perception of terrorists as 'brutal' or 'psychopathic' murderers.

The need to produce news reports has to be balanced against an ethical commitment to objectivity. As publicity is such a vital part of the terror machine both government and the terrorist have become very proficient in the years of violence in Northern Ireland at the conduct of a symbolic war with each other in and through the media. It can be argued that any reporter could become the innocent conveyor of propaganda. My experience, however, is that the sheer professionalism of the majority of reporters has been a more than adequate safeguard against this possibility.

Apologists for the IRA have long adopted the line that but for partition and the 'British presence' in Northern Ireland there would be no need for the violence: they are forced by society and the structures of Northern society in particular to continue 'the armed struggle'. They maintain that their actions are of little consequence when compared with the evils inherent in society as a whole, a direct result of that same 'British presence'. For them it is of secondary importance that, in an interview or news item, their case is supported or destroyed. They hope that the viewer or listener will be so struck by their description of reality that they will begin to question and then to doubt their own assumptions about morality and the structures of society. This is a part of the process of destabilisation. It is also essential to the terrorist who seeks to build up support among those people who feel alienated from society.

Like so many other aspects of life in Northern Ireland the role of the media has changed since 1968. It is not that its primary purpose is different. It is simply that over twenty years of serving a divided community and of describing that community to the outside world has placed pressures upon it and compelled it to confront issues in which there is no clear distinction between what is good for society and what is not. Violence, terrorism and polarisation demand integrity of reporting and comment of a high order. The conflict between absolute freedom and the restriction considered necessary in an emergency situation pose problems which go far beyond the freedom of the press. They lie close to the heart of a democracy. Confronted by complaints from those who support terrorism in Northern Ireland that they are denied access to the public through the media, an honest conclusion might be that such restrictions are a subtle recognition that society has been changed by terrorism.

Any church leader in this situation must come to terms with media attention, for the need for a comment on many issues becomes a frequent requirement. I have met many journalists over the past few years. I have had little reason to complain about the attitude or methods they have adopted, and have come to understand something of the pressures to which they are subjected. I am aware of the genuine misgivings some of them entertain on the role of the media in Northern Ireland. On balance, I lean towards trusting the integrity of the professional journalist in this situation, provided there is always the right and opportunity to reply or to clarify. Sadly, the divided society has become a community of headline readers. Those headlines do not always reflect the news story that follows.

The role of the media in a polarised society is to inform the public of facts and events, to comment on attitudes and opinions, to dig deep into circumstances and to offer a platform for differing voices. But it is in the telling of the story, a story which may not be the same as the one the actors or the groupings involved want to be told, that provides journalism with its greatest challenge and some would claim, its greatest reward. The role of the press is often defended from within in terms of, 'if we don't tell the story no one else will'. If it fails to report, there are many others who will – political figures, government agencies, the courts, pressure groups and individuals – a fact which leads us to ask if the media have another role above and beyond the duty to inform. Does that role have something to do with protecting society against itself or against those who may wish to manipulate it? Is that other role in some way to 'make society better'?

Investigative journalism has become a significant part of the role played in Northern Ireland by a profession which has become, in its own eyes, not only the objective critic of society, of its divisions, but at times outside and above it. Many journalists of my acquaintance have readily admitted that they have become more and more sceptical of the 'official statement', whether emanating from government, political parties, interested groups such as the churches, or paramilitary organisations. There is a tendency for media cover- age to become not a distinct element with recognised boundaries, but an active element, involved in and not simply reporting and observing. Yet the press is one of the few institutions which has never been subjected itself to the close analysis of investigative journalism. The possibilities of abuse of the mass media are not restricted to attempts by 'outsiders' to manipulate. Given its power to influence events here, and acknowledging the feelings and reactions of individual journalists caught up in the complexities of events, one cannot but be worried by the possibility of press manipulation. But, in my contacts with those involved in the media during the past twenty years, I have gained immense respect for their integrity and professional standards. Any criticism that has arisen seems to me to have been spasmodic and related to particular issues or events. Not everyone will agree with this observation. One can only speak from personal experience. What is of more importance surely are those broader issues about the nature of communication in a divided society and the implications such questions have for what is now undoubtedly the 'philosophy' of mass communication.

In 1787 Thomas Jefferson reflected on the American press as he knew it: 'Were it left to me to decide whether we should have a government without newspapers, or newspapers without government, I should not hesitate to prefer the latter.' Mass communication in a divided society may be at the same time both servant and master. In the particular conditions of a violent and divided society it can be the casualty.

12
SERVANT
CHURCH

'How can you people in Ireland call yourselves Christian? How can you go on killing each other in the name of religion?'

To be a church leader in Northern Ireland is to be confronted daily with both the assumption behind and the reality of such questions: the assumption that religion lies at the heart of the matter; the reality that it is the consequence of what people believe about their religion.

Simplification is sometimes helpful in understanding the complex. Over-simplification is self-defeating when it reduces the complexities of a situation so that the responsibility for what is happening can be passed to others.

It is convenient and no doubt of temporary satisfaction to conclude that, if the religious dimension is somehow removed from this situation, solutions will emerge which have been lurking on the touchline for generations simply awaiting their moment of truth. Such a scenario would be greatly welcomed by many. At least it would have the satisfaction of explaining the inexplicable and of justifying the analysis which over the years has identified religion as the root cause of our problems. To be informed abroad that a 'Protestant' has been murdered in Northern Ireland one day and a 'Catholic' a few days later must lead to a simplistic conclusion that they have been killed because of their religious tribal label alone. Tragically, this is too often true. But to live in this community and to learn the same facts is to be reminded, yet again, that such convenient labels represent far more than denominational designations.

It is a paradox of Irish history that 'the isle of saints and scholars' is also the setting for what appears to be generations of religious genocide. It is equally a paradox of this island that its history is characterised by an allegiance to the outward trappings of Christian religious practice at the same time as what have passed for inter-community relationships have taken the form of violence and human destruction.

To the man and woman of Christian faith in Ireland the 'religious war' label has in turn been viewed as an embarrassment and a judgement. Their understandable reaction has been to 'wash their hands' of any responsibility.

'It is an oversimplification and there are other much more obvious causes of division and confrontation.'

Whatever the root cause may be, whatever the real core of the problem, hidden in our history, inherited from strifes long in our past, crashing to the surface as troubles succeed troubles, the religious dimension is a reality. It is a reality which will not go away. It is a fact which confronts the Christian with questions which have no easy answers. It demands heart-searching on the part of the Irish churches: if religion is even a part of the problem, it must be a part of the solution. In a real sense the churches are on trial in Northern Ireland, for religious allegiance is a part – an important part – of much in our culture. How will the future evaluate the role of the churches in this period of conflict, a conflict which has appeared and re-appeared throughout Irish history: a conflict which is so conveniently attributable to two distinct religious groupings? Before any attempt is made to respond from within the church to such a question, the really vital issue must be addressed.

To what extent is the current conflict religious in character? When the Pope visited Ireland in 1979, although his visit was limited to the Republic, he referred to the fact that representatives of other religious communities had attended some of the functions arranged in his honour. In Drogheda he said:

> This truly ecumenical fraternal act on the part of the other churches is also a testimony that the tragic events taking place in Northern Ireland do not have their source in the fact of belonging to different churches and confessions: that this is not – despite what is so often repeated before world opinion – a religious war, a struggle between Catholics and Protestants. On the contrary, Catholics and Protestants as people who confess Christ, taking inspiration from their faith and the Gospel, are seeking to draw closer to one another in unity and peace. When they recall the greatest commandment of Christ, the commandment of love, they cannot behave otherwise.

For generations the local priest or minister has been an influential figure, particularly in rural areas. Denominational influence in education has been significant and it has been customary for the local clergy to be involved in almost all community activities. The opinions of church leaders have been sought almost as of right on many issues. Organisations such as the Orange Order have claimed a definite religious link. Interest in institutional religion has always been of a high order. As I have said, on a Saturday evening a full page of the *Belfast Telegraph* contains details of church services on the following day. City and town streets can contain several church buildings or halls.

Census returns regularly reflect a significant proportion of church membership, even if in practice such percentages are a reflection of nominal involvement. What is usually described as secularism has been, on the surface at least, slower to become an ingredient of daily life here than in other parts of Europe.

The apparent strength of the church in Northern Ireland makes its own significant contribution to the paradox of our situation. The religious can conveniently claim that, after all, those actively involved in the conflict 'don't go to church' – they're 'outside our ranks'. Yet it is just as convenient and common for a judgemental observation to be made: why doesn't *their* Church do more to marginalise the people of violence? For a Protestant 'the Catholic Church is not doing enough to give up the IRA', and for a Roman Catholic 'the Protestant churches are too closely connected to the Orange Order.' Condemnation of 'the other side' takes many forms. The frequency with which such comment is given a denominational colour reflects an almost inevitable 'religious' bias in personal perceptions of what others should do to end the conflict.

The close proximity of religious and party political identity throughout Irish history has made it inevitable that the 'us' and 'them' syndrome is a part of daily life in Northern Ireland. As I have said, to be born into a family which is Protestant usually means a party political allegiance to one of the branches of unionism. To be born a Roman Catholic is to embrace some form of the nationalist or republican philosophy. For Protestantism the links with the United Kingdom, the fact that 'Ulster is British', is much more than political aspiration: it is part, some would argue the only part that matters, of their ethos. For Roman Catholicism the reunification of Ireland is the long-term aspiration, though there is evidence that suggests most Catholics would settle in the short term for internal reform removing discrimination and injustice in Northern Ireland.

While the 'political clergy' is a more obvious phenomenon within the Protestant community, where it is not unknown for ministers of religion to be candidates in local and parliamentary elections, Protestants perceive a close identity between the utterances of Roman Catholic clergy and nationalist or republican aspirations. A minister's sympathy with political opinions and the needs of one's own flock can easily turn into too great an involvement, to the extent that the real casualty is 'pure' Christianity.

It is inevitable in such a situation that clergy are closely identified with the ethos of those to whom they minister. Some observers have spoken of clergy in terms of 'imprisonment' in the life of their particular communities. Spiritual leadership, it is claimed, is subordinated to active reflection of the fears or uncertainties of their people. It is dangerous, we have been told, for a minister of religion to step too far away from what is acceptable to his congregation; conversely it is all too common for clergy on 'the other side' to be seen in a political rather than a religious manner. Naturally, therefore, ecumenical activities produce reactions ranging from indifference to vociferous condemnation. Outward contact with members of 'the other side' of the religious divide is perceived to be some sort of betrayal. Ecumenism to many is tantamount to a political as well as a religious sell-out of principle. Extremist Protestantism thrives on opposition to ecumenical endeavour. Frequently such opposition from within Protestantism, stemming from the traditional 'fear of Rome', can adopt the outward appearance of protest rallies and speeches condemning for all time those involved in ecumenism. The depth of such attitudes and the conditions which make them possible are the visible face of the uncertainty which lies so close to the roots of the Northern Ireland problem. Within Roman Catholicism there is similar opposition to visible contacts with Protestantism, which takes the form of doubts about the nature of the religious teaching of 'non-Catholics', a phrase deeply resented within the Protestant churches.

For generations active church contact between the 'two sides' was the exception rather than the rule. Mutual suspicion prevailed and at best there was an acknowledgement of each other's existence. To that extent we have now come a very long way. Behind the smokescreen of the current conflict a degree of contact and cooperation, of understanding and mutual respect, has emerged between the churches which permits, at the official level at least, joint witness and action which would have been impossible a generation ago. The leaders of the main churches in Northern Ireland meet on a regular basis. Their joint visits to places of tension, joint encouragement of community projects, attendance at special services or occasions and joint statements on issues of community importance are commonplace. At such official levels, contacts of that nature are now a normal part of 'the scene'. Welcomed by many people and encouraged by the establishment of structures which permit regular consultation, church leadership in this way has grown in confidence.

Nor is such cooperation confined to the church leaders. Each year the Ballymascanlon Conference draws together elected representatives from most of the religious denominations for discussion and debate on social issues affecting Irish life. In many areas, members of different denominations meet to pray and study the Bible together. Clergy are unashamed and unafraid to be seen to accommodate each other in areas where a majority of their respective flocks encourage active ecumenism. Each year the Octave of Christian Unity is marked by joint services spanning the historic divide.

The faces of fear: two young rioters of the early 80s in Belfast.

ABOVE Children playing beside a burning barricade during street disturbances in Belfast of the 70s.

LEFT Normal life continues as security measures become a part of everyday life.

ABOVE 'Business as
usual' as shopkeepers
clear up following a
terrorist bombing.

RIGHT Christmas
shopping in the centre
of Belfast.

West Belfast after a night of disturbances in the late 80s.

Part of the south Fermanagh border between Northern Ireland and the Republic.

The terror of the IRA bomb atrocity at Enniskillen on Remembrance
Sunday, 1987.

Another victim is buried.

With (left to right) the Moderator of the Presbyterian Church in Ireland, the President of the Methodist Church in Ireland, Archbishop Robert Runcie and Cardinal Tomas O'Fiaich in Armagh, 1988.

The Secretary of State, Peter Brooke, welcomes Gerry Collins, Irish Foreign Minister, and Ray Burke, Irish Minister of Justice, to a meeting of the Anglo-Irish Conference in Belfast.

Peter Brooke at Stormont during a break in the inter-party talks, 1991.

With the Archbishop of Canterbury, Dr George Carey, visiting the Secretary of State at Stormont, 1991.

With the Roman Catholic Primate of All Ireland, Cardinal Cahal Daly, 1991.

Slowly but surely, in certain areas, the churches are reaching out in new ways towards each other.

However, it would be naïve and dangerous for church leadership in Northern Ireland to imagine that what is happening at such a level is either possible or welcomed throughout the Province. There are localities, frequently those in which violence or paramilitary activity takes place, where community polarisation means that such cooperation, which would be considered the norm in many societies, is impossible, even unthinkable. In the wake of paramilitary atrocities overt 'across-the-divide' activity is violently resented and opposed.

It would not be feasible either to imagine that opposition to inter-church activity is confined to the so called troubled areas. Suspicion of the 'other' religion has been passed down from one generation to the other in many a home – and the suspicion has lost little impact as it is translated to a new age group. Basically conservative in outlook, the traditional fear of the majority towards the long-term intentions of the minority, and the resentment of the minority towards the historic domination of the majority, the circle of mistrust is tragically completed. Too frequently God is a Protestant or Catholic God, the God of unionism or the God of Rome.

Sectarianism and religious bigotry are the convenient designations for much of these attitudes. Longevity, endurance and 'new evidence' of the misdeeds of the other side together with that inevitable religious/political identification create the climate in which ecumenism is a tender plant. Too often a clergyman who is perceived to be 'weak' on the basics of his tradition suffers the loss of confidence and support of his people. Fundamentalism thrives on such divisions – and itself contributes to religious alienation. Overt cooperation across the divide is perceived as weakness. 'The ecumenical clergy' has become a phrase of derision describing those who are seen to be over friendly with 'the other side'.

When there is violence and terrorism it is easy to see how divisions are accentuated and attitudes harden. The dilemmas increase and the opportunities to condemn inter-church activity multiply. The narrow line between political philosophy and paramilitary activity which has the same apparent overall aim, becomes extremely indefinite. To the extremist, the unionist philosophy can become indistinguishable from the crimes of the loyalist terrorist, and the aspirations of the nationalist or republican parties can be discussed in the same breath as IRA atrocities. Equally, if a religious denomination is perceived to be in sympathy with certain clearly identified political aims it too can be classified in the same way.

Community polarisation is the ideal breeding ground for sectarianism and prejudice which leads so easily to bigotry. It is only a short step for paramilitarism to adopt the language of such alienation and to use it to justify its actions. 'For God and Ulster' is displayed on many gable walls in strong loyalist areas. It is matched by an equal appeal to the rightness and divine justice of republican militarism. Community polarisation does not only result from paramilitary activity – it contributes the conditions in which paramilitary activity thrives.

Given such situations the dilemmas for church leadership are perhaps more easily understood. A special sort of vision of what is possible and desirable, a degree of moral and at times physical courage, and confidence in what one says or does are primary requirements. It is very easy to criticise churchmen in Northern Ireland for what is perceived as a failure to give what outsiders think of as real leadership to the community. Too frequently, what they say or do is seen to be merely a reflection of the inherent or inherited prejudice of their own community or tradition. Such criticism ignores the true atmosphere in which they live and work. As a colleague of mine once put it, 'It is not just generals who cannot go too far ahead of their troops.'

When religion and party politics coexist and are so closely identified, it is natural that the familiar path becomes a place of safety and security haven in periods of tension or uncertainty. When those conditions prevail for any length of time there is a natural desire within a community to seek solace and comfort in the known. People will retreat into areas where they feel the safety of people who believe and practise what they themselves embrace. People will welcome the familiar attitude or outlook when they feel challenged or undermined by events or leadership which is alien to their aspirations. Religion can also be used as a refuge. When Protestantism in Northern Ireland appears to be threatened it reaches out to the 'not an inch' mentality – and it is comfortable. When Roman Catholicism is faced with unionist dominance it welcomes the reference to traditional discrimination or injustice.

> It is this coincidence of political and theological factors that renders the issue so intractable. It demands both theological and political techniques for its solution. Ingenious constitutional schemes for ensuring fair treatment for the minority founder on the rocks of religious emotion, compounded by the indignation aroused by terrorism. Ecumenical endeavour to increase understanding between the churches comes under suspicion because a political sell-out is feared. To the Ulster Protestant, Catholics are seen at one moment as republicans and at the next as 'papishes', with the connotation 'rebels' lurking just below each description, and 'Feenians' available to sum up all the notions. To the Catholics, the Protestants are seen as clinging to the ascendancy, both political and religious, of days

gone by, but giving this a cloak of respectability in the form of a demand for unqualified 'majority rule'.[22]

To break this cycle of attitudes and this behaviour pattern is probably the most important task practical ecumenism faces. The evidence to date indicates clearly that it will be a long process.

Thus church leadership faces a dual challenge. First, 'to speak the truth in love' involves a process which is not always immediately obvious or acceptable to those to whom you owe the responsibility and privilege of personal identification. Condemnation of violence can tend to give the impression that it is only violence which emanates from 'the other side' which is the object of such statements. Reference to injustices can quickly take on the appearance of emphasis on what one's own people may be encountering. Sympathy following a terrorist outrage can become selective. Prophetic words about the way forward for the community as a whole can be seized upon as supportive of a sectional aspiration rather than an objective observation on society as a whole.

Recent years have seen a most encouraging development in this important respect. The voice of the churches has become a more obvious prophetic influence in Northern Ireland of late. With some exceptions, when the particular fears and anxieties of a section of the community have required particular reference or emphasis, there has been a greater willingness to see church statements and church opinions expressed in terms of society as a whole. The presence of Protestant clergy at a funeral of a Roman Catholic murdered by a loyalist gang, or the attendance of Roman Catholic clergy at a funeral service for a UDR member murdered by the IRA, would cause little comment in other parts of the world, given similar circumstances. In Northern Ireland it is a tangible though fairly recent example of a changing climate – and a most welcome change at that. The open condemnation by Protestant clergy of the actions of loyalist paramilitaries is now a frequent occurrence, while the courage of Roman Catholic priests in condemning the actions of the IRA has received great support within the Protestant community.

Secondly, church leadership in this community faces the constant dilemma of what is usually termed 'the party political stance'. There are those on each side of the divide who believe that it is normal, and should be the norm, that Church leadership will without question support the prevailing party line: Protestant churches will be unionist, the Roman Catholic Church will be nationalist or republican.

As we have already noted the line between identification and over-identi-

---

[22] Gallagher and Worrall, *op. cit.*, pp. 191–2.

fication with the views of one's own community is extremely thin. There are times when the church voice will be the only one raised on behalf of those with a genuine need to have their case heard by the outside world. In Northern Ireland, the many years when politicians had little or no opportunity to speak up for their constituents imposed on the churches the need to represent the views of their people. I recall visiting Margaret Thatcher at 10 Downing Street in the aftermath of the Anglo-Irish Agreement when church leaders, faced with the rising tide of emotional anger in the Protestant community, felt it necessary to explain the different reactions and fears of their people. There was a feeling that only extremist voices among Protestants were being listened to. Many moderates in the Protestant community at that time felt just as deeply, but turned to their church leaders for assistance in making their feelings known.

The degree to which church leadership reflects the political views of people will vary from occasion to occasion. But church leadership which is out of touch with the genuine feelings of its people will soon become irrelevant. I have always maintained that real leadership involves the church in politics with a small 'p'. Party politics is one thing; social needs, social concerns, community injustice and the need for reform are very much the substance of practical Christianity.

None the less the dangers of over-identification at the expense of objective Christian leadership remain a constant challenge for all church leaders in our community.

When inter-communal violence (soon to become the forerunner for organised terrorism) became reality in Northern Ireland in the 60s, the churches did not at once examine their part in any process which could have encouraged such a situation. There was some acceptance of the fact that the possibility of violence had long existed beneath the surface of sectarianism, and that, after all, 'it has always been the case.'

The immediate church reaction was to be seen to be 'doing something' at street level. Parish halls became refuge points for people in trouble, and street patrols of chosen volunteers operated in areas where confrontation was likely to take place. Such patrols gave an opportunity for well-meaning and often courageous parishioners to express a sense of responsibility and to reach out into the community. Undoubtedly, such efforts had a calming effect locally, but overall there was a feeling of frustration. It was as though a huge tidal wave of emotion had built up. Rumours became fact in an instant. Unease became fear and the constant uncertainty heightened tension in so many areas. There were always people available and willing to fan the flames of tribalism. Eviction from homes on both sides of the divide were common-place. Riots directed aginst 'the other side', or more frequently against the RUC, occasionally took days to quell. The naked face of sectarianism and bigotry came of age in the late 60s.

The churches became in those days a social ambulance service. It was a case of attempting to bind up freshly opened wounds and to offer where possible the cup of cold water. There was little if any coordination of street level reaction, although in east and north Belfast 'peace groups' with strong inter-Protestant identities emerged. On the Roman Catholic side, particularly in small areas which were surrounded by Protestant majorities, there were strenuous efforts made to calm fears which, not unnaturally, in many Protestant eyes identified priests with 'the views of their people'.

The monster of sectarianism had been growing steadily in the shadows. We were unprepared for its emergence with such ferocity. Inherent feelings of uncertainty and suspicion of the motives of others, fanned by the rhetoric of those who had learned how to magnify and utilise such fears, burnt like a ball of fire. Sincere and devoted pastors of their flocks were as unprepared as anyone in the community for what was to come. Their shock and disbelief was as much a comment on the sinister and corroding effects of bigotry as it was an aspect of their frustration.

A Methodist minister of my acquaintance, working in the strongly Protestant Shankill area of Belfast, was horrified to find young people from his congregation preparing petrol bombs shortly after a Sunday afternoon Bible class had ended.

I recall visiting a Roman Catholic enclave one night in east Belfast. Street lights were disconnected, windows shuttered and people moved furtively from house to house. In one home the family had been joined by some of their neighbours. The local priest sat among them sipping a mug of tea. The fear and foreboding were infectious: so far as they were concerned an invasion of Protestant mobs was no longer a question of 'if' but 'when'. The tragic irony was that, only a few hours before, I had visited a Protestant home and listened to the same words, watched the same expressions and drunk tea.

In those long dark days the common denominators of fear and rumour infected everyone – and there were those on both sides all too ready and available to turn tribal anxiety into mob reaction.

From the pulpits came exhortations for calm, appeals for restraint and requests for bedding and volunteers to man parochial and church halls in emergencies. There were condemnations of violence. But we were all so closely involved and so identified with our own community fears that identification became itself over-identification and condemnation too frequently appeared to be of 'others'.

I often ask myself now with the benefit of hindsight what more could we, the churches, have done in those days? There will be some observers who take peculiar solace from the belief that nothing more could have been done – the tide was running so strongly. Many will have felt that there had to be an explosion before sanity could return. This may well be true: normal party political activity had broken down, the police force was exhausted and had lost the confidence of an entire section of the community and government appeared to be remote and indifferent – in such a community there was only one way to go.

Behind such developments the real questions for the churches had still to be asked, let alone answered. How far had the various churches contributed to the unease and divisions which made communal confrontation on such a scale possible? Is it possible to see some connection between doctrinal disagreements and what has been termed the dogmatic isolationism of that period and violence in the community? I have often come to the conclusion that, in those days, words from a pulpit and public position may not have contributed openly to an atmosphere in which violence was the natural outcome, but they did not always help to create feelings strong enough to counter the hostilities. Was it a case of creating a value-system suggesting violence directed to 'the other side' was less despicable than when such violence was directed to one's own flock? I have said the 'us' and 'them' syndrome has never been far removed from Irish society. In those days of unease and community violence clergy were not alone in reaching out first within their own community before thinking of what was happening elsewhere. When 'elsewhere' was only a few streets away the problem became much more acute. It is so easy now, years later, to sit in judgement over what was said and done.

The fundamental issue for church leadership in such circumstances is by no means limited to a divided society such as ours alone. It is a universal problem for the church worldwide. In South Africa or South America, the Middle East or Northern Ireland, the question is the same. How close is church leadership to the *real* needs and opinions of people? The concept of the 'servant Church', which is well established in theological circles, presumes an involvement with an intimate knowledge of the actual feelings of ordinary people. In Ireland we have long prided ourselves in the intimacy of pastoral ministry and service. We claim 'to know our people'. Perhaps one of the lessons of the past few decades which church leadership here has learned and can pass on to a wider audience is that it is not always easy to be closely identified with moods and opinions, even if one's instinctive reactions or pronouncements express one's involvement. Given that a community reaction can be unpredictable at best, the gulf between reflection or representation of opinion and true leadership can be much greater than is often imagined. While the churches in Northern Ireland are undoubtedly secure in their place as a part of the culture and imagery of the community, how far can a church leader assume that the expression of an opinion is anything more than a personal view? In churches of an episcopal structure such as the Anglican or Roman Catholic tradition this is certainly a live issue. In other traditions, where leadership depends more on the committee, assembly or conference procedure, it can be argued that opinions expressed are more likely to represent the views of a majority. The problems of Northern Ireland have ensured for many in church leadership that they take seriously the obvious yet not always practised requirement of listening before speaking. Even then, the process of listening involves a decision about whom one listens to.

The events of the past twenty odd years have reminded us that there are many prisoners of history in Northern Ireland. They have also shown that the church is a prisoner too. The tasks that face the same churches are as concerned with prisoners within their structures as they are with other prisoners of other histories outside them. Yet those same events have made necessary basic heart-searching as to the real nature of Christian leadership in a polarised society. They have made many people recognise the cost of that leadership.

13
THE SECURITY
DILEMMA

From 1969 to early June 1991 283 members of the Royal Ulster Con-stabulary were murdered in Northern Ireland. In that same period ter-rorism claimed the lives of 194 members of the Ulster Defence Regiment and 430 soldiers of the various units of the British army serving in the Province. A total of 907 members of the security forces lost their lives.

From 1969 to early June 1991, 6,778 police personnel, 4,568 soldiers and 406 members of the UDR were seriously injured as a direct consequence of terrorist activity in Northern Ireland.[23] These are the horrific statistics of the human cost of the security operation for some twenty-four years.

No single feature of everyday life in Northern Ireland so concentrates many of the issues which divide her people, and nothing more clearly illustrates the practical implications of Northern Ireland's underlying tensions than the question of security policies. Security is the visible evidence of much that has happened here and continues to provide a focus for emotions and aspirations. The policies, methods, organisation and activities of the security forces, and the differing perceptions as to the purpose, role and effectiveness of community security are rarely if ever absent from debate.

While it is natural that in any polarised society there will be certain areas of particular sensitivity, the degree to which security policies and the actions of those charged with the responsibility of implementing them play a part in the day-to-day experience of Northern Ireland and its people is very sig-nificant. Given the underlying tensions between the two communities, it is inevitable that the question of law and order will be of almost obsessive interest. 'In a divided society ... the constraints on police action can be stricter, the rejection more fierce, and the cynicism proportionately greater.'[24] From the establishment of Northern Ireland this has been the case.

Questions about the nature of state security and the performance of security forces on the ground are far from academic. Law and order questions

---

[23.] Official figures issued by the Royal Ulster Constabulary, 1991.
[24.] John D. Brewer, *Inside the RUC* (1991), p. 227.

occupy centre stage. They are hotly debated and frequently given as the reasons for people's reactions to things which are often purely political in nature. The involvement of the security forces in particular incidents can become in a matter of minutes an issue of great significance for community relations. How politicians and community leaders interpret events involving the police or army has a definite and often far-reaching effect on how people view their community.

In any society law and order holds the key to the quality of life enjoyed by or denied to people. How a community is policed will always have a vital influence on how people behave and order their lives. In a divided community the degree of support any agency of security or policing can anticipate will depend on considerations often far removed from practical 'on the ground' actions. It will involve questions about the nature of security policies and the degrees of fairness with which they are seen to have been implemented. How a community sees itself is made very clear by how it responds to actions by security forces. When violence in many forms is added to the scenario and, in particular, prolonged and concentrated terrorism, the issues quite naturally multiply. The question of who should control security policy and how it should be carried out become of vital importance, not only for the good of the whole of that society, but for the quality of relations between communities themselves.

It is not my intention to present a lengthy historical analysis of what has constituted the security scene over the past twenty-five years in this part of the world. Many accounts and reports exist to illustrate the problems and dilemmas of this part of the Northern Ireland story. Nor do I write as an expert in the field of security matters. What I am concerned to do is to offer some reflections on this sensitive area of the story which I feel hold the key to an understanding of the relationship between the communities and which, from the perspective of a church leader, appear to be of utmost importance in helping the process of reconciliation in the days ahead.

First, there are surely certain definite principles which should and must govern security policies and the actions and activities of security forces.

Disagreement and controversy over anti-terrorist legislation or measures is a clear social barometer of the central position occupied by law and order questions in Northern Ireland. Such debates were highlighted in the 1968-9 civil rights campaign, emerged again with new urgency when direct rule began in 1972 and undoubtedly lay behind much of the thinking in the Anglo-Irish Agreement of 1985. Hardly a week passes when the consequences of such policies surface in some form or other.

It was reported that as the political leaders began their conversations with the Secretary of State in 1991 a police constable on duty at Stormont remarked, 'Don't fail us. We have held the line for years. Don't let us down now.' The price in lives and the price in serious injuries cannot be over-exaggerated. The 'holding of the line' in the face of paramilitary activity and, in particular, the attacks of the Provisional IRA has cost the security forces dear. In that same period I have had the sad duty of burying a considerable number of members of the security forces and, as I have remarked elsewhere in this book, the suffering, and its effects on their families and colleagues, has been immense. It is a side to the story in which statistics, facts and figures can become of secondary importance. But it is a side to the story which our society ignores at its peril. The fact that only a few days after the murder of a policeman or soldier the community moves on to think of other things is perhaps natural. But it does nothing to remove the human loss and the family tragedy which will mark widows and children for their lifetime. In a real sense, whatever is said or written about the greater issues of security policy, nothing should ever be allowed to blind society to the price which has been paid by men and women thrust into confronting terrorism. Plaques on church walls and memorial services seem at times rather insignificant testimonies to the human sacrifice which so many have made for the protection of society from terrorism. Many times I have felt genuine anger when confronted by the human consequences of terrorism. It is all too easy to accept that security forces can go on providing the buffer between what passes as normal community life and dedicated terrorist activity, to accept that there is a level which can continue to be acceptable despite the sacrifices, and to use this as some sort of excuse for failing to do anything to improve the situation. On one occasion, a police widow remarked to me 'If only we could feel my husband's murder was the last one, there'd be some point to it all, wouldn't there?' It was and is a question that still demands an answer.

I cannot help feeling that the burden of responsibility we as a community have placed on the RUC, the UDR and the army in their anti-terrorist activity has as much to say about the failure of our society to come to grips with matters of immense significance to its quality of life and political maturity as it has been a reflection of the strengths of terrorist organisations. Frequently, the human cost seems to have taken second place in parliamentary and political debate.

I have no hesitation in recording my impression, and the impression of many others I know living and working here, that as a society we have placed a burden on the security forces which ought to have been matched by our ability as a community to face up to the real needs of Northern Ireland. To that extent the remarks of the police constable on the steps at Stormont in 1991 possessed a significance outside that of the particular moment. They reflected a truth we ignore far too often.

As a law student many years ago I remember being told that if you wish to obtain a clear picture of what makes a community what it is, examine how it regards community security. That, I was informed, will tell you more than anything else about what a community wants itself to be. The concept of justice has long confronted mankind with questions about the nature of life and human behaviour. It has provoked sophisticated debate and has become the hallmark of what a nation or local community believes is important. Criticism of its absence or of the presence of 'injustices' has long been how so-called democracies have responded to other regions where human rights have been ignored or infringed. Justice has itself become a judgemental process.

In Northern Ireland issues of justice and injustice have often been the victims of perception rather than reality. It is inevitable that, when a society confronts internal divisions and internal conflicts, what one section perceives to be just will be closely scrutinised by others and not infrequently receive a completely different interpretation. The real cause of the problem, for a society under physical or moral attack from without or which endures social disharmony from within, will lie in the way in which that society gears itself to maintain justice without adopting degrees of reaction to threat which themselves erode the very basics of 'a just society'. The dilemmas, the 'grey areas', the questions abound.

Time and again as terrorism has continued here voices have been raised calling for a military solution to a military problem. The only answer to such terrorist activity, they have proclaimed, was and is an all-out military or security onslaught on the forces of terror. Measures ranging from widespread internment of anyone suspected of subversive activity and the reintroduction of capital punishment to the adoption of a 'shoot first and ask questions afterwards' policy have been called for by people whose reaction to public frustration in the face of atrocities is as predictable as it is limited in knowledge of the long-term consequences. The same people have claimed that the community is prepared to pay any price and face any inconvenience or cost if force can be met with force and terrorist atrocities met with purely military means. There is, for such people, only one answer: the defeat of paramilitarism and its adherents by military means.

There have been times, particularly in the aftermath of a brutal incident, when support for such attitudes has grown within the community. Frustration at the failure of 'the normal means' for a society to protect itself from terrorism can so easily feed such attitudes. Such frustration takes many forms. It can be spontaneous in its expression, and severe in its consequences. It can also be extremely damaging to the long-term principles of a community if it is allowed to go 'unanswered' by authority.

We have long proclaimed that there is no future for terrorism. We have often stated that terrorism cannot be allowed to succeed. People have been constantly urged to alienate the terrorist, to provide information which will disclose his or her identity, to remove the support on which he or she depends, and so on. In the face of intimidation and threat there have been countless examples of great courage on the part of individuals who have done just that.

Clearly, a majority of both communities here are opposed to paramilitary activity. This is now beyond doubt. But the defeat of terrorism involves much more than confrontation, arrest, trial and conviction. It has to do with attitudes. Writing in his Strategy Statement for 1991, the Chief Constable of the RUC, Hugh Annesley, stated:

> The Royal Ulster Constabulary is determined to provide the highest quality of service to all sections of the community; and in pursuit of this aim we are firmly committed to the concept of 'policing by consent'.[25]

This concept of 'consent' is critical in any discussion. In a polarised society how does the element of consent present itself? How does a community gauge the awareness of issues, reaction to events and expression of aspirations which together constitute consent to be policed? How far does police planning go in the measurement of what could be considered those social indicators of consent? When one section of a community, be it a minority or not, openly confronts policing, how does a police service respond to the sections of that same community who support and consent to its philosophies? Above all, how does a police force encourage consent?

It is all too easy to adopt measures and methods in the confrontation of terrorism which themselves contribute not to the defeat of such evil but actually assist the process, and do even more harm to the nature of the just society. Repressive measures can be more than justified when a community is under siege. But the balance between meeting a threat while at the same time maintaining the moral high ground of justice and even moral justification, and allowing society to descend to a level welcomed by men of violence is an extremely sensitive one. It is a balance which has not always been as clearly recognised by the divided societies of history as it might have been. In Northern Ireland it has been a constant and vital consideration where security policy is concerned.

It is essential in any polarised society that security policies receive and continue to receive the support and confidence of those they aim to protect. Justice is much more than words or aspirations: it must be seen to be done.

---

[25] The Royal Ulster Constabulary Strategy Statement (1991), p. 3.

If a society is to be protected from terrorism it must also be convinced of the rightness of the means used in the process. Terrorism is not just a challenge to community security; it is a challenge to a wide field of interests. Unless social change is reflected in the process of government, in the attitudes of people desiring peaceful change, and unless it is encouraged by all who seek protection against violence, military means alone – important though they are – will not be the complete answer. In a word, we are driven back to ask questions about society as a whole. To remove the conditions in which the terrorist can operate involves a genuine and sincere examination of what contributes to his support and encouragement. Nothing can take the place of the arrest and conviction of those who, under the guise of republicanism or loyalism, murder and maim. Nothing should be said or done which in any way makes it easier for the paramilitaries to terrorise whole communities. But, equally, nothing should be done which reduces society to a level where it is easier to justify terrorist activities.

This is the balance and also the dilemma which is faced each day by the people of Northern Ireland. Excesses by security forces, an entire community being blamed for the actions of a minority, or policies which in some way or another ignore conditions in which the terrorist can claim he is acting in the defence of a section of the community must be avoided. This is not the easy option. It is in fact the much more difficult path for society to adopt. But in the end more is at risk than temporary 'victory' or 'defeat'. The long-term nature of a whole community can be too easily jeopardised. Security measures must move hand in hand with much more. It is too easy for community leaders to place on the police or army the responsibility which is in fact rightly theirs and theirs alone.

Such a philosophy is not universally popular in a society which has endured so much at the hands of organised terrorism. Nor is it a philosophy which seeks to 'go soft on terrorism': strict and impartial security policies in which wrong is detected, society protected and wrong-doing brought to justice are essential.

It is nothing short of remarkable and sadly not always widely acknowledged in public that, given the particular conditions of Northern Ireland, so few of the security forces have fallen short of the highest levels of responsibility and duty. I do not feel they have been given sufficient credit for this. In my work I have had many opportunities to learn about the lives of members of the security forces. I have seen at first hand the pressures to which they and their families have been subjected. I have a deep and unshakeable impression of the seriousness with which they approach their tasks. I have seen something of the hopes and fears with which they live day and night. Society owes far more to them than it appears to acknowledge as often as it should.

The day for widespread street rioting on the scale of the 70s may have passed but the constant threat of inter-community conflicts on anniversaries of events, or triggered off by particular incidents elsewhere such as para-military funerals, remains. Policing such a divided community requires dip-lomacy, integrity, consistency and depends to a large extent on community support. Policing has too often become a political football: alternately applauded and reviled, depending on the other side's response. It is difficult to imagine a more complex and changing situation in which to expect any police or security force to operate and the demands on the forces only heighten the need for commitment and devotion to duty of an extremely high order. As one former Chief Constable, Sir John Hermon, once said: 'the RUC are extraordinary men and women doing an extraordinary job.'

Real difficulties have arisen for the security forces when it is perceived that their actions favour one community, or section of it, over the others. During the 60s and beyond the RUC did not enjoy the confidence of a wide section of the Roman Catholic community, when internment was seen by many in the nationalist community to be directed against them. In the aftermath of the Anglo-Irish Agreement, many loyalist voices condemned the RUC for actions particularly during parades and demonstrations which were perceived to be a consequence of 'Dublin interference' following the Agreement. It must be to the undying credit of the police in Northern Ireland that one can detect a steady improvement in this situation where professionalism, integrity and a visible ability to operate equally in Protestant areas has won much more respect for them across the community.

> The RUC have undoubtedly made sincere efforts in many aspects of policing to act and to be seen to act as a professional body, impartially serving both communities. This has been at the cost of great sacrifice to themselves. Few police forces anywhere have had to operate in more difficult conditions or have suffered heavier casualties in the call of duty.[26]

Such difficulties illustrate quite clearly the dimensions to the challenge faced in policing the polarised society. They also show how easy it is for the terrorist to seize opportunities of attacking the police.

Support for the police and the UDR has long been a sensitive issue with the Protestant community. Not unnaturally, the number of Roman Catholics serving in the security forces has diminished during the current IRA cam-paign. The reasons are obvious. Intimidation, or worse, awaits someone known to be serving in the forces of law and order and living in an area where the influence of republican paramilitarism is very strong. Loyalist

---

[26.] Cardinal Cahal Daly, *op. cit.*, p. 144.

politicians have frequently called for greater support for the police from nationalists – not just in public statements of support, but in recruitment and membership terms. How long will it be, they demand, until the 'minority community' gives active support to the RUC? The response from those they criticise is to differentiate between 'normal police duties' in the detection of crime and the use of the police in 'security operations' where actions are taken which are regarded as 'anti-Catholic'. This distinction is largely lost on many within the Protestant community. The predominance of Protestant membership of the police and UDR makes the issue more sensitive again. There are those in the loyalist community only too ready to think of 'our police', 'our UDR', and the reaction when police act against some sections of the loyalist community, as was seen some years ago, highlights these perceptions: 'How can they [the police] behave like that towards their own?' is the cry. This makes even more imperative complete fairness and impartiality from the forces of law and order.

Clearly, a significant change will take place when conditions permit greater numbers of the Catholic community to enlist in the police. The nationalist demand for a restructuring of the RUC to make it more acceptable to their community is only a part of the solution. A great deal more is necessary – a great deal of progress in the thinking and attitudes of both communities.

Undoubtedly, there have been incidents involving security forces which have raised serious questions made more significant by the willingness of politicians to interpret the details in party political terms. The so-called 'shoot-to-kill' policy which surfaces from time to time is a case in point. Here is an issue which goes far beyond acceptability or non-acceptability of security policing in a particular area. This involves the use of minimum force in the apprehending of suspects and the directives given to security forces in certain circumstances. Usually the facts of the incident are shrouded in controversy by both sides: there are often allegations that before shooting, the security forces gave no opportunity to the victims to surrender, as against the argument that the victims were dealt with in the only way feasible while engaged, or about to engage, on a terrorist mission. It is not difficult to imagine how quickly or how decisively attitudes harden following such an incident. What is clearly needed and must be demanded in all such circumstances is a full investigation as to the circumstances and that, where it is warranted, all involved are made answerable to the law. There cannot be a law for one and none for the other. Such a provision permanently available, and seen to be administered in an impartial manner, must surely be in the real interests of all communities – and certainly in the long-term interests of the security forces themselves.

It is impossible to estimate the significance to the community of policing without recognising the concern which is felt in the aftermath of incidents when it appears police and army action has gone beyond the normal response to violence or confrontation and especially when 'lethal force' is used. Nothing gives greater encouragement for criticism of the security forces, nor raises the possibility of a community refusing to accept impartial policing than the involvement of the forces of law and order in 'unlawful killings'. Amnesty International has referred on more than one occasion to 'extra-judicial executions', and the notion of those charged with the heavy responsibilities of exercising fair and lawful security measures stepping outside the very laws they are expected to enforce is guaranteed to excite controversy and community tension.

Since 1969 some 300 deaths have occurred in Northern Ireland which have been attributed to police or army action. This figure is composed of deaths occurring in situations where confrontations have taken place between security forces and crowds on the street, and during operations against suspected terrorists. In each case disputes as to the precise circumstances have encouraged the inevitable reactions.

No one will dispute the fact that it is extremely difficult, if not impossible, to disentangle the details of what occurs in many such cases from the frequently contradictory accounts of on-lookers or those involved. The only definite fact is the death of a person or persons. It is in the how, why and justification of action that the problems arise. Time and again we have seen how such incidents quickly become a focus for party political wrangling. It is all too easy to score points on such tragic occasions.

What is vital from an inter-community standpoint is not only the circumstances themselves but the ways in which these are investigated and related to the rule of law. It is in how the law covering the use of 'lethal force' is exercised that the most serious questions arise. The investigation, the prosecution in cases where the law has been broken and the timing of inquests have been the most notable examples of public concern. Any criticism of or cynicism towards the legal or political reaction to disputed killings greatly damages the credibility of and 'consent' given to the police in a divided community. If it can be proved that officers of the state are not as amenable to the judicial process as those who threaten the state or its people through terrorism or violence, untold harm is done to their credibility. It also becomes a significant obstacle to inter-community trust.

What is not always given full credit in the highly volatile and emotional atmosphere which follows such situations is the exceptional nature of the circumstances in which terrorism has compelled security forces to operate. A member of the security forces is not immune from the human reactions felt by others who do not wear his uniform. There is a clear distinction to be drawn, practically as well as morally, between, on the one hand, an incident in which a carefully thought-out plan to ambush suspects is made and, on the other, the instantaneous actions of security personnel confronted suddenly by armed terrorists. However, it must be remembered that once terrorism enters a community the dangers and possibilities of such situations arising are obvious. No one in uniform, or out of it, should be above the law. No one benefits from on-going suspicion following security operations. No one should be able to justify the killing of a human being when another course of action was possible. But, equally, no one without full possession of the facts of any case should leap into the controversy, turning the issues into another political football.

Such incidents are yet one more example of the morass of conflicting positions terrorism makes possible and even welcomes when it brings the gun and the bomb into a society. Above all else, in the battle for the hearts and minds of a community nothing should be done, or allowed to remain unquestioned, which adds any credibility to the terrorist machine. 'The perception of the police service held by the community determines its acceptability; in this respect, we recognise that our public perception remains of crucial importance.'[27]

This perception does indeed greatly influence attitudes to the entire security machine in Northern Ireland. The RUC and the UDR draw their membership from within the community in which they operate. For reasons already noted, they are predominantly composed of members of the Protestant community. Given the emotions in this community, this fact has made it more difficult for people to believe that either body can be truly impartial *ab initio* in dealings with the Catholic community. Clearly the historical process which produced the UDR has been a strong reason for this criticism. At the beginning of the century the Ulster Volunteer Force, established as a Protestant militia to resist the expressed desire of Westminster for Home Rule in Ireland was eventually succeeded by the B Specials, an auxiliary police force entirely composed of Protestants. The UDR, despite many efforts to portray itself differently, has never shaken off its earlier image. The hope was that it would become a non-sectarian force comprising members of both communities, integrated into the British army and assisting the RUC in the maintenance of law and order. Despite the heroism and devotion to duty of the vast majority of its members, their sacrifice in lives lost on active service and when off duty at home, and their steadily growing professionalism in the campaign against terrorism, the regiment continued to be severely criticised from some sources in nationalist community. Failure to live up to the ideals

---

[27]. RUC Strategy Statement (1991), p. 3.

originally expressed for the regiment, and paramilitary connections on the part of a few of the thousands who served in the UDR since 1970, have been used to support the claims of sectarianism. The decision to amalgamate the UDR and the Royal Irish Rangers in the summer of 1992 has provoked the inevitable loyalist claim that this development owes more to the influence of Dublin through the Anglo-Irish Agreement than to military strategy – a claim refuted by military and government sources alike.

Most Protestants see the UDR as a courageous and much maligned regiment protecting with great success 'all the law-abiding people' of Northern Ireland. While such support is wholesome and enthusiastic it is frequently linked to a deeply-felt resentment that the Catholic community do not appear to many Protestants to be giving wholehearted support to the regiment. Criticisms of the UDR are often matched by forceful reminders that 'they are protecting law-abiding Catholics as much as Protestants – and look at the cost they are paying and the thanks they are not getting.'

The Royal Ulster Constabulary has remained through the period of the current troubles the backbone of local security operations. It has endured periods of extreme pressure when, combined with its anti-terrorist work, it has had to contend with the problems of divisions within the community. Pressures emanating from particular events or incidents where local loyalties have brought the two communities into conflict have added to the opposing views held for many years by each tradition. The willingness and ability of the police in Northern Ireland to show an increasingly impartial and professional approach to both sides of the divide has brought a recognition, although from some people reluctantly at times, that much has changed in the administration of policing here. The integrity and discipline of the police, bearing in mind the problems they face, is remarkable. Professional estimates of their performance outside Northern Ireland have indicated an admiration which has not always been expressed in political circles in this community. But their role and their ability to act fairly and impartially will remain one of the most sensitive and vulnerable aspects of daily life for a long time yet. It will also hold a major key to the quality of inter-community relations for many years to come.

Thus the real significance of this issue lies beyond individual incidents or cases. It illustrates in stark terms the dilemmas of a society confronted by the fact of subversive activities in which the rule of law is subjected in consequence to particular pressures. Those pressures emanate not from the presence of terrorism itself, but from the desire and the will to meet a challenge, while maintaining the principles of justice which must apply to the whole of society. This is not just a question for the constitutional lawyer, the parliamentarian, or the sociologist. This is a vital question for society in its entirety. Above all, it is a moral issue.

Is society as we know it geared to meet such a challenge? Are what one usually calls 'normal procedures of law and its enforcement' able to meet the special pressures of a prolonged terrorist situation while maintaining those policies of fairness and justice which ought to be the hallmark of the normal, peaceful society?

There can be no doubt that terrorism in a society already divided on other issues threatens to erode those principles not by its activities *per se* but by the way those activities influence the reaction of law-makers. Decisions have to be made on the nature and strength of the threat and also on the restrictive policies to be implemented to meet it. The balance is precarious, the implications profound.

Perhaps one of the greatest contributions the Northern Ireland story has made in this field is to indicate to the rest of the world how very fine the balance is when normality for a majority of people must be preserved while meeting an enormous challenge to the democratic process. It is in this context that issues arising from the methods used by security forces in Northern Ireland must be viewed. It is in the interest of the law-abiding people of the Province and of vital importance to the preservation of justice for those who 'refuse consent to be policed' that these issues are constantly subjected to the scrutiny of all who long and work for true reconciliation in this community.

Chris Ryder, a journalist who has covered the troubles for several English newspapers, writes in his introduction to *The RUC: A Force Under Fire* words which capture much of the practical implications of these issues:

> In writing this book I have been motivated by a limitless admiration for the valiant men and women of the modern RUC. They represent all that is best about the good people of Northern Ireland and they are truly the cement that holds the divided community together. In saying that, however, I believe that no mature society should give the police a blank cheque, and that proper accountability and safeguards are essential for both the police and the community. In the particular circumstances of Ulster this is crucially important.[28]

I have always felt the tensions which exist for those responsible for security policies in a divided community. I have also seen at first hand something of the dilemma which confronts the policy-maker. The real crux of the problem

---

[28] Chris Ryder, *The RUC: A Force Under Fire* (1989), pp. xii–xiii.

is how to maintain the fabric of a democracy where there are divided loyalties and where subversion and terrorism are a constant threat to the law-abiding.

In those circumstances support for the forces of law and order is essential. Given the circumstances here and the pressures to which the security forces are subjected day and night I feel much more credit ought to be given to the fact that so few of their members have betrayed the trust of the community. Blanket condemnation of the police or army by some people because of the misdemeanours of the few does nothing to encourage understanding. But while the support and cooperation of the community is essential, when they are based on greater understanding of the problems and dangers the security forces face today, I do not believe the security authorities desire or deserve a blank cheque of approval. My main and lasting impression through the years in my contacts with the security forces in Northern Ireland and with their families remains one of determination to do what is right and honourable in the most difficult of circumstances and to express genuine frustration and anger when any colleague betrays the confidence and trust of those he is expected to protect.

To conclude, there can be no substitute in this community to a lawfully-constituted police force. The alternative has been shown quite clearly since 1969 to be the corrosive activities of the paramilitary, be they loyalist or republican. We have seen and endured the effects of such alternatives through the terror, thuggery, kangaroo courts and brutality they operate, often within the very districts they claim to protect. The tentacles of such alternatives to lawful policing and security policies can spread rapidly.

Yet beyond the discussion and analysis of principle we are talking about ordinary men and women who find themselves in the forefront of what those issues actually involve:

> Do not let us ever forget that so many duties taken for granted in any other community must be performed here under the constant threat of terrorist action. Society asks of its police so much without always recognising the cost of what it is asking.[29]

[29.] Extracts from author's Address, Belfast Cathedral, 14 February 1988.

14

A QUESTION OF POLITICS OR RELIGION?

I have argued that oversimplification of the root cause of Northern Ireland's problems adds to the difficult process of seeking solutions. To argue that it is a question of a religious conflict alone is to so isolate one aspect as to ignore the vital interplay of others which complicate the general picture and make it virtually impossible to define the precise nature of the religious dimension of the troubles.

As Northern Ireland and her people look to the future it must be obvious that their religious differences cannot be discussed in isolation from or to the exclusion of their differing political outlooks. Judgements and inter related tensions often merge as events in the community lead to any number of differing reactions.

Those differences are coloured by views on history, cultural expression or appreciation, national identity and political allegiance. To understand those differences one must recognise the nature of power and authority on the one hand, and powerlessness on the other. Ireland represents, as is so often stated by historians, the story of two minorities: the Roman Catholic minority in Northern Ireland and the Protestant minority in Ireland as a whole. Within Northern Ireland the fact that majority and minority status has been by tradition so closely identified with religious denominational identities is part of, if not the heart of the concept of a religious conflict.

To define what constitutes the Northern Ireland conflict involves both religion and politics. As we have noted elsewhere, it is impossible to separate the two. But they also present a unique example of how the political process and the activities of religion can be placed at points not of identification but of contradiction. The churches can find it possible, faced with apparently insoluble problems in community relations, to claim that the root of the problem is after all political, that it is there, in the political field, that solutions must be identified and expounded and that, until there is a political solution, the role of organised religion must be supportive of or even secondary to the process of reconciliation. Equally, I have often been told by politicians that their difficulties would be much more easily dealt with if there was a greater accommodation between the churches. Such attitudes illustrate how the apparently endless nature of the community divisions here creates a sense of frustration which leads to a subtle displacement of responsibility for conflict.

The role of politics has overlapped with the role of religion since Partition in 1921. Indeed it stretches much further back into Irish history. But the tensions and the disagreements have crystalised ever since the six counties separated and became the geographical and social microcosm of those tides of mythology, fact and reality which go to make up the story of the people of Ireland.

Without question the religious dimension dominates most of life and experience in Northern Ireland. Yet in other countries where historical roots have produced religious differences within a community, conflict on the scale experienced here has not been the outcome. It is, therefore, surely because of the significance of the other non-denominational issues that Northern Ireland is a place of conflict. Non-denominational factors become more negative, more emotive and more divisive because of their relationship with the religious. It is devastating socially and culturally that this mixture of interests results in such a complex problem of definition as well as such conflict in community relationships. It is also, for the churches, a stark fact that, if the religious dimension has such a paramount place in any expression of the problem, something important is being said about the nature of religion here itself.

For a churchman to look honestly at the religious process in terms of what has happened in Northern Ireland is, to say the least, an uncomfortable experience. Frequently, the real questions about the role of organised church life or witness in this divided community have come not from the churches but from without. The fact that these questions are frequently couched in judgemental tones and seek to emphasise an apparent failure to act together rather than to speak in individual or denominational ways has prompted a degree of defensiveness in the churches. Politicians have responded to critical comments from the churches by claiming that as 'elected representatives' they alone, rather than the churches, should be the judges. This tension can be illustrated from within both the political and religious arenas since 1969. But the fact remains that serious questions do need to be asked about the role of the church in the Northern Ireland story.

The truth seems to be that, irrespective of the genuineness or lack of it, in the attitudes of both political parties to the role of the churches, and irrespective of how successful the main churches feel they have been in helping to find a solution, a significant process has been occurring here within the religious sector. It is something which is not restricted to Northern

Ireland alone, but it provides a clear indicator of what more the churches could and should do to aid the process of reconciliation. It lies in the attitude of many people who adopt polarised attitudes to which they attach religious labels. It also poses searching questions for those in the churches who may feel there is little more they can do, who have become 'weary in well-doing' and who quite honestly feel that the people involved in fermenting division are outside their influence.

The truth is that for many in Northern Ireland religion is ideology. How this has come about and how it manifests itself in everyday situations is part of the tragedy. To understand it calls for heart-searching which this generation may well feel should have been engaged in many years ago. The roots run deep. The evidence today is all too visible. The consequences have had much to do with attitudes and aspirations far removed from the faithful practice of individual religious denominations.

It is possible to find evidence in the Northern Ireland story of a struggle not about constitutional or political issues but about religion itself. It is not unknown to see extreme loyalism being expressed as 'the defence of Biblical truth'. 'For God and Ulster' is a well-known loyalist paramilitary slogan. When it is realised that those who claim allegiance to such labels have little or no church identity the conclusion is obvious. Some loyalists claim that the 'defence of Ulster' is a defence of Protestant and Christian principles against the evils of republican aggression. On the other side, claims by republican activists that they are defending the Catholic population from attack by the loyalist paramilitaries make clear their belief that it is their religious denominational ethos and practice which requires protection.

Sectarian murders within both communities have become, tragically, more common of late. While it is extremely difficult to differentiate between a killing carried out under the guise of the purely political from one of a distinctly sectarian nature, the fact remains that within both communities the perception will be that the real basis of such happenings is sectarian. Attacks by the IRA on security personnel fall within the political ambit of assaults 'on the British presence', but increasingly, in my experience, the murder of police or UDR members is being interpreted by Protestants as sectarian. The diocese of Armagh encompasses a large section of the Irish border. Many Protestants living along that border have genuine feelings of isolation and vulnerability. They talk of the dangers of working on their farms when the IRA can attack at a moment's notice. For them the IRA is engaged in a policy of eroding the Protestant presence and ownership of land in that area. The fact that IRA paramilitaries loudly proclaim that their campaign is non-sectarian has little effect on that perception. To a large extent these fears can be equated with those of Catholics in other areas or districts who see in the sectarian attacks by loyalist paramilitaries an insidious attack on their community because it is predominantly Catholic rather than nationalist or republican.

Religious commentators see this situation as the ultimate example of what happens when religion becomes ideology. Northern Ireland shows what happens when Protestantism or Catholicism becomes the object of secularisation. It must not be forgotten that there has long been an extremely close identification between a process of secularisation and sectarianism.

There are many examples of reactions to events by the Protestant community which have highlighted the close identification of religious and political principles. This has occurred most often when it was felt that their culture and their religion, as well as their constitutional position, were under attack. Appeals for the 'Protestant people' to stand together in the face of challenge are common when it is thought that an assault is being made on 'their way of life'. In fact, uncertainty and lack of confidence lie close to the real causes of such a reaction – much more than a party political stance. They dictate actions and attitudes merging the Biblical with an expression of a cultural and political stance, which together are taken as the identity of a whole community. On occasions loyalists have reacted by stressing the 'rightness' of their cause and its scriptural foundation. A fundamentalist attitude to scripture emerges and is given a high profile. It becomes part and parcel of the ethos of the community.

When many thousands of loyalists protested outside the City Hall in Belfast following the signing of the Anglo-Irish Agreement, hymns were sung and there were readings from the Bible. There was an appeal to the rightness of the protest based on its 'religious' foundations. Such an association lies deep in the Protestant consciousness and is frequently invoked by the fundamentalist members of that community to justify political attitudes. To understand why this should be is to understand something of the history of Protestantism itself. To dismiss it as idolatory, or to talk in terms of an insult to religion as some commentators do, is to fail to appreciate how deep within Ulster Protestantism uncertainty or, even, 'the siege mentality' lies. Throughout its history this close identity between the rightness of the Protestant case and the assault of enemies on their religion has produced a reliance on Biblical and indeed political 'purity'. It has also resulted in the proclamation of political aspirations with such fervour that those aspirations have taken on the appearance of moral principles: one becomes reliant on the other. The danger for the churches is, of course, that they find themselves trapped in a situation where religion as practised or proclaimed in the name of a community is replaced by secularism, confronting the church with extremely significant questions including where its priorities lie when faced with the axis of the religious and the political in Northern Ireland.

It would be an injustice to loyalism in Northern Ireland to conclude that this process is limited to sections of the Protestant population. In the republican movement there is equal evidence of an alliance or merging of religious interpretation and party political stance. The 'cause' of Irish reunification, with its strong reliance on the historical details of the Easter Rising in 1916, the aspiration to a national identity, the 'one nation' philosophy and the frequent reference to the words and actions of republican leadership through the generations, has a consistent ring of commitment and rightness which comes close to religious. Such aspirations have been expressed from many republican platforms in terms of self-justification and moral values which seek to strengthen the 'armed struggle' of the IRA: the rightness of continuing that struggle is frequently expressed in terms of what has been proclaimed in the past; the rightness of the cause supersedes the iniquities of violence or terrorism. These become justified because of the overriding demands of the cause which must, in its own way, be realised. 'The cause' is, therefore, a means of translating wrong into what is justified: the ends justify the means.

Few people can deny the willingness and courage of the Catholic church authorities in areas such as west Belfast who, faced with the challenge of republicans who rely on paramilitary influence and force, engage in a battle for the hearts and minds of their community. This struggle highlights how easy it is for any church to take on the appearance, in the eyes of its opponents, of an obstacle to the realisation of purely secular political aims. Frequently in republican speeches the Roman Catholic Church leadership is blamed for identifying too closely with that social establishment which republicans recognise as the real impediment to political progress. The casualty, as in the case of militant loyalism, can be the identification of a Church not with the Gospel of justice and peace but with party political aspiration. What is called 'pseudo-mystical nationalism' may be the philosophy of a minority within the Catholic community: it remains a potent influence on paramilitary thinking and is a definite and urgent challenge to the role of the church.

Within the Protestant expression of this secularism of religion lies an underlying fear. Likewise, the fear of the Roman Catholic Church has surfaced time and again in its reaction to events and in its so-called justification of actions. Thus fear is a continuous and corrosive element of those attitudes which have allowed division and suspicion to ferment in Northern Ireland. It has been useful to extreme loyalists in their justification of their political stance. It has been a hallmark of loyalist paramilitary activity. It lies deep in much of the Protestant community's attitude towards community relations, influences the aggressive attitude of many towards genuine ecumenism and dictates basic attitudes towards cultural and social intercourse. It is a fear which has yet to be fully analysed. Yet the cost of the failure to acknowledge in honesty its presence and the failure to face up to its consequences for the future must be put right by the churches of all denominations if real and lasting understanding is ever to come to this community. Here lies much of the real task facing the Protestant churches if their contribution to community harmony is to become of permanent significance. Likewise here lies a role for the Roman Catholic Church of great significance if the churches together are to be seen to practise the real demands of the Christian Gospel.

Part of the problem for the churches of both traditions lies in the simple fact that there is comfort to be found in the maintenance of denominational teaching and practice. To observe the outward practice of worship and loyalty according to inherited doctrine, to engage in the support of one's church life alone, is psychologically reassuring for many ordinary, decent and God-fearing people. It takes effort to engage inter-church activity designed to do anything more than simply support the principles of one's own tradition.

Thus understanding of other sections of the Christian family has too often taken second place in Irish church life. Moreover, a social Gospel in which the teaching of Christ on how one relates to members of other traditions within the community has not always received the priority in church teaching it deserves. Such a conclusion is not by any means comforting. Yet it is a conclusion which events in Northern Ireland compel the churches and church leadership to take seriously. If the churches have been a part, even a part only, of the problems we face, then they must indeed be a part of any solution.

The answer to ignorance is knowledge. If ignorance of each other's denominational teaching is at the root of inter-church tension, then greater knowledge of each other is clearly a necessity. Such a demand cannot be isolated or removed from any process of community reconciliation where religious concerns play a negative part! Yet removing fear of each other demands something more than basic knowledge. It involves the growth of confidence and trust. In that process a way will have to be found to separate mythology from fact. The degrees of honesty demanded are high. The extent to which such honesty can be encouraged to overcome inherited doubts will depend as much on a desire to succeed as it will on a basic belief that such effort is worthwhile. At present there is cause to wonder at the extent to which this willingness exists at what we term 'grassroots levels'.

The notice-board outside a church building usually identifies the denomination which meets there. In Northern Ireland it is difficult to find a street or road which does not possess a church or church hall, a worship centre for some sect or a building used 'for a religious purpose'. In rural areas villages are grouped around a church. In cities and towns the skyline is dotted with spires and towers. No better advice can be offered to the stranger who seeks to identify the religious/political make-up of an area than that they should read the church notice-boards: the denomination can be identified at a glance.

Membership of the four main denominations, Roman Catholic, Presbyterian, Anglican and Methodist, whether active or nominal, makes up 90 per cent of the total population. That membership will dictate how people live, with whom they associate, how they vote at elections – often the way they talk.

> ... the Churches are integral to the experiences and understanding of people in Northern Ireland. They are places and groups which channel, shape and direct the experiences of life in Northern Ireland. Of course this reality cannot be separated from experiences outside the Churches in economic, social and political life and in family and community structures.[30]

As we have seen, people in Northern Ireland are defined both politically and denominationally. Being born into the Protestant community means acquiring the 'Protestant unionist' perspective: being born into the Catholic tradition leads to a nationalist/republican outlook. Whether the churches are prepared to acknowledge it or not they are a part of the process, and an important part, which dictates the rhythm and strength of social and community movement. Equally, they are a part of the conflicts of power which have often played a negative part in community relations. We have seen that if the churches are a part of the problem they must be a part of the solution. Such a statement may be simplistic and provide an easy formula for the observer of the conflict. The distinction between the institution and the individual adherent, a vital part of the explanations or the excuses given by churchmen as they grapple with events in a violent society, is equally important. 'The churches' are very frequently the faces and voices of church leaders, church assemblies or synods. Policies are formulated by officialdom: the lives of individual members are an entirely different matter.

Thus it is impossible to give any accurate estimate of the real influence of the church in a state such as Northern Ireland. Spokesmen for the churches frequently voice opinions about or comment on the media. Statements of condemnation following an incident of terrorist activity are commonplace.

[30] Duncan Morrow, *op. cit.*, p. 111.

Interviews of churchmen on TV and radio are also frequent. While this reflects the presence of the churches in Northern Irish society it is difficult to gauge the net effect in changing the views of a society such frequent appearances or comments may have. Comments from church leaders have often been given great prominence. The impression that comments from churchmen are welcome and expected by the media is widespread. 'We've heard enough from the politicians' is often part and parcel of an invitation to take part in a programme. Equally, there have been occasions when people who are presenting a case or petition, appealing for public support or seeking community approval for some cause, have found it useful, if not essential, to include the support of church leadership. In all honesty it must also be said that church leaders have become wary of the approaches of government and party politicians when some scheme or programme of reform is envisaged: the feeling of 'being used' is not uncommon in church leadership. A desire to maintain independence for the voice of the church is a sign of institutional religious maturity. But it demands a clear intention and understanding of the way others perceive the workings of a community, for while it is advantageous at times for a politician to feel he has the support of a church voice for some point he wishes to make, it is also advantageous for the support of the churches to be visible when some scheme or programme of social reform is launched. It is surely of equal importance that the church does not allow itself to become the willing or unwilling vehicle through which credibility is gained as of right. Independence for the Christian church is a plank on which much more than credibility in any given circumstance depends.

Party politics and the whole panorama of government overlap with much which could be termed 'the social Gospel', being concerned with people, their persuasions and influences, the encouragement or change of attitudes, the long-term goals people will seek. There will therefore be instances when tensions exist. This is inevitable. It is surely healthy for the body politic and the Christian church to be seen to be actively engaged in the struggle to bring about peaceful change in society which is for the good of all. It is equally important to recognise that if that tension is to be healthy and productive for the greater good of society then the integrity so often demanded by the churches in the actions of their members (and others) must be visible in the ways the churches themselves make use of their opportunities to influence society.

Reconciliation is the cry of the moment in church life in Northern Ireland. Yet, as with the word 'ecumenism', it is a term subject to a great variety of interpretations. It is a convenient word to cover a spiritual and practical aspiration when all other words fail.

I remember visiting a school on one occasion and being faced with the question of a sixth-former: 'How will I recognise the day I wake up and reconciliation has happened?' Reconciliation is, of course, a process. It is a process involving a new understanding between people and a new willingness to find ways in which that understanding can be to the mutual benefit of all communities. What it does not mean is uniformity of aspiration, attitude or practice. In Northern Ireland it is all too frequently accepted as the equivalent of surrender or weakness. I cannot accept that true reconciliation involves any surrender of deeply-held convictions or principles of conscience. A person is not any less a Protestant or any less a Roman Catholic by being involved in this process. The churches themselves have not always made this plain. Sometimes the fault has lain with those who in taking ecumenism seriously have given an impression that 'ecumenism' is some sort of new denomination. The real ecumenist is surely the person who takes what is vital and best in their doctrinal stance with them into the experience of meeting others equally committed to their principles. It is in the meeting of minds and hearts and in the recognition of their honestly-expressed differences that common ground emerges.

We have seen that fear of each other's religion may find its roots in Irish history – a history which can give a dismal vitality to incidents and wrongs, real or imagined, which continue to divide people today. However, we have also seen that fear of each other's churches is to some degree encouraged by what people today misguidedly believe of each other. A clear declaration by churches that they have no wish to overcome or to submerge each other's witness or principles must become the bottom line in inter-church relationships at any official level. Mutual respect, in which sectarian attitudes become irrelevant to a desire in both words and actions to share responsibility for the good of the community, is the only long-term policy which ought to dictate our attitude to each other.

Theologians recognise that there are fundamental differences in the teaching of individual churches. Indeed, they recognise that there are fundamental differences of approach to the nature of what constitutes 'the church'. To group denominations as is the case in Northern Ireland, into Protestant and Roman Catholic, is itself to gloss over differences of tradition and emphasis within the Protestant family. This fact alone can cause problems across the religious divide. The 'Catholic' and 'Reformed' nature of Anglicanism must understand the differing emphasis within the Reformed traditions of Presbyterians and Methodists, to say nothing of the large numbers of other denominations existing in the Province. But this ecclesiastical fragmentation must never be allowed to remove the importance, in an inter-community sense, of the distinctions between the two main groupings.

Within all our denominations there is an urgent need for a programme of inter-church understanding. This should not be a luxury or optional extra in a polarised community. It should be an essential part of church planning if we are to provide some degree of mutual awareness to the community. The question ought to be asked as a matter of form whether what we are teaching or expecting our adherents to accept about other churches is an accurate description of what is important to other denominations. Too frequently, I feel we tend to emphasise what separates the doctrinal teaching of churches at the expense of understanding the points in common. Superiority in religious terms must never be confused with sincere acceptance of fundamental beliefs which have historic denominational importance.

It would be wrong to give an impression that the differences between the churches can be overcome in an instant without close examination of the practicalities. There are concerns within Protestantism over Roman Catholic attitudes to the upbringing of children born following an inter-Church or mixed marriage. There are concerns within Roman Catholicism over the connection between Protestants and the Orange Order. There are difficulties for many Protestants in their perception of the power and influence of the Roman Catholic Church within the Republic of Ireland. There are worries on the part of Roman Catholics about anything which erodes the importance of the control and support of their schools. Many Protestants harbour suspicions about the attitudes of the Catholic Church to the constitutional position of Northern Ireland, just as the traditional links of Protestantism to unionism cause critical comment from within the Catholic community. From each side there have been criticisms of 'selective denunciation' of violence, denunciation of paramilitary activity only when 'one's own' community has been the victim. The importance of joint Christian witness by the churches of Northern Ireland can never be overemphasised. There are occasions when society needs the united voice of the churches. Opportunities abound here for such action. Too frequently, those opportunities have been lost, to the detriment of all our churches.

In the late 60s it appeared that a united church stand on major issues went by default. The reasons were obvious. Pressures in a sharply-divided community made it much more likely that the official voice of the church would reflect the identifiable needs or complaints of sectional interests. In this as in many other ways we have moved a long way. Denunciation of paramilitary atrocities is now much less selective than once was the case. Examples of injustice now call forth much more 'general' comment from churches. Church leadership encourages joint action to a much greater extent.

We are learning in refreshingly new ways what it means 'to do together what conscience does not demand we do separately'.

It is a source of amazement to churchmen from outside Northern Ireland to discover how much contact and cooperation exists here between the churches. They had been led to assume by the violence and media attention to incidents of bigotry that contact was if anything minimal. But for the churches in this situation having come in many ways so far since the 60s there is the temptation to lose the incentive to push on and to increase the lines of communication and understanding. What used to be called 'tea-cup ecumenism' has long passed. Now we ought to be at a stage where trust is sufficient at most levels to face up honestly to what continues to divide us.

It will take time, much patience, immense integrity and courage in the face of vociferous and often violent opposition. But the path to greater inter-church understanding, and indeed charity, is an essential road for the churches throughout Ireland. It is, above all, a road they must travel if their collective contribution to a new dawn of reconciliation is to be more than a pious hope.

> Religion and the Churches … have a crucial part to play in inter-community relations but this cannot be forced. Policy and practice can only be successful if the change is desired.[31]

Reconciliation may be a process – but it cannot be enforced. In human terms reconciliation in a divided community becomes a priority when sufficient numbers of people across the divisions see the advantages it can bring. Institutions and those who represent them may spell out the need for reconciliation; it is in the hearts and minds of people that that process gains its real momentum. And until sufficient numbers of ordinary people want it to happen it will remain a vision on the horizon.

[31] Duncan Morrow, *op. cit.*, p. 119.

15
JUST A HOPE ...

The atmosphere and experience of Ulster has emphasised church divisions. And nonetheless, given the actual divisions of world Christianity, one is left to ponder whether Ulster was not an accident waiting to happen to the churches.[32]

Church leadership is a leadership which is aware of parameters to the expression of its opinions, policies and comment. Such is the theory. But in the particular inter-relationships of Northern Ireland this is often seen not to be the case. Much though a church leader may seek to confine his leadership to the spiritual and moral sphere, he will be perceived to be speaking and acting 'on behalf of his community'. The political-social-religious sphere in which his leadership is exercised will lead to his being judged within society at large by criteria far removed from the spiritual. Judgements will be made and comment encouraged on what a church leader says or does which will be as much related to the political identities of his flock as to the spiritual strengths of his denomination.

The tensions generated by this situation are constant. A church leader may see himself as a spiritual leader. But, whether he likes it or not, approves or disapproves, he will be taken to be speaking as a leader of a community, often in ways which will themselves encourage reactions far removed from the purely religious. Self-analysis, self-criticism and self-discipline in his public role will become his most vital considerations. It will also make necessary serious thought on the role and purpose of church leadership in a divided community.

After some sixteen years in such a position in Northern Ireland I cannot but be acutely aware of the nature of such dilemmas. The degree to which one achieves and maintains any separation of function in the exercise of such leadership will be a matter for the community to decide, but, in the exercise

[32] Duncan Morrow, 'Pastors and Politics', *Fortnight Magazine* (June 1991), p. 4.

of such responsibilities, certain priorities, which are as much a concern for the churchmen as for the politician, become clear.

After years of conflict it is comparatively easy to conclude that peace is the prime need for this community. Few could argue with such a statement of the obvious. Peace has been longed for, prayed for and planned for over the years – evidence the demonstrations, the movements, the legislation and the statements. In the past few years it is clear that the vast majority of people long for peace. But what is not as clear is the nature of the peace they seek, the nature of the structures they will support to bring it about and the extent to which they are prepared to see changes in society which will make it a reality.

'Peace' is itself open to such a variety of interpretations. Each community, and almost each individual within it, will present a variation of what is acceptable as well as what is possible. The vision is as conducive to conflicting ideas as it is desirable to so many. Does peace mean only an absence of violence? Does peace mean the recognition of what one community sees as injustice to the exclusion of a full recognition of what constitutes grievance for another? Are there degrees of peace in which agitation for reform will continue to blight social progress for many more generations? Are those who claim you cannot resolve the aspirations of two groupings which disagree on fundamentals of constitutional structures for Northern Ireland in fact stating what the 'peace-makers' prefer to ignore? Above all, has society here really faced up to the meaning of compromise and what it will involve if agreement is to be a reality?

A divided community will always be able in time to identify what divides it. Once real efforts are made to separate fact from fiction, and the real from the imagined, and fear is recognised for what it is, the issues which make division possible, and even in some eyes desirable, will become clear. There will always be areas of doubt, but time and determination, changing social conditions and often a social weariness will create a situation where the real issues will become clear. This will not always result in a settlement of the difficulties. Recognition may be an end in itself. But to isolate and define what causes division is to make a major step along the road to peace. Sometimes asking the right questions is just as valuable as supplying answers.

Outwardly, Northern Ireland appears a resilient and more tolerant society than it was, a Province where there is greater equality of opportunity, cooperation between the majority and minority and a growing awareness that what concerns unite rather than divide are important to more people. This is the positive side of the picture. Visitors who come expecting to see in Belfast a city like western Beirut are disappointed. Many of them cannot believe what they see. The warmth of the people and the progress that is visible in new building projects, improved housing, recreation facilities and tourism are in stark contrast to their expectations. To talk of division and alienation, prejudice and violence, paramilitary influence, intimidation and lawlessness, injustice and social grievances, is to use language which seems very far from the normality and spirit of much they see.

The truth is that Northern Ireland has come a very long way since 1969. But the real issues which have made possible the years of community unrest, terrorism and sectarian violence, social inequality, perceived injustice – the divisions and suspicions – continue to be the obstacles to a stable society.

Complaints about the action of the security forces continue in the national-ist community, terrorism emanating from both sides continues to claim lives, grievances about job opportunities, housing and social amenities surface regularly in certain districts, local politicians continue to emphasise a lack of compromise in councils although there have been excellent examples of cooperation in some. Chiefly, basic attitudes towards members of other communities appear to have changed little.

Frequently, claims of growing 'normality' and great hope for the future are made on the basis that much has been endured. There is wide recognition that the events of the past twenty odd years have not destroyed the basic fabric of this society. The violence has not changed life for everyone. The terrorism has not brought the community to its knees. The communities have so often come to the brink and yet have always, somehow, drawn back. The essentials of life, though threatened and disrupted from time to time, have survived. Many people have prospered. Many people have had their standard of life enriched. Many social agencies and programmes have expanded and become the envy of other countries: indeed, much of what has been accomplished here in social welfare, community action and commercial enterprise has been adopted elsewhere.

But the lessons of the Northern Ireland story are still to be learned. The real issues of a divided community remain. The questions which deeply affect human lives and the way in which those lives relate to each other, the principles of what constitutes the stable and just society and the ways in which different traditions can find structures which will make living with difference a positive and wholesome experience remain.

Dialogue in its widest sense is the key. And the process of dialogue involves much more than involving various parties in discussion. It involves a willingness to listen, to build up trust and to indicate those degrees of understanding that are vital to the interests and aspirations of others. Divided communities by their nature suffer from a lack of communication. Reality is often the victim. Wrong questions are asked – and wrong answers given.

At every social, political, cultural and religious level dialogue remains a prime necessity if greater understanding is to emerge. No means of breaking down barriers or meeting those elements of ignorance which breed prejudice and distrust will be more effective than a concerted effort at dialogue. Already there is much evidence of such activity throughout this society – but much more is needed.

Serious questions are being asked about the value of the political process in Northern Ireland, not because of any inherent disenchantment with the principle but rather as a consequence of the apparent ineffectiveness of the process to meet the actual needs of ordinary people. We cannot ignore the dangers of such a conclusion. Political failure or political vacuum is a constant encouragement to the men and women of violence from within both communities.

Many hopes were raised in 1991 when attempts to encourage the leaders of the political parties to engage in worthwhile discussions appeared to succeed. For years church and community voices had been calling for 'political dialogue'. Such calls became insistent and claimed the support of a majority of the people in urging politicians to reach the conference table. The efforts of the Secretary of State, Peter Brooke, and the encouragement of both the British and Irish governments finally succeeded to the extent of a prolonged period of 'talks about talks'. The obvious 'smoke signals' which owed as much to the feelings within the various political camps as to the reservations of the politicians themselves gave an impression of a willingness to move forward. Preconditions occupied much time and effort. The fact that this initial dialogue came to an end early in the summer of 1991 still left the hope that much had been gained and much remained on which another attempt could be built.

These attempts at political dialogue were based on the possibilities of a new Anglo-Irish Agreement. The *Irish Times* was not alone in describing the occasion as 'the most significant attempt to address relations within and between these islands in 70 years'.[33] For the first time participants would include the constitutional parties in Northern Ireland and the Irish and British governments. The same structure would include discussions on relations within Northern Ireland and would be followed by analysis of North-South and Anglo-Irish relations. After eighteen months of preliminary and often tentative discussion the air was filled with talk of 'historic opportunity'.

There were varying degrees of hope, cynicism and expectation when the talks began. Here was the opportunity to bring together those political figures who led constitutional parties, elected by people who represented themselves

---

[33.] *Irish Times* (18 June 1991), p. 5.

the diverse attitudes, hopes and fears which make up this divided community. Here were leaders whose words and attitudes were as much dictated by the people they represented as they were conditioned by the realities of party political exchange.

What was possible was much more than 'political agreement'. There was the possibility that, if political progress could be made, other issues within the wider community would become easier to address. Political problems demanded political solutions. The question was more to do with possibilities and nerve than with details of political niceties. Much was at stake.

For a tired and weary community it was natural that expectations were high. The hope that agreement, whatever it contained, would end the violence was widely canvassed. The reality was, and is, that political talks alone would not end violence. In fact, as events proved, any progress on the political front presented a threat to the 'men of violence'. Undoubtedly, political progress would be a major and historic step towards community stability and an improvement beyond words to political understanding between both parts of Ireland and Britain. But to place responsibility on the political leaders alone to end violence and terrorism was for many of us unrealistic. Indeed, the pressure such hopes generated on the parties to the discussions was counterproductive.

James Molyneaux, leader of the Ulster Unionist Party, sought to prioritise the 'Union' of Great Britain and Northern Ireland ahead of the 'three sets of relationships'. His opposition to the existing Anglo-Irish Agreement was equalled by his refusal to accept executive power-sharing in any developed legislature. He favoured parliamentary reform at Westminster, to bring about legislation for the Province by the normal bill procedure rather than the present 'Order in Council' method with a Select Committee on Northern Ireland, and a return to 'modest' administrative powers for 'one or more' regional councils. He had suggested on occasions that the Anglo-Irish Agreement would be less objectionable if the consultative role of the Irish Republic could be extended to cover concerns of the Irish community in Britain. But he regarded any relationship with Dublin conditional on the withdrawal of its constitutional claim to Northern Ireland.

The Reverend Ian Paisley, leading the Democratic Unionist Party, strongly supported devolved government in the United Kingdom as a whole. He did not regard reform of procedures at Westminster as fundamental to the alternative agreement he sought. For him a legislature at Stormont with real powers, including some security responsibilities, was needed. He opposed 'executive power-sharing' and could not accept participation of the main Catholic constitutional party, the SDLP, as of right. A new assembly would for him have to reflect majority rule through the inclusion of 'an executive'.

Like James Molyneaux, he vehemently opposed the Republic's claims to jurisdiction over Northern Ireland.

Thus there were traditional similarities in both attitudes of the unionist family representatives. The opposition to the Irish Republic's jurisdiction or claims to the Province remained. The degrees to which recognition could be given to the nationalist standpoint varied, but both parties continued to emphasise the cementing of the Union.

Dr John Alderdice, leading the non-sectarian and middle-of-the-road Alliance Party, also accepted the priority of the Union with Great Britain. While he had originally accepted the Anglo-Irish Agreement he now felt it had failed to achieve its objectives and required at least some significant change and development. He favoured partnership, regional government in Northern Ireland and a tripartite structure to promote North-South and East-West interests. Any links between Northern Ireland and the Republic should be institutional but not constitutional. He visualised power in any new assembly for the Province to be allocated proportionately, with the exclusion from government positions of any party which supported violence.

John Hume, leader of the SDLP, approached the talks as a firm supporter of the Anglo-Irish Agreement. Any alternative to the Agreement he saw as something which would 'transcend' in importance the 1985 treaty. While his long-term aspiration remained Irish unification this had to be based on the consent of the majority of people in Northern Ireland. For him a prerequisite of any discussion of solutions must be agreement on the precise nature of the problem. That problem he saw as revolving around the relationship between unionists and the remainder of the island of Ireland. He saw endorsement by Dublin of any new agreement as the only way unionist objections to partnership in the Province could be met. The details of agreement which would then emerge should be put before the people, North and South, in a referendum. He had no 'ideological commitment' to devolution and was prepared to consider the possibility of several alternative structures for institutions of government.

The extent to which these positions could represent a basis which would satisfy the hopeful expectations emerging for the talks from within both communities was doubtful. The hidden agenda was not to do with political institutions alone, but with how far compromise was possible at a political level and could lead to hope that such a spirit would overflow into community relations outside the Stormont discussions. It also had to do with how far political leaders felt they could go to change a situation where political progress was nevertheless seen by some people to be a vital element in restructuring the relationship between Protestant and Roman Catholic, unionist and nationalist, Ireland and Britain. What was being attempted was much more than a ritualistic statement of well-known positions, and it had to do with the survival of any hope that there was and could be a place for the political process in true reconciliation. When the preliminary discussions ended we were assured that, despite the difficulties, some progress had been made – all had not been lost. The hope was that a way could be found to continue the process in some form later.

The emergence of another feature of Northern Irish society became increasingly clear as the talks began, a factor which cannot be ignored when one attempts to see the way forward in community relations in Northern Ireland. For a considerable number of people the party political process appeared to be increasingly irrelevant to the main issues which confronted them. It was not that they had become totally disillusioned with sectarian politics: sectarian attitudes were too much a part of daily experience to permit that. What they were finding was that life could go on, standards could be maintained and personal well-being could be realised despite any 'stop-go' performance in the political field. Granted, there were those who spoke of local politics as an on-going feature of life and continued to regard progress 'as desirable'. But the way they lived and their prosperity were increasingly matters which no longer depended on 'political progress'.

Within both communities, but in my opinion particularly obviously amongst Protestants, there has been an 'opting-out' of community involvement by a large section of what can be loosely regarded as 'the middle class'. For a growing number of people who have so much to offer in ability, leadership and influence, there has been a deliberate (or subconscious) reaction to events here since 1969 which has led them to decline any overture to 'become involved' in inter-community relations or progress. As one person put it to me recently: 'if your home, or family is unaffected by the troubles, if your business or work is surviving you don't want to know.'

There are many reasons for this attitude. A feeling of *déjà vu*, a belief that after so many years nothing is going to change, an outlook that sees intransigence as continuing, and a belief that society's weariness with violence and the failures of the political process means that individuals can do little or nothing to bring change – all this contributes to the growing number of people who effectively present a challenge to the process of reconciliation. Such attitudes are no longer on the periphery of the situation. I believe they are a growing reality. How many who have so much to offer can be motivated to become more involved in community consciousness has become vital in Northern Ireland. Their role in the dialogue cannot be ignored. Their existence is as much a comment on the failure of community relationships as it is a subtle part of the puzzle to be solved:

... important, too, is an end to the opting out which has characterised all too many of the well-off and comfortable – doing very nicely, thank you very much – in Northern Ireland, unwilling to raise their heads above their own garden walls in case they are confronted by unpleasant realities outside.[34]

As the community watched the attempts to make political progress in 1991, there was talk among commentators of 'people power'. What they meant is doubtful. Did not the population have an opportunity to express its wishes at the ballot box? Did not successive general and local elections indicate the preoccupation of the people of Northern Ireland with the 'constitutional issue'? How far had attitudes changed? How far did the stated attitudes of the political leaders as they approached the Brooke initiative in fact indicate a willingness to move forward beyond traditional positions? When reference was made to 'people power', how far had such opinions really moved beyond what many accepted as the continuing 'will of the people'? In fact, had anything really changed?

The crucial question remains. Have attitudes changed sufficiently to permit chosen political leaders to feel a new confidence, a new ability and a new freedom to see compromise as anything other than abject surrender? Dialogue alone will determine the answers to such questions. But dialogue which involves personal integrity and a willingness to move out beyond the trenches of what represents past failure is essential for many more than elected politicians. Too often within our divided society the responsibility for progress had been passed 'to others'.

Politicians are not just elected leaders. They are a part of the community. It is very easy to criticise them and to leave it at that. The constituencies they represent alone can provide the latitude and at the same time set the limits to what they can be expected to achieve:

It is time for that constituency to raise its ambitions – to exert a direct impact on the 'big p' political arena. Even if, least plausibly, the talks succeed, popular support will be needed to make any new institutions work. If, as is more likely, the talks drag frustratingly on and on, popular pressure will be needed to spur them to a conclusion.[35]

As long as violence is a feature of life in Northern Ireland no progress and no institutional reform is going to achieve real stability. Violence is a part of the spiral, a part of the sinister circle, which is the chain we must seek to break. The fact that it is frequently claimed that violence is the consequence

[34] Robin Wilson, 'Spare us the pious platitudes' *Fortnight Magazine* (November 1991), p. 5.
[35] Ibid.

rather than the cause of our divisions makes the problem more urgent. On the other hand, the sectarian outlook within both communities makes violence possible. Somehow, the chain has to be broken.

If, as has been argued, there is no military solution to the violence in this community, other considerations become vital. The chain of reaction and counter-reaction will continue as long as situations exist which permit some people to see violence as the only way of making their aspirations known. Violence is as much an indication of a failure of society to address its root causes as it is an evil to be met. It is as much a political and social statement as it is the cause of needless human suffering, even though one resents and abhors its presence.

It cannot be without significance that violence has emanated most clearly from within those areas and from within those social classes which have over the years been the real focus of social deprivation in this community: the ghetto areas, the estates which house people who have moved from traditional 'tribal' districts and people who in other generations have made up 'the working class'. There is a social dimension to Irish violence. Attitudes may be reflected throughout the length and breadth of the community, but the experience of sectarian violence has a strong social connotation.

If it is argued that there is no justification for terrorism as an expression of political ideology, and if it is maintained that violence places its instigators and supporters beyond the political or social process which is essential for reconciliation, the question remains – what is to be done to end it? From within Irish republicanism came the call that no political progress could be made at the Brooke talks if Sinn Fein was to be excluded. It was stated that by alienating republicanism from that process any results would be irrelevant for a large section of the Catholic population. From within constitutional unionism and nationalism came the rejoinder that people could not bomb or shoot their way to the conference table. From government came the response that as long as terrorism continued there was no place for Sinn Fein in the process of political dialogue. But that if terrorism ceased, 'a new situation' with new possibilities would exist.

Time and again church leaders have been at the forefront of calls on the paramilitaries to cease their reign of terror. At the funerals of victims, in public addresses and in frequent statements, Protestants and Catholic leadership has been united. Condemnation of violence has become the common denominator of church comment on the situation. In a report 'Violence in Ireland', jointly commissioned by the Protestant and Roman Catholic churches in Ireland and published as far back as 1976 there was a categorical conclusion:

In spite of the complicated historical and social issues involved and without prejudice to any legitimate political aim, we find unanimously that there is no justification in the present situation in Ireland for the existence of any paramilitary organisations. It follows that we see no justification for the campaign of bombing and killing being carried on in Northern Ireland, in the Republic of Ireland and in Britain. We uphold the right of any group to express its views in peaceful demonstration and in seeking electoral support.[36]

This has remained the view of church leadership ever since. But it is in the connection between the expression of legitimate political philosophy through paramilitary means that the real questions for society arise.

Within the loyalist community condemnation of the IRA has reached fever pitch following atrocities, and in party manifestos for years unionism has spoken of the 'futility of violence'.

What remains to be considered when paramilitaries are urged to end violence is what will replace violence if it ends. Have those who condemn violence given real thought to what the situation will involve for them if and when paramilitary-inspired violence ceases? For example, if constitutional parties refuse to have any contact with the supporters of violence, have they thought out the implications of dealing with those who 'once supported terrorism' in a new political process which would emerge once violence ended? If and when terrorism ends there will be a vacuum in Northern Ireland which something must fill. I wonder at this stage what our society, which has suffered so much because of violence, envisages as the political, social and indeed cultural character of that same society when the pressure of terrorism no longer exists. Appraisal and reappraisal of a future situation cannot await its arrival.

While there is unity of attitude among constitutional political parties and the official stance of the main churches, that until terrorism ends there can be no dialogue with those who engage in it or support it, there must, surely, be serious and considered analysis of the cost of peace. It remains to be seen if both the constitutional parties and the churches have given sufficient thought to this.

Undoubtedly, there is at this time debate within Irish republicanism on the way forward. I cannot accept that, while calls for an end to terrorism have been refuted, those involved in 'the movement' are unaware of the calls so often made for an end to violence. The cost of an unconditional ceasefire for republicanism is great. Historically, they can point to failure in their terms

---

[36.] *Violence in Ireland. A Report to the Churches* (1976), p. 90.

to provide any realistic response by the rest of the community to temporary cessation of terrorism.

However, I have no doubt that if terrorism were to end, and renunciation of the bomb and the bullet became somehow a reality, the dismantling of the machinery of terrorist violence would create for all of us a new situation. Legitimate political aspirations exist in Ireland. Dialogue can be a reality, but dialogue can never be forced on people by the threat or reality of murder and destruction. Too much is at stake in the long term for this society. The moral issues involved exist quite apart from the reactions of whole communities which dwell on the injustice of terrorism. For there is hypocrisy in the ways republican terrorism has sought to 'justify' much of its activity. To argue that its violence is a consequence of injustices perpetrated on the community it claims to defend seems to ignore the real injustice the IRA inflicts on its victims. Can there be any greater injustice than killing another human being under the guise of a political or religious cause?

If a process of dialogue is to involve those who until now have presented to the world both the visions of 'the armalite and the ballot box' serious questions arise for republicans and the remainder of Irish society. If there is 'another way' who will be able to spell it out in ways which will give permanent peace a real chance? Who will make the first move in breaking the chain of violence and the inevitable reactions to violence. How will society organise itself to grasp the opportunities a permanent ceasefire will bring?

These issues all point the way to community dialogue. They also show how high the mountain is we have to climb.

16
FACING
THE COST

It is almost a quarter of a century since 1968. In that period the contrasts in terms of what people have actually experienced here have been huge and significant. Days of heightened tension and confrontation have been followed, in time, by weeks of comparative peace, despite the underlying uncertainties and instabilities. Incidents which have raised the social temperature to boiling-point have contrasted with courageous efforts to build bridges and seek understanding. Calls for the removal of injustices and social deprivation have continued alongside sweeping reforms in administration and social amenities. On the one hand, community awareness of social need has grown immensely since 1968, but, on the other, there continues to be definite limits to cross-community cooperation. The widespread street confrontation of the late 60s and the 70s has been replaced by the terrorism and sectarian conflicts produced by paramilitarism. The levels of violence have fluctuated with peaks where the taking of lives and the destruction of property have raised fears and brought tragedy for many families, and with troughs where an uneasy peace appears to prevail – only to be shattered by actions and the inevitable retaliation. While the 'normality' enjoyed by a majority of people causes amazement for visitors to the Province, tensions and fear of physical violence continue to be experiences of people living in particular areas. Attempts to achieve political dialogue have begun with a new sense of urgency, only to face the historic obstacles of intransigence and preoccupation with constitutional issues which prevent progress on questions actually affecting day-to-day lives in the community.

In the past twenty-four years much has changed here – yet it is all too obvious and tragic that so much has remained the same as it was in the late 60s. Stability and reconciliation remain a dream for a community which continues to suffer the consequences of fears, suspicions and division and, despite the changes we have seen in that same period through much of Europe, continue to bear the outward appearance of a society in which too many doors remain closed and movement towards genuine community understanding seems so reluctant.

The human cost of those divisions has been stated so often, and the changing levels of violence have become so much a feature of life, that there is a very real sense in which the people of Northern Ireland have become desensitised to the full significance of what has been happening. If one's own family circle has not been directly affected, the genuine feeling of powerlessness to bring an end to the violence has produced even in this community the attitudes of weariness and incomprehension we find in other people towards Northern Ireland. A large majority of ordinary people in both communities opposed to violence continue to be the victims after twenty-four years of a minority of people from the same communities, and this is perhaps one of the most striking features of the troubles. But it is to the matter of inter-community relationships that the real questions must be addressed. It is at that level that the issues which one day must lead to reconciliation and peace should be viewed. It is there that so much remains to be done.

It has become fashionable of late to conclude that there is no real answer to the problems of Northern Ireland. Weariness among neighbours who have seen little they can recognise as progress, and disappointment at the results of efforts to produce change have been reflected in varying degrees of disenchantment in mainland Britain and further afield. Dublin has become steadily more involved in the affairs of the Province since the Anglo-Irish Agreement was signed but has faced a proportionately increased degree of opposition from loyalists. Political writers have expressed something of the exasperation felt in the corridors of Westminster at a problem which has become for many a 'situation': a problem can be solved, a situation has to be accepted. There are many who would agree today that 'perhaps there is no solution to the Northern Ireland problem except to accept it and live with it.'[37] Certainly, simple solutions, naïve in their formation, lacking sensitivity and a sense of history in their application, will never meet the intensities of 'our situation'. The lesson that we cannot legislate for or enforce reconciliation is being accepted by many who are aware that the only solution is in the basic attitudes of people towards themselves and towards each other.

None can doubt the intensity of the efforts to define and state the nature of the problems. Much intellectual and practical effort which has been as prolonged as it has been costly has been applied to the definition of what needs to be achieved and what has to be done to speed a resolution of historic division. But I am often reminded of the words of Benjamin Disraeli: 'I want to see a public man come forward and say what the Irish question is.' These days one might well say that once a problem is solved an Irishman

---

[37] James Hawthorne, BBC Controller, Northern Ireland 1981.

moves the goalpost so that the answer no longer fits the question. The spiral of action and reaction and the continuing inability of the community as a whole to reach the level of harmony and understanding which the vast majority longs for remains the cause of the question, irrespective of whether one talks in terms of a problem or accepts a situation. Just as there should be no such concept as 'an acceptable level of violence' there cannot be 'an acceptable level of inter-community tension'.

Many have indeed tried to solve the 'insoluble': such failures have added weight to the conclusion some people have reached, that the effort involved in seeking a lasting solution is too great. Certainly, we must acknowledge that the price of failure makes many people unwilling to attempt any long-term solution. There have been too many casualties among people who have tried, and failed. Not surprisingly the corollary – the people of Northern Ireland do not really want a solution – has appeared more than once. At times, I have found this most commonly expressed in the sentiment 'what's the point of trying? It's always been like this. There's nothing we can do about it.' This has too often been the perception: but, as we have remarked before, the perception becomes the reality in an instant in this society.

While one community looks back to 1690 and enshrines the triumphalism of an ancient battle in its folklore and finds in it so much which justifies how it sees itself, the other turns to 1916 and expresses a continuing reliance on principles which have given the commitment to the concept of national identity an intensity akin to religious fervour. How the ideals and aspirations of the two communities relate to each other has become wedded to questions of power and powerlessness, authority and subjection, majority and minority syndromes and the continuing unease of where their future lies, together or apart. The fact that expressions of identity have encouraged a belief that the only worthwhile change must come about within 'the other community' rather than within one's own has removed some if not all of the real dimensions of a solution. Neither community cannot change what it really is. What must change is the attitude so often expressed in intolerance, prejudice, bigotry and violence that the totality of justice, the totality of 'rightness' is contained within one tradition to the exclusion of any other. The real impact of the terrorists has lain in the belief that they would achieve what constitutionalism and moderation appear to them to fail to accommodate: the ultimate triumph of one belief, aspiration or tradition over the other. Triumphalism, whether it be republicanism, nationalism, unionism or loyalism, Protestantism or Roman Catholicism, violent method or peaceful reform, is the real issue for Northern Ireland. We have seen that attitudes can be just as violent as historic divisions. We have also learned to our cost that the triumph of one tradition over the other is the ultimate defeat.

Difference has almost always been the ultimate negative in Ireland, North and South, but difference as a productive and positive tension must be the ultimate goal. For one tradition to say 'you must change because we cannot' is the attitude which lies at the root of so much which is wrong in our community. To acknowledge the limitations of that attitude must surely be the first real step to reconciliation.

It is there, at that point of recognition, that the Christian churches of Northern Ireland face their real challenge. For such a recognition of the problems of attitudes must stem from toleration, charity and Christian understanding. To reach a situation in which differences can be accommodated not only by community structures but by the way people regard each other is the basis of reconciliation.

In writing I have tried to examine what I understand to be those issues which each community sees as vital to its well-being and future. I have been aware that to live and work in Northern Ireland involves a subjectivity in these issues which itself indicates the depth of the feelings the on-going tensions have instilled in each of us. I will have made assumptions which themselves indicate something of the problems of understanding we all face. But there are surely certain principles in one form or another at the heart of both traditions which must transcend even inherited prejudice.

Can the political process be shown to have the willingness and ability to address the differences between the communities, or must it remain, at best, the politics of confrontation and, at worst, the politics of irrelevance for a growing number of people? Can organised religion transcend the inherited identities of one tradition to produce an understanding of what matters most to others, in the knowledge that Christianity is about a way of life in which what unites people under the one God is more important than what divides them? Can a new generation, in which an increasing number see their future outside Northern Ireland, glimpse possibilities and opportunities which will make the effort to build a life here worthwhile? Can the structures of government and the ways relationships are institutionalised gain the support of enough people that stability, recognising difference, is attainable? Is there a strong enough desire for peace and the advantages it will bring to convince enough people that the bullet and the bomb should have no place in our dealings with each other? Above all else, is the price of a lasting peace a cost sufficient numbers of Protestants and Catholics are prepared to pay? For there is a price to be paid – which tells us where we have come from as a community and indicates the road ahead.

First, there are questions of recognition. Each community and each tradition has to recognise certain inalienable and basic rights. Protestants and unionists have a right to a full expression of their ethos and way of life. They have inherited as many obligations as they have privileges. They have a right to effective and realistic political, symbolic and structural recognition of their identity. Their British-Irishness, their natural affinity with a way of life which identifies with 'Britishness' is perfectly legitimate as an aspiration. The true nature of that identity may continue to be a matter of discussion and may indeed be open to various interpretations, but remains legitimate. Likewise, Roman Catholics and nationalists possess the right to maintain their cultural, religious and political ethos in this community. They too have an inalienable right to this recognition. This too may provoke debate, but theirs remains and must remain a vital and legitimate way of life. Republicanism throughout Ireland's troubled history has maintained certain principles which have too encompassed the religious-political link. As a political aspiration, republicanism is a legitimate and justified principle. What has happened to republicanism and loyalism has been that a process of hijacking has taken place, in which the real principles of each has been subjected to manipulation, causing wounds in each community which will take a very long time to heal.

Each community must also recognise that no solution will come through any process of victory of the one over the other. Too often the difficulties faced by one community have been the consequence of attempts at total victory over the other. It has seemed that nothing less will satisfy. Moderation, in the sense of compromise or accommodation, has been squeezed out of a process in which it has a vital role to play. The recognition that we do not talk at each other but with each other, that we no longer see confrontation as the real way to achieve progress rather than listening to each other's legitimate grievances, and the recognition that the real hope of accommodation of difference lies in structures in which those differences can coexist to the benefit of all must remain the first real steps to community reconciliation. The deep fears each tradition has inherited from the past will only be met by dialogue in its widest sense.

Behind all this lie questions which have to be addressed with new urgency and to be faced in a new spirit of openness if either the 'problem' or the 'situation' is to be resolved. Is there a real desire across the communities for change to the extent that people will actually want it enough to make it happen rather than complain in private? Is the desire for progress matched by a willingness in both communities to face the compromises that this will inevitably involve? If political structures to permit productive and positive coexistence of the two communities are possible how far can ordinary people, many of whom feel not just alienated from each other but from the institutional process necessary to attain those structures, become an active part of the process?

I have written as a Churchman. My conviction is, and must remain, that the churches, while a part of the problem, must contribute to the solution. My faith and belief point me to the hope that good ultimately triumphs over evil and that the day of the peacemaker will come. My abhorrence of violence in all its forms has been strengthened by the suffering I have seen in this community. My conviction remains that the path to peace must involve all the people of this community: for I believe Protestant and Roman Catholic, unionist and nationalist must acknowledge that, in fact, they have more that unites than divides them.

The frustration felt by so many Christians of goodwill, that they appear to be unable to overcome violence in this community, is understandable. But they must come to see more clearly that the attitudes which have contributed to the divisions on which terrorism thrives are matters for each individual. Heart-searching is as necessary for the individual as it is for the community. No greater challenge faces the Church than to present peace for Northern Ireland as a realistic probability, rather than merely an alternative possibility. The task is far from hopeless, and the prize awaits the people of hope. In God's name we must all ask, not how, but why not?

17
WHERE NOW?

It is hardly surprising that many people have come to regard the Northern Ireland problem as insoluble. Over a long period of twenty years, various proposals have been put forward and various efforts made, but the hopes that inspired them have been followed by disillusionment and continuing violence.[38]

This pessimistic conclusion is not shocking when one reflects on all that has happened in Northern Ireland since 1968.

It is understandable if one accepts that Northern Ireland has two distinct communities locked in an intense and volatile conflict. It is almost inevitable if one has been watching and listing to reports in the media since 1968. One will think of violence, division and confrontation, of devastation and endless atrocities, of the apparently futile attempts to gain peace through agreement or legislation. The long duration of the conflict, as much as the perceived refusal of the people of Northern Ireland to move forward as so many have done elsewhere in Europe in recent years, has made many observers lose hope of a solution.

Yet to speak of two totally polarised communities is to fall into the trap of generalisation which has marked so many of the efforts to define and understand the precise nature of the Northern Irish problem. If there is one clear lesson to be drawn from this story, then it is that to generalise is to misunderstand its true complexity.

The last twenty years give the appearance of having been dominated by extremist views, views which were expressed with such conviction that there seemed little or no real area of cross-community agreement. The possibilities of compromise through which some agreement and some definite progress towards stability and harmony could be achieved have for a long time seemed elusive.

Is there a middle ground? Are there 'middle people'? Does moderation

[38.] Tom Wilson, *Ulster, Conflict and Consent* (1989), p. 250.

exist in Northern Ireland? For anyone who is a victim of a conflict it is not easy to give 'moderate' views credibility. This is partly due to the difficulties of definition, for moderation is always a relative concept in unstable situations where changing events are bound to provoke a range of reactions. Moderate voices are also squeezed out by the sheer pressure of public reaction to happenings in which the loudest voices and the most extreme attitudes which are often emotional and irrational dominate. Division fosters extremism and places on any moderate burdens which are at times intolerable: against such a background moderation, like ecumenism, has been interpreted as weakness, surrender and a loss of principle. This is true not only in Northern Ireland: it is the experience of any community with (historic) internal divisions.

After 1968 moderate voices were largely suffocated by sectarian attitudes and behaviour; and following on from this, moderates were adversely affected by the consequences of terrorism. For many years there have been people who have supported the moderate approach. Their influence has varied as tensions and attitudes have produced outpourings of anger and resentment within both communities. For many years moderate influence has depended on individual witness rather than collective power: if there was a middle ground, it was very unsteady.

But now, looking back over all that has happened, there is reason to believe not only that a middle ground has appeared but that it is a part of the community which holds definite promise for the future. At present, it is still difficult to quantify. It is evident in the many positive reactions to the first signs of a new way forward, and the steps taken in this direction. It is far from a great wind of change, far from great institutional agreement, far from any radical alteration in party political outlook. But it is there in the words and longings of a growing number of people in both main communities.

In both communities there are very large numbers of people who do not see themselves as extremists. Their roots lie in the unionist or nationalist traditions, but they do not regard either their attitudes or their actions as extreme. They do not welcome confrontation either in political or religious terms. They do not support the use of violence, have fears and uncertainties, experience anger and frustration and suffer the consequences of polarisation. But their lives and their aspirations and beliefs are far removed from the divisions many outsiders have come to accept as the only face of Northern Ireland. Election trends continue to suggest that the communities can be divided sharply into one or other of the two camps, and reactions to terrorism and other events continue to be sharply divided. But contrary to what is all too often assumed outside the Province, the middle ground which recognises that there is an alternative to confrontation, and that peace is attainable through greater understanding across the divide, exists here. That fact, which is remarkable in the light of all that has happened, and remarkable in the face of the attitudes inherited on both sides, cannot and must not be ignored.

I have the impression that people beyond these shores see nothing in Northern Ireland but intransigence, confrontation and conflict. Living and working in Northern Ireland one must face the differences which exist and the violence which produces nothing but a deepening of traditional enmity, but one must also recognise that the Northern Irish are a people whose generosity, warmth of expression and attitude and perseverance are without equal. These qualities have a negative side to them – in that religious identities, party political alliances and interpretations of history are often expressed with a passion which contributes to the sense of a divided community. Thus people have retreated since 1968 into more recognisable 'party' districts. But that is only a part of the story.

The active nurture and encouragement of the middle ground I have been speaking of, composed of both Protestants and Roman Catholics who seek peaceful and positive coexistence, holds the real key to the future. The degrees of stability such as process will bring will not be the result of political or inter-church progress alone. It will involve every area of community activity and expression. It calls for vision, but it involves immense courage at every level of society – a courage to see the current situation is untenable and the future could be much brighter.

'History is a nightmare from which I am trying to awake,' wrote James Joyce. In recent times Northern Ireland has continued this process. A sort of fatalism has encouraged memories of past pain and injustice. 1690 and 1916 each held their own particular message for Protestant and Catholic. The images of those events have continued to cast their spell on succeeding generations. Yet such images do not have to be entirely negative. They can be positive in as much as they contribute to the development of community ethos. It is in the acceptance of those two traditional outlooks and in the recognition of a level of mutual understanding that so much of the way forward depends.

My own view is that cultural diversity enriches and strengthens a society, that a society is strong in proportion to the number of disparate elements which it can contain without actually blowing apart. The figure I like to use is of a bubble – where there is just enough surface tension to keep the entity intact and to keep it floating, but where undue pressure either from within or without will fracture the fragile construction.[39]

[39] 'Whither Cultural Diversity?' Speech by Dr Maurice Hayes, Chairman of the Cultural Traditions Group of the Community Relations Group (29 November 1991).

That bubble can be threatened by the imposition on everyone of the majority culture, which erodes the legitimacy of that culture precious to the minority. It can also be threatened by a minority culture which ignores the majority. In the end we must return to the facts of Ireland: the Roman Catholic minority in Northern Ireland and the Protestant minority in Ireland as a whole.

Given the happenings of the past, it is nothing short of remarkable that this community and its people can and do enjoy the degree of normality which is the real paradox of Northern Ireland today. The visitor is often confounded by what he or she sees of daily life here. The ability to rise above the tensions and to lead normal family or commercial lives appear to deny the presence of problems or conflicts which have dominated the media image of Northern Ireland. For there is another side to the story, a side that is all too rarely portrayed. It is one which speaks of good neighbours, good local relationships and a new equality of opportunity for people irrespective of background. It speaks of decency and humour, depth of character and a magnificent determination to rise above the darkness of sorrow and loss. It speaks of a people who have time without number shown a resilience which could be the envy of many another community beyond our boundaries.

This is in no way to minimise what remains to be done. Feelings of injustice continue, housing and employment opportunities remain priorities in many districts and we continue to be reminded of the needs of the younger generation in areas such as west Belfast. But it would be wrong to give the impression that nothing has happened to meet social need. The sense of community awareness and community influence has never been greater. Expressions of community togetherness in both the voluntary and statutory fields are far reaching.

No greater challenge faces the Christian Church than to find its role in healing the divisions of Northern Ireland. No greater challenge confronts the political process than to find structures which will allow real human problems to be faced with reasonableness and integrity. No greater opportunities exist for people brought up in an atmosphere of pride in their identity to find accommodation with each other.

For the real questions of our situation are ones of relationships, of relationships at every level of life. The degrees of trust which are so essential to making the process of community reconciliation a reality depend on fragile considerations – so fragile that the roots for trust can be destroyed in an instant by word or action. Here so many are prisoners – prisoners of their past, prisoners of their fears and uncertainties, but above all else prisoners of perceptions. It is to break that chain of fear that the efforts of good people of faith in themselves and in each other are needed. Such people exist in Northern Ireland. Their cry for peace and progress must have its day. Irrespective of political structure or religious understanding, the issues are human in nature. In the end they are about how people who have inherited so much can discover in that inheritance that what really unites them is far more potent and lasting than what divides.

If we can agree to regard differences as a positive rather than a negative factor, we will have made a major step forward. How can the message that freedom from fear holds the real key be grasped by a community which has come through so much? The fear of reaching out to each other while not losing political and religious identity; the fear of regarding compromise as betrayal; the fear of being overcome by events or agreements over which ordinary people feel they have no control, and the fear that to make concessions to others will mean alienation from a proud heritage – these are the barriers to real understanding.

I have suggested that at the root of almost all the problems in Northern Ireland lies a profound and destructive fear. People fear terrorism, the consequences of paramilitarism and what others will think of them, if by word or action they are perceived to have 'let down their own side'. People fear the loss of their influence or control, they fear that the opposition will abuse power and that 'they' cannot be trusted to exercise that authority any more now than in the past, should it be returned to 'them'. People fear the real intentions of the other community, their 'hidden agenda'. People fear what they think is happening to their community identity because they lack the power to do anything about it. There is a deep fear of the unknown and of change to traditional attitudes, change to structures which will encourage reconciliation.

There are many answers to fear. Confidence, trust, cooperation, integrity, dialogue most readily come to mind. Yet the story of this community since 1968 has indicated quite clearly that hope which cannot be spelt out in practical and acceptable terms for a sufficient number of people will remain simply that – hope.

I have argued that dialogue holds an important key to the future. Yet while we think of political or inter-church dialogue, there are other demanding needs which are so related to the political and the religious that they cannot be ignored. Ways must be found of encouraging social dialogue.

Dialogue – a process of listening as well as speaking – in this divided community is essential for political parties and the various churches and also across the social groupings and between the generations. It is sometimes argued that terrorism in Northern Ireland continues to exist because it is, to some degree, an expression of social anger at deprivation or injustice. It is true that the term 'men of violence' can most easily be applied to men who come from districts or areas which have known social deprivation. It is frequently said that it is not the people of the affluent areas who are engaged in terrorism: they may share the same attitudes, but they are not involved in violence. It is equally true that commentators on the situation here have tended to overlook the different ways in which the divisions have been fostered. I have referred to the 'opting out' by many people whose lives have been relatively untouched by the violence. Are there ways yet untried of permitting a greater understanding across the classes and generations of Northern Ireland?

When criticism is made of the role of the churches in Northern Ireland's troubles, they are often accused of having failed to capture the hearts and minds of those most deeply involved in the violence. We are told that the churches have become largely middle-class and spend too much time speaking to the 'converted'. Such comments pay little regard to the superb and courageous work within the communities of committed Christian clergy and laity. But the point remains. Have the established churches lost the real ability to influence where it matters most? Are they giving sufficient attention to community projects in deprived areas? Are they providing real succour to those who face daily and nightly the ravages of paramilitary activity? Where now a social Gospel for the churches of Northern Ireland?

These are devastating issues for the church leadership, and questions which individual denominations cannot tackle alone. If the church has allowed itself to become 'too respectable' in Northern Ireland, it must look hard at its own structures before it really possesses the moral right to tell others what they ought to be doing.

It is imperative that the main churches here place the practical implications of a programme of reconciliation high on their individual agendas. Inter-church activity and ecumenism are subject to real and genuine pressures within each denomination. The uncertainty felt about the outcome of increased inter-church cooperation which could possibly erode denominational principle and practice is really the result of ignorance and, therefore, doubt about each other. Ecumenism must not become 'another denomination'; it has to be as much an attitude as a practice. In the social field there is immense strength in the adage that we must do together what conscience does not demand we do separately. None the less those who see ecumenism as a priority must be more aware of and sensitive to the suspicions and doubts which some people have of such inter-church contact.

Undoubtedly, the violence of the past years in Northern Ireland has built up divisions and exaggerated historic tensions. But equally it has forced the denominations to identify in a common cause, the best example of this has been the united condemnation of terrorism. Such condemnation must continue to be united. The voice of the Christian church must speak to mankind in all its conditions. If it is said that, after all, church condemnation of violence is predictable to the point of becoming ineffective, so be it: such criticism cannot be allowed to challenge the evil of murder and terrorism by default. From the Christian standpoint, there can be no justification for the taking of human life.

Equally, as we look ahead the churches must be unafraid to be the voice of the powerless and of those who suffer injustice. The effectiveness of Christian witness committed to the individual churches will be diminished for all the churches if attention is drawn only to the needs of one community or denomination. There must be no line of demarcation where social need or injustice exists.

Not unnaturally, there are many people here who wonder 'will it ever end?' On the whole they are thinking of the violence, but the question should just as readily refer to the root causes of mistrust and alienation which contribute so much to the vicious circle of prejudice and bigotry.

Bringing our community to a stage where the goodness and charity that we know exist among many people in every level of society extends to even more people will be a slow and difficult process. At times, it seems to be a case of 'one step forward and three back'. Good community relations, patiently achieved with courage and initiative, can be destroyed in a few hours of confrontation or manipulation. Yet I have seen many examples of how readily people are prepared to pick up the pieces, to rebuild lives as well as buildings, and to go on. Such attitudes deserve so much more recognition than they usually receive. Such resilience is an answer to those people who seek to entrench divisions; such determination is the basis of hope for our future.

I have attempted to express the feelings of the two communities on a wide range of issues as fairly as I can. In so doing I am only too well aware that involvement in life in Northern Ireland makes objective assessment difficult. I have been privileged to see at first hand great courage, faith and vision from within the Roman Catholic community. But it is only natural that my deepest impression will come from the feelings, attitudes and emotions of the Protestant people.

I believe that Protestantism needs a new confidence in itself in Northern Ireland. I do not mean a confidence in terms of domination but a confidence in what Protestants believe about themselves and about others. This is a confidence that Protestantism has a real and not an imaginary role to play in building a better community for all; a confidence that it has an equal right to a place in the life of this community. It is a confidence that what it believes about itself has given it both direction and a future role, but a confidence which recognises the dangers – the real dangers – of seeing its future unrelated to the well-being of others. The fragmentation of churches and sects within Protestantism stems from many historical factors, but does not explain the uncertainty of so many people within that community with regard to ecumenism or reconciliation. I believe that the communities, whether linked to a political or religious label in Northern Ireland, need each other even in ways which are not immediately apparent. Yet the entire process of meeting that need demands an integrity which is itself the forerunner of openness. We cannot change what we are. We should not have to. But we can and must see what we are able to do to combat the fears of the Northern Irish: foremost is a need to recognise that no community has a monopoly of the truth, just as no community has a monopoly of pain.

It has become increasingly apparent that Protestantism perceives itself to be the victim of the troubles. This is not always recognised by others in Northern Ireland or people outside the conflict and it helps to explain many of the attitudes many Protestants have towards inter-community activity – the defensiveness of spokesmen for the Protestant community in the past which I believe needs to be replaced by confidence.

The Northern Ireland problem is classified by some not as a problem but as a situation. Such a definition assumes acceptance of the inevitable, and this generation is compelled to ask *how* inevitable the tensions and divisions are.

I have already said the Province has come a very long way since 1968. Each community has suffered and each community feels deeply its pain, and the ways in which its customs and beliefs have been interpreted by others. Each community has buried its victims of violence – and each has lived on. Each has passed through periods of hopelessness – and each has produced its voices of hope. Such is the speed of events that between the time of writing and actual publication, incidents will occur and, inevitably, much will remain the same.

When travelling abroad, it is a sobering and valuable experience to see the Northern Ireland story from a new perspective. To live and work here is to be confronted by the problem, the suffering and the difficulties. Such factors become paramount. To move away, even for a short time, is to realise that the troubles of this community pale into relative insignificance compared with the experiences of other people in other places. The death rate from

Northern Ireland terrorism it not very different from the consequences of urban violence in many a city in the United States. The religious and political divisions of Ulster seem minute compared with the horrors of the inter-tribal feuds and wars of the Middle East. The tensions of our communities are dwarfed by the racial problems of the southern states of America some years ago. More lives are lost through road traffic accidents in Northern Ireland than as a consequence of terrorist activity.

Nevertheless, these perspectives tend to magnify as well as diminish the problems of our local scene. When one contemplates the examples in history when human rights issues have been addressed, when the whole ethos of peoples have been transformed and dramatic reforms produced in a short space of time, one confronts yet again the apparent inability of a small part of the earth to move forward and away from historic emnity. We cannot isolate Northern Ireland and its attitudes from what is happening elsewhere. We are not a special case.

Moreover, it is becoming clear, slowly but surely, that the new Europe which is emerging will have little patience with this conflict. It may not be possible to legislate for reconciliation or to enforce inter-community understanding, but economics have a habit of concentrating the mind. Parochialism cannot survive very long if economic reality demands otherwise. Of course, the extent to which this may be the experience of the people of Northern Ireland remains to be seen.

For I remain convinced that the end of sectarian violence holds the key to Northern Ireland's future. All that has been achieved in the past few years would take on a dimension of immense and lasting worth if violence were ended. And violence will end when that section of the community which at present makes it possible withdraws its support – active and passive. It is for the rest of society to show what will accompany an end to violence. It will not be history that somehow produces a neat and satisfactory solution to the problems of Northern Ireland: elsewhere we have seen 'people power' has proved stronger than institutions and the catalyst for social and political reform. It is now Northern Ireland's turn.

As a Christian I have to believe that goodwill which has the Christ-like ingredient of redemption and which is expressed without recourse to violence in any form will ultimately triumph. In any situation of human conflict that must be for a Christian the ultimate hope, the ultimate reality in which he finds good stronger than evil, love greater than hatred and justice more powerful than injustice.

If there is one word which must be spelt out clearly as we look to the future then surely it is toleration – not toleration of the evils of a divided community, such as violence, for there must never be an acceptance of violence in Northern Ireland, but toleration of each other's deeply-held convictions and beliefs. That toleration must become strong enough to withstand the fears and uncertainties, to overcome the violence and gain greater weight than the voice of hatred. There should be no surrender in true toleration: no winner nor loser. There must be a new awareness that the two communities can maintain their separate identities, but maintain them with mutual respect.

The gun and the bomb can subject whole communities to fear and render them seemingly impotent for a period. At times the gun and the bomb have appeared to dominate. They can hold lives and hearts in their fearful grip and produce reactions which run deep. But they do not and cannot change the deepest longings of peoples' hearts and minds, nor can they quell the greatest desires of a people who reach the conclusion that there is another path and another way.

When that point is reached it may not be easily recognised. History will judge it more clearly than those who are living through it. But there is a new confidence today that what is needed to reach that point has never been more plain than now for the people of Northern Ireland. So much common ground exists and is being recognised. We have the opportunity to grasp that peace for which many people yearn and to translate desire into reality. But 'a stable, peaceful, kindly Northern Ireland is not a cost-free option'.[40] The cost is real and expensive. The hour demands much courage, vision and honesty; it demands that the yoke of terrorism no longer burdens people; it demands a new look at how we think of each other, and it demands that each community recognises with greater honesty what it has contributed to the conditions and attitudes of the other. One day the people of peace will come into their own in Northern Ireland. One day reconciliation will have become the consequence of patient and faithful endeavour and the suffering of so many will have to take its place in history.

The Christian must always be the voice of hope. That hope which, stemming from faith and belief, must be related to the actual experiences of ordinary people. It will be prompted and encouraged by belief, but it must be reflected in the influence and example given in real life situations.

The presence in Northern Ireland of so many people who claim that faith and belief, and the courage of those who are prepared to stand up to be counted because of it, must be the real basis for hope for the future of this community.

The influence of good people of faith has been severely tested since 1968.

[40.] Dr Brian Mawhinney, Minister of State, 4 September 1991.

And the years ahead will demand more testing if belief is to be translated in practical ways of removing those barriers and breaking those chains which have for too long held people prisoners in Ireland.

SELECT
BIBLIOGRAPHY

ACKROYD, C., MARGOLIS, K., ROSENHEAD, J., AND SHALLICE, T., *The Technology of Political Control*, London, Penguin, 1977.

AKENSON, D. H., *Education and Enmity: The Control of Schooling in Northern Ireland 1920–50*, London, David & Charles, 1973.

ALL PARTY ANTI-PARTITION CONFERENCE, *Discrimination: A Study in Injustice to a Minority*, Dublin, 1954.

AMNESTY INTERNATIONAL, *Report of an Amnesty International Mission to Northern Ireland*, London, Amnesty International, 1978.

ARTHUR, P., *The People's Democracy*, Belfast, Blackstaff, 1974.

ARTHUR, P., *The Government and Politics of Northern Ireland*, London, Longman, 1980.

AUNGER, E. A., 'Religion and Occupational Class in Northern Ireland', *Economic and Social Review* 7, 1, 1975.

BARBER, S., AND HILL, M., (eds.), *Aspects of Irish Studies*, Institute of Irish Studies, Queen's University, Belfast, 1990.

BARRITT, D. P., AND CARTER, C. F., *The Northern Ireland Problem: A Study in Community Relations*, Oxford, Oxford University Press, 1962.

BECKETT, J. C., *A Short History of Ireland*, London, Faber, 1952.

BECKETT, J. C., *The Making of Modern Ireland*, London, Faber, 1966.

BELL, G., *The Protestants of Ulster*, London, Pluto, 1976.

BOYD, A., *Holy War in Belfast*, Tralee, Anvil, 1969.

BUCKLAND, P., *Ulster Unionism and the Origins of Northern Ireland, 1886–1922*, Dublin, Gill and Macmillan, 1973.

BUCKLAND, P., 'The Unity of Ulster Unionism, 1886–1939', *History*, 60, 1975.

BUCKLAND, P., *A History of Northern Ireland*, Dublin, Gill and Macmillan, 1981.

BURTON, F., *The Politics of Legitimacy: Struggles in a Belfast Community*, London, Routledge and Kegan Paul, 1978.

BREWER, J. D., *Inside the RUC*, Oxford, Clarendon Press, 1991.

CAIRNS, E., *Caught in the Crossfire: Children and the Northern Ireland Conflict*, Belfast, Appletree Press, 1987.

CALLAGHAN, J., *A House Divided*, London, Collins, 1973.

CAMERON COMMISSION, *Disturbances in Northern Ireland*, Cmnd. 532, Belfast, HMSO, 1969.

CAMPBELL, J. J., *Catholic Schools: A Survey of a Northern Ireland Problem*, Dublin, Fallons, 1964.

DALY, C., *The Price of Peace*, Belfast, Blackstaff Press, 1991.

DARBY, J., *Conflict in Northern Ireland: The Development of a Polarised Community*, Dublin, Gill and Macmillan, 1976.

DARBY, J., (ed.), *Northern Ireland: The Background to the Conflict*, Belfast, Appletree Press, 1983.

DIPLOCK COMMISSION, *Report of the Commission to Consider Legal Procedures to Deal with Terrorist Activities in Northern Ireland*, Cmnd. 5185. London, HMSO, 1972.

FLACKES, W. F., *Northern Ireland: A Political Directory*, Dublin, Gill and Macmillan, 1980.

GALLAGHER, E. AND WORRALL, F., *Christians in Ulster 1968–1980*, Oxford, Oxford University Press, 1982.

GREER, J., *A Questioning Generation*, Belfast, Church of Ireland Board of Education, 1972.

HARBINSON, J. F., *A History of the Northern Ireland Labour Party, 1884–1949*, Belfast, unpublished Queen's University MSc. thesis, 1966.

HARBINSON J. F., *The Ulster Unionist Party, 1882–1972*, Belfast, Blackstaff, 1973.

HAYES, J. AND O'HIGGINS, P., *Lessons from Northern Ireland*, SLS Legal Publications (NI) School of Law, Queen's University, Belfast, 1990.

HUNT COMMITTEE, *Report of the Advisory Committee on Police in Northern Ireland*, Cmnd. 535, Belfast, HMSO, 1969.

IRISH COUNCIL OF CHURCHES, *Violence in Ireland*, Dublin, Christian Journals Ltd, 1976.

LYONS, F. S. L., *Ireland since the Famine*, London, Weidenfeld & Nicolson, 1971.

MCCAFFERTY, N., *The Armagh Women*, Dublin, Co-op Books, 1981.

MORROW, DUNCAN, *The Churches and Inter-Community Relations*, The University of Ulster, Centre for the Study of Conflict, 1991.

MAGEE, J., 'The Teaching of Irish History in Irish Schools', *The Northern Teacher* 10, 1, 1970.

O'MALLEY, P., *The Uncivil Wars*, Belfast, Blackstaff Press, 1983.

O'MALLEY, P., *Biting at the Grave*, Boston, Beacon Press, 1990.

NELSON, S., *Ulster's Uncertain Defenders*, Belfast, Appletree Press, 1984.

PALLEY, C., 'Evolution, Disintegration and Possible Reconstruction of the Northern Ireland Constitution', *Anglo-American Law Review* 1, 1972.

PATTERSON, H., *The Politics of Illusion*, London, Hutchinson and Radius, 1989.

QUIGLEY REVIEW TEAM, *Economic and Industrial Strategy for Northern Ireland*, Report by Review Team, Belfast, HMSO, 1976.

ROBBINS, K., *Cultural Traditions in Northern Ireland*, Institute of Irish Studies, Queen's University, Belfast, 1990.

RYDER, C., *The Ulster Defence Regiment*, London, Methuen, 1991.

RYDER, C., *The RUC: A Force Under Fire*, London, Methuen, 1989.

ROWTHORN, B., AND WAYNE, N., *Northern Ireland, The Political Economy of Conflict*, Cambridge, Polity Press, 1988.

ROYAL ULSTER CONSTABULARY, *Chief Constable's Report*, Belfast, RUC, Annual.

SAVAGE, D. C., 'The Origins of the Ulster Unionist Party, 1885–1886', *Irish Historical Studies*, 12, 1961.

STEWART, A. T. Q., *The Narrow Ground: Aspects of Ulster, 1609–1969*, London, Faber, 1977.

Ulster Year Book, Belfast, HMSO, Annual.

WILSON, T., *Ulster, Conflict and Consent*, Oxford, Blackwell, 1989.

INDEX